MERCHANTS AND PROFIT IN THE AGE OF COMMERCE, 1680–1830

Perspectives in Economic and Social History

Series Editors: *Andrew August*
Jari Eloranta

Titles in this Series

1 Migrants and Urban Change: Newcomers to Antwerp, 1760–1860
Anne Winter

2 Female Entrepreneurs in Nineteenth-Century Russia
Galina Ulianova

3 Barriers to Competition: The Evolution of the Debate
Ana Rosado Cubero

4 Rural Unwed Mothers: An American Experience, 1870–1950
Mazie Hough

5 English Catholics and the Education of the Poor, 1847–1902
Eric G. Tenbus

6 The World of Carolus Clusius: Natural History in the Making, 1550–1610
Florike Egmond

7 The Determinants of Entrepreneurship: Leadership, Culture, Institutions
José L. García-Ruiz and Pier Angelo Toninelli (eds)

8 London Clerical Workers, 1880–1914: Development of the Labour Market
Michael Heller

9 The Decline of Jute: Managing Industrial Change
Jim Tomlinson, Carlo Morelli and Valerie Wright

10 Mining and the State in Brazilian Development
Gail D. Triner

11 Global Trade and Commercial Networks:
Eighteenth-Century Diamond Merchants
Tijl Vanneste

12 The Clothing Trade in Provincial England, 1800–1850
Alison Toplis

13 Sex in Japan's Globalization, 1870–1930: Prostitutes, Emigration and Nation Building
Bill Mihalopoulos

14 Financing India's Imperial Railways, 1875–1914
Stuart Sweeney

15 Energy, Trade and Finance in Asia: A Political and Economic Analysis
Justin Dargin and Tai Wei Lim

16 Violence and Racism in Football: Politics and Cultural Conflict in British Society, 1968–1998
Brett Bebber

17 The Economies of Latin America: New Cliometric Data
César Yáñez and Albert Carreras (eds)

18 Meat, Commerce and the City: The London Food Market, 1800–1855
Robyn S. Metcalfe

19 Merchant Colonies in the Early Modern Period
Victor N. Zakharov, Gelina Harlaftis and Olga Katsiardi-Hering (eds)

20 Markets and Growth in Early Modern Europe
Victoria N. Bateman

21 Welfare and Old Age in Europe and North America: The Development of Social Insurance
Bernard Harris (ed.)

22 Female Economic Strategies in the Modern World
Beatrice Moring (ed.)

23 Crime and Community in Reformation Scotland: Negotiating Power in a Burgh Society
J. R. D. Falconer

24 Policing Prostitution, 1856–1886: Deviance, Surveillance and Morality
Catherine Lee

25 Narratives of Drunkenness: Belgium, 1830–1914
An Vleugels

26 Respectability and the London Poor, 1780–1870: The Value of Virtue
Lynn MacKay

27 Residential Institutions in Britain, 1725–1970: Inmates and Environments
Jane Hamlett, Lesley Hoskins and Rebecca Preston (eds)

28 Conflict, Commerce and Franco-Scottish Relations, 1560–1713
Siobhan Talbott

29 Drink in the Eighteenth and Nineteenth Centuries
Susanne Schmid and Barbara Schmidt-Haberkamp (eds)

Forthcoming Titles

A Global Conceptual History of Asia, 1860–1940
Hagen Schulz-Forberg (ed.)

Mercantilism and Economic Underdevelopment in Scotland, 1600–1783
Philipp Robinson Rössner

Commercial Networks and European Cities, 1400–1800
Andrea Caracausi and Christof Jeggle (eds)

Jewish Immigrants in London, 1880–1939
Susan L. Tananbaum

Consuls and the Institutions of Global Capitalism, 1783–1914
Ferry de Goey

Insanity and the Lunatic Asylum in the Nineteenth Century
Thomas Knowles and Serena Trowbridge (eds)

Philanthropy and the Funding of the Church of England, 1856–1914
Sarah Flew

MERCHANTS AND PROFIT IN THE AGE OF COMMERCE, 1680–1830

EDITED BY

Pierre Gervais, Yannick Lemarchand and Dominique Margairaz

Translated in part by Darla Rudy-Gervais

LONDON AND NEW YORK

First published 2014 by Pickering & Chatto (Publishers) Limited

Published 2016 by Routledge
2 Park Square, Milton Park, Abingdon, Oxfordshire OX14 4RN
711 Third Avenue, New York, NY 10017, USA

First issued in paperback 2015

Routledge is an imprint of the Taylor & Francis Group, an informa business

BRITISH LIBRARY CATALOGUING IN PUBLICATION DATA

Merchants and profit in the Age of Commerce, 1680–1830. – (Perspectives in economic and social history)
1. Europe – Commerce – History – 18th century. 2. America – Commerce – History –18th century. 3. China – Commerce – History – 18th century. 4. Merchants – Europe –History – 18th century. 5. Merchants – America – History – 18th century. 6. Merchants –China – History – 18th century. 7. International economic relations – History – 18th century.
I. Series II. Gervais, Pierre, 1962– editor of compilation. III. Lemarchand, Yannick editor of compilation. IV. Margairaz, Dominique editor of compilation.
382'.09033-dc23

ISBN-13: 978-1-138-66317-6 (pbk)
ISBN-13: 978-1-8489-3482-5 (hbk)

Typeset by Pickering & Chatto (Publishers) Limited

CONTENTS

ACKNOWLEDGEMENTS

The present volume is published with the help of ANR MARPROF and University PARIS 1 Panthéon-Sorbonne. It contains the first results of a five-year-long research project funded by the French Agence Nationale pour la Recherche. Along the years, supplementary financial or organizational support was generously granted by Centre National de la Recherche Scientifique, Maison des Sciences de l'Homme Ange-Guépin de Nantes, LEMNA and Nantes University, IDHE and University Paris I Panthéon-Sorbonne, REDEJHA, LARCA and University Paris-Diderot in France; Sheffield University and the British Group for Early American History in England; and University of Chicago. Project MARPROF, as it was called, benefitted greatly from the tireless work of Camille Amat, Mathieu Beaud, Manuel Covo, Toby Frajerman, Cécile Robin and Martine Sennegond-Meslem. The project was a success in part thanks to the expertise of Nora Petit de la Villéon, who conceived and built the databases we used, and Jacques Bottin, who provided guidance in the first stages of the research. A presentation of the programme can be found at http://marprof.univ-paris1.fr. Our thanks also to Darla Rudy-Gervais for ensuring a speedy process of translation at the very last minute, and to the editors at Pickering & Chatto for their warm support and guidance.

LIST OF CONTRIBUTORS

Boris Deschanel attended the Ecole Nationale des Chartes, and is *professeur agrégé*, currently employed as ATER at the University of Limoges, France. He is also working on a thesis at University Paris I Panthéon-Sorbonne, and, as a doctoral candidate, is member of the research group IDHE – UMR 8533. The topic of the thesis is 'Négoce, espaces et politique. Les commerçants dauphinois dans la Révolution (années 1780–années 1820).'

Robert DuPlessis is Isaac H. Clothier Professor Emeritus at Swarthmore College, Swarthmore, Pennsylvania, USA. He has published extensively on early modern capitalism, manufacture and trade, most recently 'What did Slaves Wear? Textile Regimes in the French Caribbean', *Monde(s)*, 1:1 (2012); 'Mercadorias globais, consumidores locais: texteis no mundo atlantico nos seculos XVII e XVIII', *Afro-Ásia*, 41 (2010); 'Cottons Consumption in the Seventeenth and Eighteenth Century Atlantic World', in G. Riello and P. Parthasarathi (eds), *The Spinning World: A Global History of Cotton Textiles 1200–1850* (2009); and *Market Makers and Market Takers: A History of Natural Fibers Textiles in the Central Apennine Region (the Marche and Umbria)* (2006).

Pierre Gervais is Professor of American Civilization at the University Paris 3 Sorbonne-Nouvelle in Paris, and member of the research centers CREW (EA 4399) and IDHE (UMR 8533). He was coordinator of the ANR Project MARPROF from which the present publication was derived. He has published extensively on the market economy in North America and France, in *Annales Histoire Sciences Sociales, French History, History of European Ideas, Revue de Synthèse, Common-Place* and *Oxford Bibliographies Online*. His book, *Les origines de la Révolution industrielle aux Etats-Unis* (Paris: Ed. de l'Ehess, 2004), has been awarded the Willi Paul Adams Prize of the *Organization of American Historians* in 2006.

Frederic Delano Grant, Jr, a practising lawyer, has written extensively on the business and legal history of early Western trade with China. He received a BA from Bates College in 1976, a JD from Boston College Law School in 1983 and a PhD in history from Leiden University in 2012. His Leiden doctoral dissertation, 'The Chinese Cornerstone of Modern Banking: The Canton Guaranty System and the Origins of Bank Deposit Insurance 1780–1933', is now being revised for publication. In his dissertation, in the essay submitted to this volume, and other current work, he applies insights developed over thirty years' active practice as a lawyer specializing in guaranty and insolvency matters to produce new understandings of the workings of the Canton System (1684–1842) and the development of modern bank deposit insurance programmes.

Xabier Lamikiz is Assistant Professor of Economic History at the University of the Basque Country (UPV/EHU). He earned his PhD in history from Royal Holloway, University of London, in 2006. In February 2010, after a two-year postdoctoral fellowship at University College London, he was appointed Assistant Professor of Economic History at the Universidad Autónoma de Madrid. In 2012 he was Visiting Fellow at the École des Hautes Études en Sciences Sociales, Paris. He moved to the UPV/EHU in September 2012. His articles have appeared in *Revista de Historia Económica*, *International Journal of Maritime History*, *Hispanic American Historical Review* and *Colonial Latin American Review*. He is the author of *Trade and Trust in the Eighteenth-Century Atlantic World: Spanish Merchants and their Overseas Networks* (2010). At present he is working on commercial credit in the Spanish Atlantic.

Yannick Lemarchand is Professor Emeritus in management sciences at the University of Nantes, and member of the research group *Laboratoire d'économie et de management de Nantes Atlantique* (LEMNA – EA 4272). His research focus on the history of management knowledge an practices. He co-founded in 1995 the *Journées annuelles d'Histoire de la comptabilité et du management*, and he is President of the *Association pour l'histoire du management et des organisations*. His most recent publications include, with Ludovic Cailluet and Marie-Emmanuelle Chessel (eds), *Histoire et sciences de gestion* (2013); and with Cheryl McWatters 'Merchant Networks and Accounting Discourse: The Role of Accounting Transactions in Network Relations', *Accounting History Review*, 23:1 (2013).

Dominique Margairaz is Professor of History at the University of Paris 1 Panthéon-Sorbonne, and member of the research group IDHE – UMR 8533. She has published extensively on eighteenth-century economic history and the history of economic ideas. Her most recent publications include 'City and Country: Home, Possessions, and Diet, Western Europe 1600–1800', in F. Trentman (ed.), *Handbook of Consumption* (2012); 'Produits et circuits du commerce', in C. Maitte et al. (eds), *La pluralité des mondes industriels* (2012), and 'Qualité et fiscalité dans l'économie d'Ancien Régime', in J. Vögle and R. Salais (eds), *Qualitätspolitik. Die Qualität der Produkte in historischer Perspektive* (2013).

Cheryl Susan McWatters is Full Professor and the Father Edgar Thivierge Chair in business history at the University of Ottawa. She is associate editor of *Accounting Perspectives* and a member of the editorial boards of the *Journal of Operations Management, Accounting, Auditing and Accountability Journal, Accounting History Review* and *Accounting Historians Journal.* Professor McWatters has published in a diverse set of journals including *Accounting, Organizations and Society, Accounting, Auditing and Accountability Journal, Journal of Operations Management, Droits, Accounting Historians Journal, Accounting History* and *Accounting History Review.* Recent work focuses on seventeenth- and eighteenth-century mercantilism in which accounting acts as an integrative and facilitating mechanism across space and time. In 2012, she was appointed by the French government to the Board of Directors of the *Réseau français des instituts d'études avancées* (RFIEA).

Laure Pineau-Defois holds a PhD in early modern history from the University of Nantes ('Les plus grands négociants nantais du dernier tiers du XVIIIe siècle. Capital hérité et esprit d'entreprise, fin XVIIe – début XIXe siècle'). She has published several articles on the social and commercial practices of the Nantes merchant elites in the eighteenth century, including 'Sphères d'approvisionnement des grands négociants nantais en denrées d'exportation (fin XVIIIe siècle)', *Histoire Urbaine,* 30 (2011); and 'Une élite d'Ancien Régime: les négociants nantais dans la tourmente révolutionnaire 1780–1793', *Annales historiques de la Révolution française,* 359 (2010).

Steven Sarson is Associate Professor in History and Classics at Swansea University and is a member of the Scientific Committee of the European Early American Studies Association. He is the author of *British America, 1500–1800: Creating Colonies, Imagining an Empire* (2005), *The Tobacco Plantation South in the Early American Atlantic World* (2013), and of articles in the *Journal of the Early Republic,* the *Journal of Economic History,* the *William and Mary Quarterly,* and other periodicals. He has also edited with Jack P. Greene an eight-volume documents collection on *The American Colonies and the British Empire, 1607–1783* (2010–11).

Julien Villain has attended *Ecole Normale Supérieure* and is currently *professeur agrégé,* while completing a doctoral dissertation on 'Aires et structures du commerce dans le bassin de la Moselle 1670/1790', under the direction of Prof. Dominique Margairaz, at the University Paris I Panthéon-Sorbonne. As doctoral candidate, he is a member of the research group IDHE (*Institutions et Dynamiques Historiques de l'Economie*) – Unité Mixte de Recherche 8533. His publications include 'Espaces et filières d'un commerce de gros et de demi-gros au XVIIIe siècle: les activités commerciales des "marchands-magasiniers" lorrains (années 1750 et 1760)', in C. Maitte, P. Minard and M. De Oliveira (eds), *La gloire de l'industrie XVIIe–XIXe siècle. Faire de l'histoire avec Gérard Gayot* (2012), and 'Privilèges douaniers et profits marchands. Le cas de la Lorraine et des Trois-Evêchés, provinces de "l'étranger effectif" (1718–1791)', to be published in 2014 in the Acts of the Frankfurt-am-Main colloquium 'L'économie du privilège/Ökonomie des Privilegs'.

LIST OF FIGURES AND TABLES

INTRODUCTION: THE MANY SCALES OF MERCHANT PROFIT: ACCOUNTING FOR NORMS, PRACTICES AND RESULTS IN THE AGE OF COMMERCE

Pierre Gervais, Yannick Lemarchand and Dominique Margairaz

The present collection is the result of a concerted, negotiated effort between all its contributors to better understand merchant profit (or should we say more broadly market-based profit?) in the early modern period. The question may seem meaningless, since profit is at first glance one of these self-evident notions which everybody naturally understands. Bring in some capital, apply it to some activity, harvest whatever monetary value is generated thereby, and *voilà*! Some profit is made, usually summarized by the simple subtraction of the original layout, plus liabilities and costs incurred, including opportunity costs and depreciation ideally, from the final proceeds including whatever assets are acquired. Accounting details may differ, but the basic mechanism is fairly transparent. It is often presented as such in the literature, with most historical accounts of merchants in the early modern era assuming that when a profit was made here and there, it was hardly necessary to detail how it was made.[1]

This inquiry was born out of the hypothesis that reality was more complex, that a close study of merchant practices, focused on the various constitutive parts of profits, would perhaps lead to a historical narrative in which early modern merchant profit in particular, and therefore early modern merchant practice in general, would take a more historicized colouration. Every time 'profit' was mentioned in the early modern period, should we accept that the meaning was the same, that everybody had the same common object in mind, regardless of variations in scale, period and point of view? Were all agents seeing the same profit, whether they were individuals, groups or institutions, whether they were acting on their own or as agents of a city or a state, whether they were working on producing it or merely intent on understanding it in theory, as economists?

What we were looking for was a chronology of profit, an approach of it in time, which would account for both the surroundings of its pursuit, the historical environment, the cognitive constructs the agents doing the pursuing had to or wanted to use, and also the inner baggage of this pursuit of profit, the practices and organizational approaches already accepted, and the varied sets of cognitive artefacts inherited from the past, present in the memories of these agents, within which they would reframe their action and from which they would derive their tools. This meant focusing on discrepancies, on discontinuities in the heroic tale of business endeavours: looking for differences, as it were, and thus raising, again, the issue of the 'spirit of capitalism'.

There is little doubt that there were practices, activities and representations, a system of production, a legitimizing structure, characterizing the older, merchant capitalism, during what we have chosen to call the 'Age of Commerce'. The issue is whether these were specific to this 'old' capitalism, as opposed to the 'new' one postdating the Industrial Revolution. The answer to this question has direct consequences for our ability to understand profit in each of the two frameworks. To what extent can we assume that the vocabulary and syntax of 'profit' remained constant through this line of divide? Shouldn't we at least check our instinctive assumption of continuity against the historical record?

Profit: What Was It?

Asking what 'a profit' meant exactly is thus far from pointless, especially since, even if one leaves aside the differences between the learned use of the term and its popular accepted meaning, there is no one accepted way to understand profit even today. The accountant's profit, the change in the net value of the firm over a given period of time, is not the profit of the economist, who will want to break it down into its component parts so as to understand its sources and its distribution. Indeed there is no one accountant's profit, since the precise accounting rule used varies with the country and the period one considers. And there are several ways to account for it in economics as well: is it a function of innovation, in the Schumpeterian tradition? Or is it rather Knight's positive result of an anticipation in a context marked by uncertainty? Should we see in it a legitimate return on the capital invested productively by its owner, granting that some unearned income may arise from situations of imperfect competition? Or should we insist that profit is merely that part of the surplus value forcibly taken from its producers by the owner of the means of production, to the extent that naked power relations allow them to do so?[2]

Thus definitions of profit are essentially plural, and they raise issues which were already discussed in the eighteenth century. Should profit be defined as a particular kind of income? In the *Encyclopédie*, for instance, 'profit' was defined as the gain derived from a commercial transaction over goods in a subsection of a more general comparative article on 'Profit, Gain, Lucre, Emolument, Bénéfice', in which the very same word was presented as meaning only a secure profit linked to landed income, for instance, hence *not* merchant income. The latter was described in this comparative entry as in the nature of a 'gain', based on luck – but in a third, earlier comparative entry on 'Bénéfice, Gain, Profit, Lucre, Emolument', profit was described as both more secure than the gambler's gain and as a term characteristic of merchant income. Such wavering definitions show conclusively that the notion was far from being well defined. Indeed there were only two technical subentries, for 'Profits de fief (Jurisprud.)', describing the charges that a feudal tenure would generate to the benefit of its lord when a new vassal took over, and 'Profit avantureux (Marine)', explaining bottomry loans.[3]

In the early modern period the word 'profit' still belonged mostly to a non-technical vocabulary, with rather neutral, descriptive value in popular use (gain, benefit) sliding easily into more negative ones (lucre, theft). In its general, accepted usage, it could point to any income, from commerce, from land and from any kind of human 'industry', i.e. any useful activity. It was used as an equivalent to a 'benefit' in the field of banking, or to an *émolument*, what officers of the Old Regime derived from their offices either as wages (*gages*) or otherwise. There was also a propinquity to the notions of game, luck or risk; a merchant was not that far from a gambler. And there was a closer link to trade, as shown by the aforementioned subentry 'profit', which immediately proceeded to load the word with moral considerations. For merchant profit and for that type of profit only, 'illicit' and 'legitimate' profit (*profits illicites* and *profit légitime*) were explained with reference to a social norm controlling quantitatively the gain achieved, with a fixed gross margin on goods, akin to a tariff duty, aimed at holding the merchant's income down to what would be 'fair' profit.[4]

The nascent science of political economy also dealt with profit, with many of its proponents trying to conceptualize the origins and reproduction of wealth and its application to more or less useful pursuits. At a more abstract level, the nature of value was the real topic, in combination with the causes for market price fluctuations and the influence of monopolistic or competitive settings thereon. Political economists thus developed the idea of a *prix fondamental*, equivalent to Adam Smith's natural price, in which production factors, capital included, were paid for at cost (including a cost of subsistence for all involved). Surplus profit would then appear either temporarily due to an accidental scarcity or more permanently because of a monopoly situation. But there would be a certain amount of income credited to productive activities – a profit perhaps – even in a perfectly competitive situation. We should therefore expect to meet some sort of profit category, identified as a particular species of income, in the works of Pierre le Pesant, sieur de Boisguilbert (1646–1714), Richard Cantillon (*c.* 1680–1734), Anne-Robert-Jacques Turgot (1727–81) or Adam Smith (1723–90).

This is simply not the case before Adam Smith. Cantillon considered as entrepreneurs 'all those who endeavor at a fixed price to sell at an uncertain price', a definition which covered a variety of social groups, merchants certainly, but also farmers, manufacturers and craftsmen, and generated a view of profit which did not distinguish between the rent gained from landed property, interest on investments or loans, income of the entrepreneur or whatever 'net profit' remained once paid the costs of production and of living for the entrepreneur. Similarly, Turgot jumbled together, under the same heading of 'profit', land rents, more or less along the Physiocratic lines of a net product 'given freely by the land to he who cultivates it, as an independent and available part beyond what he advanced and the wages of his labors'; the income of the manufacturer which 'compensates his advances, his cares, his risks and his talent'; and the wages of 'mere crafstmen, who have no other capital than their arms, and advance only their daily labor, [and] have no other profit than their wages'.[5] Indeed even in Smith, profit was seen as the price of stock advances to labour, and a deduction from final output, which generated only enough to refund the original investment and to ensure the basic subsistence of the investor – any income beyond this rather limited, 'natural' profit was seemingly the result of non-competitive or extraordinary conditions.[6]

Overall, 'profit' was far from being a rigorously defined analytical concept among pre-classical economists, even though they did try to penetrate the mysterious ways in which a surplus was generated whether at the micro, entrepreneurial or macro level of the states. They knew that there was a certain something which did appear over and beyond the consumption of currency, raw materials or labour which led to its creation, a surplus that could be accumulated, and also reused, not only to initiate a new cycle, but also to prevent any *dépérissement* or 'wasting away' (Turgot's formula) of the funds one held. These authors felt, indeed knew, that there was what we call growth, but they never saw it in terms of innovation or fixed capital investment. On the contrary, what counted, as Smith insisted, was the circulating capital of merchant activity, of exchange, of consumption. What Physiocrats, Turgot and Smith all called 'annual advances' were precisely that – purchases of labour and raw or semi-finished material which underpinned a view of profit as the price differential between what was bought and what was sold.

All these authors do give us a picture of an economy which is not altogether the one we are used to. Landed property was its focus, and made up most of the wealth. Industry, such as it was, required little fixed capital; similarly, a relatively small amount of capital would command a large quantity of labour; so that industrial 'advances', what had to be invested to ensure production, went mostly into raw materials. This underpins Cantillon's contention that commercial credit and long-term loans were really one and the same from the point of view of the availability of capital, so that both a water-bearer and the owner of a textile manufactory could equally be seen as entrepreneurs.

Profit, in this world, was a gain on exchange, on the difference between buying price and selling price. This held true even for apparently highly capitalized branches such as calico factories. Oberkampf remained primarily a merchant and described his activity in merchant terms, claiming that the key to success was his ability to buy unbleached cloth cheap and sell it printed at the highest possible price, wherever demand was highest. His job, he explained, was to collect information efficiently, through a network of informants, to find out where there was a large offer at given levels of quality and price, and buy there, and at the other end find expanding markets on which marketing his products would bring in the best result.[7] In other words, this early manufacturer, at the beginning of the nineteenth century, was still illustrating what Cantillon saw as the 'uncertain' operator. Indeed, the separation between labour and capital was limited at best, and formalized primarily through, again, merchant relationships, such as leasing agreements or fixed-price contracts, in which many labourers were what Cantillon calls *entrepreneurs d'eux-mêmes* (self-entrepreneurs).[8]

Profit was also linked to gambling and very early so, with the speculations on shares of monopolistic chartered companies, which multiplied from 1680 to 1720 in the Netherlands, England and France. Unfettered speculation ended with the Law disaster in France and the South Sea Bubble in England, but never disappeared, and sovereign debt in the meantime had grown exponentially. The latter generated fruitful experiments with stock markets and various securities, standard as well as stemming from tontines or lotteries. In London or Amsterdam, such securities were traded in what Isaac de Pinto called a 'game of shares',[9] frantic trading which already involved anticipations and futures markets, and short and long trades on stocks.

This was not a separate financial sphere; then just as now, financial transactions were linked to the so-called 'real' economy, not only through the Companies and Nations, the shares and sovereign debt of which were traded, but also because of the widespread use of securities as collateral for credit, and because financial players were also more often than not big traders: Hope, banker to the Kings, was also the man who provided Necker with emergency shipments of grain out of the Baltic in 1789. Indeed through exchange discounts the financial markets were present at the heart of every international commercial transaction. The 'artful' money changer was hard to separate from the international merchant articulating skilfully his payment flows, and arbitraging between the various places where he could send remittances. As Charles Carrière and his co-authors showed for Maison Roux in Marseille, exchange profits were closely intertwined with commercial profit.[10]

Logically, both commercial and financial profit was subjected to a process of religious, ethic and legal objectivation, providing standards for the legitimacy and acceptability of profit. This process was at the heart of the work of auditing Courts throughout Europe, such as the French Chambre de Justice or the post-Law debt reduction operation of the Visa; it underpinned the work of magistrates enforcing Assizes of Bread and other price controls for basic necessities in times of scarcity of grains or meat; it legitimized the decisions of clerks of the Contrôle Général or of the Navy Department reviewing and assessing the bills presented by war suppliers; it justified rescissions of contracts handed down by tribunals based on fraudulent intent. From the condemnations of rent buybacks at low price to the denunciations of monopolies and forestalling, the questioning of the origins of profit, of its legitimacy, of its possible reliance on an excessive gap between buying and selling prices, was a common thread which opened the way to the differentiation of legitimate and illegitimate profit, adding a new layer of complexity to the word.

Profit: How did it Work?

All this is what we know, what historiography tells us about the mental and material framework within which profit was deployed by the actors. What is missing is a detailed account of the operations and tools through which this apparently rather amorphous category took concrete shape in the minds and in the activities of the women and men who actually did 'make a profit', defined here provisionally the way Weber famously did: there is profit if, 'at the close of a business period, the balance of the enterprise in money assets (or, in the case of a continuous enterprise, the periodically estimated money value of assets) exceeds the capital, i.e. the estimated value of the material means of production used for acquisition in exchange'. As Weber also pointed out in the same paragraph, this implies 'always that a calculation of capital in terms of money is made, whether by modern book-keeping methods or in any other way'.[11] A final balance is, at some point, compared to a beginning balance, and the difference is what profit (or loss) has been made.

There lies the rub. For, as the preceding pages show, in the early modern period, in spite of what seems to us its straightforwardness, such a calculation did not give rise to an equivalent notion, which would clearly contain and express it. This is hardly surprising for historians of accounting, who have long confirmed that profit calculations, even widely defined in a Weberian way as a closing balance compared to an opening balance, were far from universal then. Even when they did take place, they did not necessarily lead to a calculation of a rate of profit; again, specialists in accounting history point out that the 'profit' calculation can be the calculation of a residual income (net profit minus the original capital), enough of an indication if the only issue is what is earned, as opposed to the calculation of a rate of profit (net profit divided by original capital), which must be calculated if one is interested in measuring one's profit as a rate of return, rather than an absolute value. And the second kind of calculation is not even enough to constitute a 'modern capitalist' computation, which has to take into account not only the capital originally invested, but all incomes, expenses and depreciations incurred, and the assets and liabilities at the end of the period. Each of these elements is necessary in order to unpack the profit-making process and thus be able to maximize the rate of return, not just to measure it (and to maximize it through productivity increases, which implies cost controls, if one wants to go further and stick to the Marxist definition of capitalism).[12]

By these more stringent standards, profit calculations were almost non-existent in the early modern period. Most economic agents did not even use double-entry accounting, and merely recorded incomes and expenses, and not even systematically so outside of the charge and discharge accounts of the stewards of great landholders. Double-entry bookkeeping did exist, but calculations of the return on original capital even for the few large operators who did use this kind of advanced accounting method were extremely limited, with no balance sheets drawn for several years on end, or when they were drawn, no obvious attempt at calculating a rate of return. A basic calculating mentality, with the simple calculation of income minus expenditure, with little regard to the original capital invested, was indeed widespread from the sixteenth century onwards, at least in England and increasingly in France. The slow transformation of this income into 'interest', a rate of return on the capital advanced originally, was an evolution characteristic of the seventeenth and eighteenth century. But there is not one instance of calculations allowing investors to know what accountants today call the return on investment before the nineteenth century, and such an elaborate form of control did not become widespread before the twentieth century.[13]

There were structural reasons for such a situation. As Basil Yamey has pointed out, wholesale trade at the time

> was subject to wide, frequent and largely unpredictable changes. Commercial conditions, more notably, but not only, in long-distance trade, were in large measure unstable. The experience of the recent past had little if any relevance for decisions to be taken in the immediate or near future; and there was often a long interval between the ordering or acquisition of goods and their eventual resale.[14]

Thus the very concerns which would have been most expected to trace profit, large firms with high levels of capital dealing in large quantities of goods, had little incentive to do so from a purely managerial point of view. As for smaller businesses, they were highly dependent on largely unpredictable long-term customer credit and dealt in relatively limited flows of value, so that profit recording would have seemed even more pointless.

Most cases of calculations of the simple return on capital originally invested, with no regard for the niceties of a return on investment, stemmed from the 'socialized' nature of the original capital of a firm, that is, its belonging to a partnership or a joint-stock company. This raises another issue: what Jean Bouvier called the 'declared profit' computed and made public to the partners or stockholders was an accounting representation constrained by the strategic choices of the managers with respect to the dividends/ reinvestment ratio, and thus not necessarily identical to the 'original profit', what the economists would want to know in order to build a proper model of the dynamics whereby profit in the firm was generated in the first place.[15] And of course the complete lack of fiscal pressure, with taxes conceived as either flat rates or even more frequently flat fees, always based on one's holdings, especially landholdings, meant that the main other motive for recording profits besides sharing them with partners or stockholders did not appear before the twentieth century either.

Profits were talked about, especially in the advertisements for various get-rich schemes from the sixteenth century onwards; most notably colonization overseas, and later on a number of joint-stock companies. But these 'declared profits' in Bouvier's sense, or rather promises thereof, could not be linked to any attempt at regulating the relationship between net profit in the modern sense and distributed dividends, to the point where the practice of paying dividends out of the capital was outlawed only in 1856 in France. In common law, it came under fire from the end of the nineteenth century onwards, but was entirely banned in Great Britain in 1980![16] On the whole, even within so-called 'socialized' capital, there seems to have been no tendency to set up tools enabling investors who were not managers to exert any kind of control over the costs and generally the strategies and choices through which these managers generated 'declared' profit. As long as the latter was forthcoming in the shape of dividends, nobody really cared how this positive result was achieved, and in case of repeated losses, investors just put an end to the concern and redistributed whatever was left of the original capital.

Another point of entry into the practical uses of profit in the eighteenth century would be the search for 'good practices'. These could be formalized through some legal-institutional rules, which, even if not enforced, would set a standard for practitioners. Another possible source would have been a generally accepted community standard, what these same practitioners themselves would have held to be necessary and proper, and which would have been enforced through some sort of Greifian community pressure. The first possibility at least can be dismissed fairly easily. In France, the *Ordonnance de 1673* was entirely focused on the prevention, or at least easy adjudication, of conflicts between practitioners. This royal regulation took its cue from government accounting practices, stressing the control of both receivables and disbursements through proper maintenance of a set of books, but ignoring almost entirely the general balance sheet, which merchants were required to draw up once every two years. English practice was even less demanding, since no balance at all was required, merely a set of account books which could be presented in conjunction with the oath of their owner regarding a given debt.[17]

The professional standards upheld through community pressure are harder to assess, but can be approached through the textbooks on double-entry book-keeping which started to multiply in the eighteenth century. Presumably, such textbooks would tell us what 'good practice' was according to people who considered themselves cognizant enough of the matter to write a textbook in the first place, and who would probably have avoided to run counter to the received wisdom of their intended audience. Of particular interest in this regard are the textbooks which enjoyed several print runs, a sign that they were widely taken as reasonably serious in their approach. However, there again we meet a rather ambiguous record, in which the obvious 'profit' motive turns out not to have been as central to bookkeeping promotion as one would expect.

A recent analysis of two of the most widespread textbooks in France and Great Britain, John Mair's *Book-Keeping Methodiz'd* (1736) and Mathieu de la Porte's *La science des négocians* (1783), concluded that on both sides of the Channel, accounting was primarily seen as a way to track credit; profit and loss calculations were more of an afterthought, a way to clean the accounts from the increases or decreases in capital stock with which each successful or failed operation was balanced. While many authors may have offered double-entry bookkeeping 'as a means of measuring profitability and changes in financial position', or of 'calculating profit and loss' on given merchandises, this was merely a potential usefulness, not a realized one, and there was remarkably little thought given either to calculations of rates of return, as opposed to gross residual income, or to how the components of a gain or loss on a particular account could be properly identified.[18] Indeed Mair himself, in spite of his apparently modern proposition that one could calculate 'the Gain or Loss upon the Sale' of a particular merchandise, systematically debited his profit and loss account with all operating expenses, with no regard to the link between these costs and the profit on a given sale.

All in all, the most prominent functions given double-entry accounting by textbooks were primarily as *ex post* tools of control, enabling an economic actor to assess his or her 'true position' at regular intervals, particularly what was owned to and by whom within the framework of an economy in which what really counted was circulating capital. The complexities of this circulation made necessary a careful tracking of this circulating capital, which constantly morphed into new ventures and accounts; this was the main justification. Even the overseeing of agents rarely appeared as a separate issue, which makes sense since the usual relationships were partnerships or commissions, and only a few large joint-stock companies dealing in overseas trade had to manage large numbers of autonomous employees, and therefore check their accounts.

As for the costs and return rates, these were mostly ignored; at least as long as the business was not stopped for some reason, such as dissolution, bankruptcy or death. But the ever-present threat of such a business death made it necessary to have one's accounts in order, to present them to the rest of the community and prove one's good faith – this was a moral obligation much more than an accounting one, akin to the necessity of presenting oneself for the Last Judgement with one's soul properly cleansed and ordered. And such an occasion for taking global stock of the business was rare. While the best authors[19] recommended a yearly balancing of the accounts, few of the economic agents of the time were as scrupulous in that particular subfield of their spiritual life.

Conclusion

To sum up: the way profit was generated, which would arguably be the core of the way merchants operated, is not obvious upon close examination. The theoretical record is confused at best, with none of the self-evidence with which 'profit' is endowed at least in popular discourse today. Which is less of a surprise when one turns to practice: neither the actual bookkeeping practised in the early modern era nor the private standards and public norms governing them then, point to a consistent view of profit as the core goal of merchant activity. While the necessity of a 'gain' was almost everywhere upheld in principle, it seems to have been surprisingly detached from actual calculation, almost as if this gain were not a simple mathematical issue of addition and subtraction. Would there be something more to early modern profit than adding and subtracting revenues and expenses? This is the question we ended up with, and the following essays attempt to answer it.

Assuming, as we do, that there was profit, but that this profit was not merely a matter of calculation with the proper data, how can we go beyond the relative silence of the most obvious sources, scholars, textbook authors and regulators? How can we capture a practice, the contents of which was not made clear by the agents themselves (leaving for the conclusion of this work the discussion of the reason why this was so)? Merchant profit was linked to a limited set of merchant artefacts, which made it possible and recorded it to a certain extent, essentially account books and merchant correspondence. By analysing closely and/or combining them, can we throw light on what 'profit' meant, or at least on why its meaning seemed so vague? Can we recapture the larger set of practices within which these artefacts were inserted, and with which they interact, and by rebuilding this material and mental system of reference, access its meaning better? Can we go beyond the affirmation of embeddedness, of some sort of moral economy or networking dimension which would impinge on an otherwise standard, rational-choice profit, and reach an integrated analysis of both moral and economic attitudes to profit as part and parcel of a socio-economic whole, as a *praxis* rather than a mere practice?[20]

Each of the essays in this collection addresses this core goal in one way or other. Part I, 'Understanding Merchant Transactions', focuses on accounting processes, and on the contents of the images they build. Yannick Lemarchand, Cheryl McWatters and Laure Pineau-Defois examine merchant archives of the eighteenth century and argue that the current account was the critical mechanism in linking merchants across space and time. The impressive administrative material, enabling merchants to manage complex and diverse networks, was not relied upon for strategic decision-making or for the calculation of profits; hence its value resided elsewhere in its role in establishing and maintaining co-operative exchange relations. Pierre Gervais, using both accounting textbooks and examples of double-entry accounting, also argues that the profit and loss account was actually not focused on profit measurement; rather, it was primarily a cleaning tool, which enabled the owner of the books to keep track of credit flows proper, while profit was rather seen as a holistic, non-quantitative result. Part II, 'The Credit Nexus and its Pitfalls', aims to describe the way in which profit or loss was a factor and/or a result in the credit interface which linked economic actors to their peers, thus exploring networking consequences on profit in a quantitative, rather than qualitative way. Julien Villain offers a detailed account of the way medium-sized traders in eastern France in the eighteenth century had to thread their way between the temporally contradictory demands of their short-term creditor suppliers and their long-term debitor customers, and how debt *per se* took a variety of shapes and paths according to the actors involved. Fred Grant, Jr, confirms in a very different setting that the nature and value of a debt was heavily time- and place-specific, and could change dramatically with the legal-institutional arrangements underpinning it. The highly variable value of Chinese debts to Europeans in Canton thus underscores the difficulties of building a robust creditor–debtor relationship. This naturally leads to Part III, 'Beyond Price Signals: The Institutional Framework', which looks at the way the institutionalized frameworks of reference which constituted an integral and necessary part of the functioning of the merchant economy could be commonly built. Xabier Lamikiz shows how in a transatlantic world in which price signals were actually of little use, apparently highly inefficient institutional organizations such as the Spanish *flotas* could actually serve as a basis for complex processes of negotiation and decision-making aimed at reducing risks and uncertainties, operating just as well (or just as inefficiently) as private flows of information in other periods. Dominique Margairaz points to the categories of goods and their underpinnings in public policies as again more essential than price signals and similar classical manifestations of markets in structuring merchant transactions. Part IV, 'Diversification and Risk Management', explores how various social and institutional tools were brought to bear on these same merchant transactions to alleviate further the risks and uncertainties inherent in them, as well as the limits of these tools. Boris Deschanel studies the Pinet family of Gap, in the French Alps, and the way it created and maintained its dominant regional position before and through the French Revolution by combining political and economic power, showing yet again that mere quantitative, or even mere economic, assessments of profit missed a good deal of the mechanisms through which this profit was generated. Similarly, Steve Sarson points at the vagaries of the tobacco markets and shows how a business-savvy slaveholding planters's wife in the South of the United States ended up using merchant techniques such as speculative hoarding, product diversification, insider trading and also social networking as conscious tools for economic success.

We will leave the assessment of the overall result of these various scholarly efforts to the general conclusion Robert S. DuPlessis kindly accepted to provide, in which he offers his own reading of merchant profit and the study thereof. As for the us, we do believe that the time has come to reassess the very notion of profit, and to recapture it into a historicizing process which at the very least would prompt historians to better qualify its use and take better care to point to the period to which they want to refer to when using it. While merchant profit in the eighteenth century was undoubtedly a core focus of merchant activities, it neither referred to the contents nor to the processes which we too often blithely ascribe to this notion on the basis of twentieth- and twenty-first-century experiences. Rarely computed *ex post*, even more rarely predicted *ex ante*, always mixed with other, qualitative business processes which made such computations futile anyway, early modern profit was a set of beliefs, much more than a set of figures. Recapturing its operations has required us to forget our preconceptions, and we hope that this volume will help other readers to discover in turn the unexpectedly exotic intellectual territories of merchant profit in the Age of Commerce.

1 THE CURRENT ACCOUNT AS COGNITIVE ARTEFACT: STORIES AND ACCOUNTS OF *LA MAISON CHAURAND*

Yannick Lemarchand, Cheryl McWatters and Laure Pineau-Defois

Introduction

For more than sixty years, the controversy concerning the role of double-entry bookkeeping in the emergence and expansion of capitalism, initiated by the works of Werner Sombart and Max Weber, has played itself out in the accounting literature. This debate, as noted by W. Funnell and J. Robertson,[1] has centred primarily on developments in England to the neglect of those elsewhere. Funnell and Robertson examine Dutch and German accounting texts of the sixteenth century to test Sombart's thesis, concluding that at this time 'a capitalistic form of double-entry bookkeeping was a curiosity in the north Netherlands, notably Amsterdam'.[2] While in broad agreement with their argument with respect to the desirability of expanding this energetic debate to other contexts, our approach differs from their study in two significant ways: context and critique. First, our research context is the eighteenth-century French trade. Second, our story has a distinctly different angle in that we are not so much debating the adoption or non-adoption of double-entry bookkeeping to test Sombartian claims or more recently, those of R. A. Bryer.[3] To the contrary, our analyses indeed confirm that double-entry systems were utilized and these techniques highly developed, a feature that we have confirmed in other archives of this period. Instead our preoccupation resides elsewhere: if double-entry accounting was not employed for purposes of profit determination *à la* Sombart, what were the purposes for its adoption and development? Our investigations into this puzzle focus on the archive of a major family of *négociants*,[4] *les Chaurand*, established in Nantes, France in the second half of the eighteenth century and the accounting methods used by these merchants.[5] The overarching objective of our research, based on our examination to date of accounting data along with a variety of other archival documents, is to better comprehend what the Chaurand family might have been able 'to discern' in their account books, the information that they might have found there and perhaps more speculatively, to offer insights into the information that they might have been seeking.

Despite our inability to respond definitively to these last points, it is possible to identify what they apparently were not seeking, once one establishes that they dispensed with several of the possibilities provided by tools at their disposal, chiefly those tools that would have permitted the calculation of their annual profits. This observation, which has led us to question the role that these merchants *did* assign to their accounting, is all the more pertinent given the enduring dominance of the double-entry discourse in accounting historiography. While differing in degree, Sombart[6] and Weber[7] have considered the properties of double-entry accounting, which the Chaurand brothers apparently neglected, to have played a defining role in the birth and rise of capitalism: utilizing a capital account, establishing a balance sheet, calculating financial results.

Nevertheless, despite this 'sub-optimal' use of the techniques at their disposal, *les Chaurand* developed their business affairs to great success. Moreover, if their accounting did not correspond in totality to the ideal type promoted by bookkeeping treatises, it was far from being rudimentary. Their archives reveal instead a very elaborate administrative and accounting apparatus, going well beyond what was prescribed by the *Ordonnance du commerce* of 1673 yet well suited, it seems, to the variety, scope and complexity of their business affairs. The management of multiple operations in which they were implicated, as well as the tracking of accounts opened with their partners and those of their trade and investment portfolio, constituted undoubtedly the principal mission assigned to this accounting system.

The arguments advanced by Sombart and Weber have been thoroughly and enthusiastically discussed, including the capacity of double-entry accounting to furnish a pertinent aid to decision making. Our examination of the Chaurand account books[8] presents an opportunity to renew this debate but also to re-focus it. Our deep immersion into the tangible reality of these merchant practices fosters a better understanding of the underlying issues related to the utilization and potential contribution of double-entry accounting in the pre-industrial era. Allowing for the odd exception, profit determination has always been the privileged question in these discussions; its being the principal point of demarcation between double-entry bookkeeping and other less sophisticated accounting methods. However, many other aspects, considered secondary or relating to routine practices and devoid of interest, have been neglected.

Such neglect has been the fate of the functioning of the commonplace current (debit and credit) account. The role of this elementary yet fundamental accounting 'object' deserves to be reconsidered by going beyond the narrow perspective of accounting at the service of rational calculation for a single actor. By moving from the individual to the collective, from the unilateral to the multilateral, our aim is to comprehend it as an instrument for establishing relations across a set of multiple actors undertaking among themselves various transactions all the while pursuing their own individual objectives. In this vein, we adopt the concept of 'cognitive artefact' defined by D. A. Norman as 'an artificial instrument conceived to retain, make evident or act on information so as to serve a representational function'.[9]

After an initial presentation of *la Maison Chaurand* in the context of eighteenth-century commerce in Nantes, we return to our main themes relative to the cognitive artefacts, the theses of Sombart and Weber, and finally conclude our story by developing the role of the current account.

The Material: The Archives of the Maison Chaurand

Eighteenth-Century Trade in Nantes

The port of Nantes managed to maintain its place as the second-ranking French port of the eighteenth century after Bordeaux, and to overcome the competition posed by Marseille and Le Havre, thanks not only to the entrepreneurial spirit of Nantes merchants but equally due to its favoured geographic position.

From the outset, the geographic situation of the city of Nantes conferred upon it a strategic advantage in terms of commercial development. This location enabled it to exploit readily the French maritime and colonial system, centred on the Atlantic, and by the same logic, to take advantage of its relations with an immense hinterland, structured by the hydrographical network of the Loire and its tributaries. The Loire was one of the principal communication routes of the country, taken by thousands of vessels and which assured the Nantes–Paris link via the canal of Orléans and the Loing River.

Beginning in the early thirteenth century, Nantes turned its gaze to the Atlantic. The Newfoundland cod fishery first played an important role in capital accumulation, supported and then surpassed by its relations with the Antilles beginning in the 1680s.[10] In effect, the growth of the port rested largely on its relations with the colonies in the Antilles, principally Saint-Domingue; shipping known as *la droiture antillaise*[11] as well as the slave trade represented two complementary pillars of the city's prosperity. Nantes occupied the position as the principal French port for the outfitting (*l'armement*) of ships during the first half of the eighteenth century but saw itself gradually distanced by Bordeaux.[12] Nevertheless, at the eve of the Revolution, Nantes remained the first-ranked port in terms of the slave trade and second in importance for colonial trade.

Maritime outfitting continued to be the linchpin of commercial enterprise in the city throughout the eighteenth century and all the major families, the new port elites, participated en masse. These elites were *négociants-armateurs*.

Yet as noted by J. Meyer, 'the outfitting of vessels was only one form of commerce amongst others, certainly essential but encompassing only a part of it'.[13] The other branch was *le négoce* and all of the activities that it incorporated: commission sales, consignment of merchandise, chartering, re-exporting. Thus, in a global sense, the *négociants* participated in the circulation of merchandise by practising trade in all its forms. In the eighteenth century, a major *négociant* at Nantes was also a major *armateur* who also owned plantations in the colonial islands. Nonetheless he worked equally to maintain relations with the hinterland of Nantes, of France more widely and with other parts of Europe to stock up on merchandise for export, along with the practical necessity of finding outlets for the colonial staples that he imported.

The world of *le négoce* was characterized by three principal features: its international dimension, its network functioning and the versatility of its operations.[14] It is often not straightforward to distinguish the activities involved especially as they were superimposed and intermingled, but one can state that the *négociant* was an intermediary, an essential link in the commercial chain of the eighteenth century, providing the bridge between the place of merchandise production and that of its consumption. The *négociant* dealt in both the importing and exporting of merchandise, played the role of commission agent equally for buying and selling and acted as a consignor for trade goods. What we hope to tease out in more concrete terms is the professional reality to which these activities referred.

If we attempt to define these activities technically, here is what we can say: in commercial and maritime law, the commission agent was a *négociant* who undertook commercial operations on account of a third party known as *le commettant*, receiving thereby a commission that represented his remuneration; the consignor for his part was a *négociant* to whom one addressed merchandise that he received in stock and/or took care of selling. The consignor therefore also represented a commission-agent intermediary. As one can quickly see at the level of definitions, the approaches were divided neatly into sectors but one would be hard pressed in fact to draw the fine line between commission and consignment activities. It appears, from the analysis of our sources, that the *négociant* did not undertake either the role of commission agent, or that of consignor, but rather often filled concurrently these different functions as opportunity arose.

On the one hand, *négociants* found themselves acting simultaneously as purchase commission agents, when they contacted their suppliers of fabrics, wines or other merchandise; as sales commission agents and as consignors when they received colonial staple goods from the Antilles. On the other hand, the most important *négociants nantais*,[15] following the example of the Chaurand family studied here, were property owners in the colonial islands. Thus, beyond the commissions earned on merchandise bought and sold for third parties, they also marketed their colonial production, as well as simply purchasing goods to resell 'as is' on their own account. Finally, as their account books reveal, they were highly versatile. They acted as insurers, invested in bottomry loans[16] and undertook banking operations such as the discounting and collection of commercial bills, as well as participating in a diverse set of speculative activities in conjunction with other merchants. The profits of the *négociant* – *armateur*, planter, insurer, lender, banker, etc. – stemmed from the multiplicity of functions and activities that he fulfilled.

The Chaurand Family

With ancestral roots in the Alps of Haute-Provence and descended from the *bourgeoisie de robe*, Honoré Chaurand settled in Nantes during the 1740s. His marriage to Marie Portier de Lantimo in 1748 signalled the beginning of his economic and social ascension. This alliance with one of the most notable families of *négociants nantais* was most certainly because he already possessed a personal fortune of consequential size. The marriage contract concluded between the couple indicates that Honoré possessed 150,000 livres that belonged to him on his own account.[17] This significant sum derived from real estate that he owned in Provence, at Valensole, and also a plantation in la Martinique, La Jambette, of which he held a one-half share interest with a certain Sieur Bérard. In fact, Chaurand had already started to interest himself in colonial trade, founding a company in la Martinique in 1744, with Antoine Bérard and Louis Rateau, *négociants* from Bordeaux, and Joubert and Boimafour, probably *négociants* in the colonies. Despite its being organized in la Martinique, company operations actually were established at le Cap in Saint-Domingue.[18] Even if the origins of Honoré Chaurand's fortune remains somewhat blurry, it is clear that once he arrived in Nantes, he was able to integrate himself easily into the milieu. On a final note, Jean Meyer estimated the fortune of Honoré Chaurand in the 1750s to be as much as 500,000 livres, after the integration of his wife's dowry established at 106,000 livres.[19]

Honoré Chaurand purchased a *charge anoblissante*[20] in 1751 and some landholdings in the following years. Scarcely ten years after his arrival in Nantes, he was elected *juge consul* by the *négociants nantais* and was counted henceforth among the most powerful members of Nantes society. An interesting question is the facility with which Honoré Chaurand was assimilated into this merchant world; it appears, in the final analysis, that until the 1770s he devoted only a minor portion of his activities to trade strictly speaking. Instead, Chaurand acted above all as an investor before actually being a *négociant*. His investment strategy led him to take share interests in a number of vessels outfitted *en droiture* and for the triangular trade. Of his thirty-two such investments made between 1752 and 1771, seventeen were in slaving voyages.[21] When the voyages in the long-distance trade – from France to the îles Bourbon as well as to the East Indies

– became open after the suspension of the monopoly of la Compagnie des Indes in 1769, Honoré Chaurand placed investments in these areas of endeavour. The variety of his financial investments bear witness to a truly speculative mentality: he held interests in tax farms (le Minage,[22] les Fermes de Bretagne), the Indian Ocean both in terms of exports and redistribution, *cambies*, purchases at Lorient, the slave trade (vessels from Nantes and La Rochelle), *la droiture*, and in the redistribution of goods to Northern Europe as well as Spanish America.

In short, Honoré Chaurand was a *brasseur d'affaires*, in today's parlance, a big businessman, the quintessential example of the country land-based fortune redeployed into large-scale commerce. From the investments in the Antilles in the 1740s, arrival in Nantes and then the alliance with les Portier in 1748, the financing of tax farms, and ultimately to the share interests in trading vessels beginning in 1751 – the completion of a picture-perfect process – he immersed himself in the world of *le grand négoce*. The final touch was his becoming an *armateur* on his own account from 1771. However, this latter activity was only really developed by his sons beginning in 1774 with Honoré being content to participate in a more moderate fashion in this sector – he outfitted his own vessel *La Comtesse de Menou* for Saint-Domingue only four times. The objective, it seemed, was to leave his sons on a solid financial footing and with some experience of the sea. Honoré Chaurand did not grow up in the merchant milieu and the training that his eldest sons were given rather confirms this fact in that it privileged formal studies over maritime experience. In all likelihood it was this gap that he wished to fill in embarking on the outfitting of ships and in encouraging his sons to follow his example.

The training followed by the Chaurand brothers was in keeping with that given to all young gentleman of the period. We focus on the two eldest as it is the archive of their company that we have studied. Honoré-Anne pursued his studies at the Oratoire de Nantes then completed sojourns in Lisbon, London, Hamburg and Paris. As for Pierre-Louis, whose education was entrusted to one Henry Casthaing, he assumed the responsibility for outfitting vessels for the trading house and reserved the right to manage dealings with banking houses.

Honoré-Anne and Pierre-Louis founded their commercial enterprise on 20 September 1774 under the name Chaurand Frères. The articles of incorporation indicated, among other conditions, that the duration of the partnership was for nine years and that each partner would provide one half of the capital funds.[23] The two brothers had participated financially in the last vessel outfitted by their father in 1774 and the profits earned from this venture enabled them undoubtedly to raise the necessary capital, which amounted to 140,000 livres when the partnership was created.[24] Despite a rather unpromising start, due to the bankruptcy of the Babut trading house in Amsterdam, the operations carried out by the two brothers proved to be profitable as some data from their accounts will later demonstrate. In the 1780s, Chaurand Frères further developed their trade and their network extended from one side of Europe to the other and across the Atlantic to Saint-Domingue, so much so that their firm capital had grown by 1785 to 2,000,000 livres.[25] The war of American Independence proved highly lucrative for *les Chaurand*; between 1776 and 1784 they appear to have earned the greatest profits. Encouraged by the good results of their business affairs, the two brothers came to regular agreement to extend the duration of their partnership. In 1783, the deadline date for the first nine years established by the initial contract, they signed a new one for seven years, then for an additional ten years on 1 January 1790.[26] At the end of 1793, the firm of Chaurand Frères had assets in the millions. Notwithstanding all of this apparent success, the firm went into liquidation in 1806; the definitive loss of Saint-Domingue and the return to war against England eventually won out and got the better of the previous glory days of the Atlantic trade.

The Archive – the Fonds Chaurand

The composition of the archive is interesting in itself as it provides initial tangible evidence of the administrative and accounting organization put in place by the two brothers, well beyond the documents required by the *Ordonnance du commerce* of 1673. The requirements that concerned them were presented in articles I and VII of titre III (*Des livres et registres des négocians, marchands et banquiers*):

> Article I. *Négociants* and merchants, both wholesale and retail, will have a book that contains all of their trade, their bills of exchange, their active and passive debts and the funds used for the maintenance of their household.
>
> Article VII. Every *négociant* and merchant, both wholesale and retail, will put in bundles the missive letters that they receive, and record a copy of those that they write.[27]

Beyond this book, which article V made clear was referring to a journal, and the registers and bundles of correspondence, *les Chaurand* utilized most certainly a general ledger, within the framework of double-entry bookkeeping. Their administrative tools included a series of other registers, some of which were specific to certain activities:

> *carnets de caisse* (cash book)
> *comptes de vente* (sales accounts)
> *brouillards de factures* (invoice blotter)
> *livres de factures* (invoice books)
> *livres de magasin* (warehouse book)
> *lettres et billets à payer* (letters and bills payable)
> *livres d'armement et désarmement*[28] (ledgers for vessel outfitting and laying up)
> *livres des assurances* (insurance books)

In total, there are more than eighty volumes covering the period 1774–93, though with a few gaps.

The entries recorded in the journal of the firm of Chaurand Frères from 22 October 1774 to 31 December 1775, then for the first three months of 1784, were collected and integrated into a relational database. This chapter reports results based on our manipulation of this data set, as well as our analyses of various other archival elements.

Capitalism and Accounting

Weber, Sombart and the Ongoing Controversy

Beginning with the early articles of Basil Yamey,[29] many authors have examined and re-examined the relationship between capitalism and accounting: S. Pollard,[30] J. O. Winjum,[31] K. S. Most,[32] B. G. Carruthers and W. Espeland,[33] M. Nikitin,[34] Y. Lemarchand,[35] R. A. Bryer[36] and most recently but rather indirectly, Yamey;[37] not to overlook E. Chiapello,[38] J. R. Edwards et al.,[39] S. Basu et al.,[40] J. S. Toms[41] and Funnell and Robertson.[42] Rich discussions of these debates can be found elsewhere, for instance Chiapello,[43] Toms[44] and Funnell and Robertson.[45] We do not attempt to re-state this literature or to repeat the exercise but instead frame the debate in more general and condensed terms.

Weber raised this topic in *Wirtschaftsgeschichte Abriss der Universalen Sozial-und Wirtschaftsgeschichte*, translated by F. H. Knight as *General Economic History*.[46] The original volume published student notes from a lecture series presented by Weber in 1919–20, shortly before his death (14 June 1920), texts initially collected at the request of his widow Marianne Weber. It linked and connected four concepts that have since engendered much controversy, capitalist rationality, double-entry, capital account and profit calculation:

> Capitalism is present wherever the industrial provision for the needs of a human group is carried out by the method of enterprise, irrespective of what need is involved. More specifically, a rational capitalistic establishment is one with capital accounting, that is, an establishment which determines its income yielding power by calculation according to the methods of modern bookkeeping and the striking of a balance.[47]

Depending on one's persuasion, one could consider that Sombart in *Der moderne Kapitalismus* had been much stronger in his opinions and gone even further in affirming:

> The essential characteristic of double-entry bookkeeping had undoubtedly this objective: to track the complete cycle of the capital of an enterprise, to quantify it and to record it in writing ... For the first time, thanks to these two new elements ['profit and loss' account and 'capital' account], double-entry bookkeeping allowed for the understanding, without a break, of the complete cycle of capital: from the capital

> account to the stock accounts, then to the profit and loss account, to return lastly to the capital account.[48]

Yamey was one of the first to issue an opinion radically opposed, based first on the study of British manuals of the seventeenth and eighteenth centuries,[49] then on the examination of a set of merchant archives dating from the same period.[50] His first judgement is unequivocal:

> The evidence is largely against the view that the merchants of the period required anything more from their ledgers and journals than a clear and ready record of transactions for easy reference, and descriptive details of their cash, merchandise, and other assets bought and sold. Double-entry bookkeeping, to the extent that it was adopted in practice, could bring order and system to such records and so contribute towards the 'methodising' of business life ... However, this role of systematic bookkeeping, important as it is, is considerably more circumscribed than the other roles ascribed to it by some.[51]

He reiterated his argument with equal force fifteen years later: 'In fact knowledge of the total profit of an enterprise for a period, either absolutely or in relation to the amount of capital in the enterprise, is rarely necessary or useful for business decision-making within that enterprise'.[52] Then further:

> The business man wanted to have an accounting reminder of the existence of his claims (even if their effective enforcement were doubtful), and was well aware, from the descriptions in the asset-accounts and from his knowledge of his firm's affairs, of the real nature and probable value of these assets. Calculation and quantification were less important than the availability of records for ordinary administration.[53]

This debate 'for and against' Sombartian claims, the extent to which Weber supported or moderated them, and the various challenges beginning with those of Yamey has met with renewed interest in the past decade especially in the reaction to the seminal papers by Bryer.[54] Funnell and Robertson recently have challenged Bryer's thesis and broadened the horizon by shifting the discussion to the Dutch context.[55] Thus, one might reasonably ask what further contribution could be made to this controversy. Our response is two-fold and one which we believe the evidence of the Chaurand archives corroborates. First, as argued by Yamey, profit calculation was not a characteristic of double-entry systems of this period, but as we intend to indicate, double-entry was a requisite once commerce attained a certain scale and scope.[56] Second, notwithstanding that merchants hardly ever called upon double-entry accounting as a tool for providing profit calculations or for making strategic decisions, it did not preclude its otherwise playing a fundamental role in the birth and expansion of modern capitalism. We later explore the second point through the concept of cognitive artefact.

The Accounts of les Chaurand and Profit Calculation

The Diversity of Operations

To underscore our earlier comments concerning merchant activities, the list of the types of operations recorded in the Chaurand's journal during the first year of the firm's existence (1774–5) offers an initial glimpse into the diversity and importance of their own operations. The latter would multiply over the next ten years, notably the outfitting of vessels, for both the trade *en droiture* and the slave trade. One significant characteristic of the port trade, namely risk diversification, also stands out. This diversification was pursued through joint participation such as merchandise held in common, vessel share interests and *les pacotilles*,[57] but evident also in the speculative protection against the risks assumed by others, such as insurance syndicates and bottomry loans. Any number of ways existed to grow one's capital by dividing it to shield oneself as much against commercial risks as the hazards at sea.

Commission operations

- *Purchases on account of a third party and shipment* (brandy for Amsterdam).
- *Sales on account of a third party* (coral from Marseille).

Joint Operations

- *Merchandise in common, one-half, one-third, etc.* (principally with *négociants* from Amsterdam).
- *Outfitting of vessels in co-proprietorship* (*La Comtesse de Menou*, ¼).
- *Share interest in vessels outfitted by third parties* (*Le Lion*, 1/12; *Le Dominique*, 1/24).
- *Insurance* (insurance on account of a third party).
- *Pacotilles* (*pacotille* on account of a third party with Berthomé, captain of the vessel *La Comtesse de Menou*).

Operations on one's own account

- *Bottomry loans* (4,000 livres on *La Bricole*, 5,000 on *La Comtesse de Ségur*).
- *Insurance* (on the vessel *la Brune* of Bordeaux).
- *Exchange operations* (foreign exchange gains on drafts drawn at Amsterdam).
- *Banking operations* (negotiation, discounting and collection of trade paper).
- *Financing operations* (issuances of drafts and promissory notes).

Initial Observations

Our first question was to establish from the Chaurand accounts the information that they might have found in terms of profit understanding and thereby, to tease out the accounting perception of profit. We can state right away that there was no effort to calculate a periodic and global profit result, contrary to what the accounting manuals of the time advocated. Opened in 1774, the accounts were not closed and transferred to a new general ledger until 31 December 1783, at the expiration of the initial partnership agreement, when the partnership was extended for another seven years. Only a variety of partial results were calculated, considered perhaps to be the only ones pertinent. Several net results, such as profits on speculative activities – the interest on bottomry loans in situations where the vessel for which the loan had been made returned to its home port safe and sound – were transferred to the profit and loss account once identified. This treatment was also the case for losses on active insurance agreements. The debit and credit entries were made from time to time to the profit and loss account, without any specific periodic recapitulation, other than a summation at the end of each page when moving to a new one. In April 1777, the balance of the commissions account was transferred to the credit of the profit and loss account but why at this particular time and for what particular reason are not evident.

Certain operating accounts never seem to have been closed. Expenses and revenues continued to accumulate in the debit and credit columns of many accounts. This situation was sometimes the case with vessel share interests. We know that such accounts often remained open due to the anticipation of further returns, nonetheless it does not rule out their apparent lapse for other reasons. While our answers remain provisional, a general impression emerges. Despite the scope and size of the administrative and accounting apparatus produced and of which a few figures next will illustrate, the calculation of profits was not a dominate preoccupation of *les Chaurand*. Thus, in our view, the utility of accounting resided elsewhere.

A Paint-by-Numbers illustration of *les Chaurand*: Business Volume and Partners

The data collection to date covers two periods: the early beginnings of the firm Chaurand Frères from 22 October 1774 to 31 December 1775, then the first three months of 1784 after the prolongation of the firm. 1,530 lines of entries have been captured for the first three months of 1784 compared to only 970 for the fourteen months of the first period. The average monthly volume of administrative work therefore had increased by 7.5 times. In the same interval, the average total of the monthly flow of funds recorded in the accounts (total debits and total credits, which obviously are the same) had multiplied by fourteen. The total flows recorded at the end of 1775 had grown to approximately 2,050,000 livres in fourteen months, compared to 4,700,000 livres in the first three months of 1784 alone. These figures indicate not only a net expansion of activity but that this activity was accompanied by an almost doubling of the average unit volume of transactions.

The operations dealing with financial paper – issuance, negotiation (purchase or sale), discounting, presentation for collection or endorsement of bills of exchange and promissory notes – also provide an indication of the intensity of the firm's activity. In 1774–5, almost 400 drafts were handled, either inflow or outflow, at an average amount of approximately 2,800 livres. Eliminating Sundays and other holidays, roughly one draft per day was received or issued at the trading house of the two brothers. At the beginning of 1784, the figure was roughly four drafts per day that were handled for a slightly higher average amount of 4,000 livres. On 1 January 1784, the portfolio of bills and letters of exchange receivable contained fifty-five instruments for a total of 512,520 livres, whereas it also included ninety-eight letters and bills payable totalling 814,200 livres. One final important detail, there were at the same date 853 *billets de prime* to pay, that is premiums corresponding to that number of maritime insurance contracts taken out by *les Chaurand* on their own behalf or on account for a third party.

The various partners of Chaurand Frères are present in two different ways in the accounts. First there are those for whom a nominative account was opened. If on 31 December 1775, only thirty-six accounts of this type existed, there were 132 by 1 January 1784, as outlined in Table 1.1. A quick analysis of this table allows one to appreciate the importance of credit tracking *vis-à-vis* their partners in the Antilles. While the latter comprised 30% of the debtors, they also represented 70% of the credit outstanding with third parties. This figure is moreover revelatory in terms of the fragility of the enterprise, whose prosperity was overly linked to the fate of the Antilles and would be liquidated with the irrevocable loss of Saint-Domingue in 1806.

Yet many other actors – individuals and corporations – were in direct or indirect contact with the two brothers within the context of their business activity, without as far as we know having an account opened in their name. One finds approximately 260 actors in the journal entries in the first year and another 170 who intervene during the first three months of 1784. They were a diverse group, quite probably small-scale suppliers or clients, and the transactions in which they were involved also were handled through 'sundries' or 'miscellaneous individuals'. These actors were often intermediaries involved in the shipment of merchandise – consignors, ship captains, bargers or common carriers – and finally other *négociants* implicated in one capacity or another in finance operations as a drawee/er, beneficiary, endorser or discounter of trade paper, or acting in the role of insurers.

Our intention is not to provide a micro description of the extensive operating situation of *la Maison Chaurand*. Instead delving into the accounts and the numbers can enrich our perceptions and understanding of the important administrative and accounting techniques that such an organization required. This tracking of accounts and the players involved also provides a greater appreciation for the role assigned to accounting *at this point in time*. It is certainly difficult, after having examined in detail accounting records such as those of *la Maison Chaurand*, to accept the earlier reasoning of Yamey, that a 'system of single entry, with personal accounts for debtors and creditors as well as a cash account, provides a large part of the information necessary in routine administration'.[58] In our view, once activities surpassed a certain scale and scope, one could do without neither operating and asset accounts nor double-entry accounting if one wished to disentangle the resulting maze of relations among multiple actors.

Table 1.1: Distribution of partners for whom nominative accounts were open on 1 January 1784.

Types of partners and location	Debit balance		Number of partners		Credit balance		Number of partners		Total	
	Amounts (*livres*)	%	No.	%	Amounts (*livres*)	%	No.	%	No.	%
Plantation owners	589,460	54	9	11					9	7
Colonists, *négociants*, brokers	175,136	16	16	19	52,697	15	5	10	21	16
Partners in the Antilles	*764,596*	***70***	*25*	***30***	*52,697*	*15*	*5*	*10*	*30*	*23*
Foreign *négociants*	*54,466*	*5*	*5*	*6*	*1,182*	*0*	*4*	*8*	*9*	*7*
French *négociants* (beyond Nantes)	110,978	10	27	33	94,327	26	21	43	48	36
Négociants nantais	59,422	5	10	12	25,498	7	6	12	16	12
Family-related accounts	13,410	1	5	6	128,283	35	4	8	9	7
Metropolitan trade	*183,810*	*17*	*42*	*51*	*248,108*	***68***	*31*	***63***	*73*	*55*
Banking houses	*4,105*	*0*	*3*	*4*	*56,037*	*15*	*5*	*10*	*8*	*6*
Unspecified	*92,850*	*8*	*8*	*10*	*4,834*	*1*	*4*	*8*	*12*	*9*
Total	**1,099,827**	**100**	**83**	**100**	**362,858**	**100**	**49**	**100**	**132**	**100**

Refocusing the Debate

Beyond the apparent indifference for the utilization of accounting tools for the purposes of calculating financial results, what the Chaurand archive reveals to us (and as other similar accounting archives do also) is that accounting could not be reduced solely to the technical device and specific mechanisms of double-entry bookkeeping. It was accompanied by the construction and development of a series of auxiliary books and ledgers designed for the capture and elaboration of data, which were then recorded in the journal, synthesized or not depending on the situation, or originated from this same journal and intended to be processed in a specific context.[59] These registers might also have provided for a more detailed tracking of certain elements, for example trade paper, letters and bills payable/receivable, and insurance premium notes. Moreover, French bookkeeping manuals of the period made reference to them, following the example of Mathieu de La Porte[60] or those books which deal more specifically with maritime commerce such as those authored by C. F. Gaignat de l'Aulnais,[61] E. Degrange[62] and P. B. Boucher.[63]

Thus it is the administrative apparatus in its entirety of this 'information system' that must be considered if we wish to appreciate the utility of accounting in the development of commerce and thereby the later development of industrial capitalism. This analysis shifts the debate from one centred on the utility of accounting for the specific individual (or entity) who maintained it to one focused on the role it might have played in the emergence and functioning of merchant networks, which became increasingly complex and ramified, and in the expansion of commercial activity. In our opinion, this approach requires moving from an individual or unilateral view to a collective or multilateral vision of accounting.

The Account as Cognitive Artefact

As noted at the outset, a 'cognitive artefact' is as an 'artificial instrument conceived to retain, make evident or act on information so as to serve a representational function'.[64] Acting as an external memory for its users, this cognitive instrument facilitates the development of operations and influences, additionally, the perceptions that actors will have of each other. While reminding each other of his or her obligations, it establishes confidence through the possibility for scrutiny and mutual control that it provides them. We introduce the concept of the cognitive artefact by first looking at a relatively primitive 'accounting object', the tally stick, before moving to the more complex (yet seemingly commonplace) current account.

Tally and Counter-Tally

Tally sticks are among the oldest 'accounting objects' known, if not the oldest,[65] and were still used in France in the middle of the twentieth century in certain retail shops such as bakeries. The *Thrésor de la langue francoyse* defines the tally in the following manner:

> A small piece of wood, on which with notches or incisions one records the count and the number of something; and comes from the Latin word *Talea*. Accordingly one speaks of taking bread, wine, and other things by the tally, *Taleae caesuris ac crenis amphorarum vini, panum, modiorum alteriusve rei numerum notare*. And from this meaning comes tally, for the tribute imposed on the people to be paid to the Prince, as much perhaps as tax collectors, assessor or distributors of some subsidy previously had granted on each tally holder, his tribute quantity marked or notched on these small sticks. Accordingly, one says, to impose or to tax the tally and the tally-holder – he and she who are subject to paying the tally.[66]

More concretely, a stick of wood is split into two symmetrical halves, one of which – the tally or stock – was retained by the shopkeeper, whereas the other – the counter-tally or foil – was given to the client. At each sale, the shopkeeper would juxtapose the two halves, and then carve them simultaneously, making as many notches as necessary depending upon the size of the transaction.

This accessory object to credit operations – it was not indispensable – symbolized the underlying relationship. Adopting the terminology of S. Jubé,[67] the object served a function of *rappel* or 'recall', of one's rights on the one hand and of one's obligations on the other. Buyer and seller knew at any time the amount of credit agreed upon. In the case of litigation, the tally or the counter-tally constituted a means of proof: a non-written contractual proof which the French Civil Code has maintained in that article 1333 devoted to it remains in effect. In the chapter entitled 'of the proof of obligations and of that of payment', this article is worded: 'The tallies corresponding to their counter-tallies bear witness between individuals who are in the habit of declaring in this way the supplies that they make or purchase'.[68]

Yet litigation was expected to be the exception; what was expected by both the seller and the client was that this relationship would be long-term in nature and that after each payment, a new period of credit would unfold. Thus, other than the fact that it saved the seller the trouble of memorization, an effort that quickly could become onerous, the object and its successive manipulations participated in the construction of confidence between the two partners. As Jubé notes, 'the institution of confidence – of *credit* – presupposed that each party would be reminded of the fair execution of his obligations'.[69] The current account (and the statement of account prepared from it) operated in the same manner between two merchants. This object, however, possessed one additional property: it could play the role of money.

The Current Account

For accountants and accounting, the current account has long ceased to be the focus of attention. The common debit or credit account, whose balance changed along with transactions that were recorded in it and which was the foundational element for single-entry, double-entry or even mixed systems (those which combined charge and discharge accounting with debit and credit accounts). Although the term now has a more restricted sense, particularly in the banking sector, we adopt the expression 'current account' for the account in debit or credit opened on account of a third party, in accordance with earlier usage as it was referred to at the beginning of the nineteenth century by the jurist Dalloz: 'There is a current account between two *négociants*, as soon as there is a credit or debit between them for commercial affairs. There is some basic knowledge needed about this matter and for this one need only consult the first bookkeeper to come along'.[70]

However, this account was not simply a framework for recording accounting entries. It was an accessory of the credit process, following upon the example of the tally; it also was a payment instrument. With origins in banking practice, the current account provided a means to complete payments without the physical movement of funds, either through the transfers from account to account, or more readily, between partners, who were at the same time both supplier and client one of the other; this scenario being a frequent one in commerce of the period. All that was necessary was the rudimentary clearing of the account. By its very functioning, it effected novation, in the legal sense of the term,[71] by converting a set of debt or credit obligations into new ones, the value of which corresponded to the account balance at time *t*. While the legal theorization is relatively recent – the mid-nineteenth century in France – the practice dates back to the middle ages and no doubt much earlier.[72] What is evident from its multi-faceted role is that it cannot be understood simply from the perspective of a given enterprise but instead in terms of a 'mediating object', one between two partners, and as a central element in their exchange relations over time.

This single observation is all that is necessary to appreciate the importance that this tool quite possibly had in the development of commercial exchange, in the same capacity as a bill of exchange, in a world long portrayed as one in which hard currency was in short supply and in which transportation was relatively insecure. One must, however, delve more deeply into the logic of its use to grasp all of the implications. Freed from the necessity of proximity that the utilization of the tally assumed, the current account enabled by means of written communication the undertaking and tracking of transactions between partners geographically removed from one another. In the accounts of two merchants in a business relationship together, once all the operations that linked them had been correctly recorded at their respective trading house, one should have found reciprocal and symmetrical current accounts with opposite balances. Periodically or on demand, it was possible to calculate the balance of an account open on account of a third party in order to inform the latter of his debit or credit position by issuing him a detailed copy of this account – extract or statement – such that he would be able to compare it with his own ledgers. As outlined by Ricard in 1724, a current account was based on the fundamental principal that it was not sent unless the correspondent could verify and see that all the entries matched those in the account that he maintained at his own establishment. Such verification would be quite difficult if such entries were not specified in detail, making it necessary to distinguish all debit and credit amounts such that the third party could verify that they matched those put down in writing in his account books.[73] The forwarding of such statements followed standard format.

> We have just closed, sir, as per our custom at the end of the year, our account with you, you will find it enclosed and after its examination if you would be so kind as to credit us once again for £ 68 833. 11. 9 including the interest balance of our advances which we have carried at 5% as per the account also enclosed.[74]

Depending on the circumstances, the current account could carry interest *agios*, whether they be sums which the *négociant* had advanced or on funds that he had temporarily at his disposal. In other words, these interest amounts were calculated in proportion to the time elapsed, on the successive account balances. The statement of account always included equally the detailed calculation of this interest amount. M. de La Porte[75] provided an example of the calculation method, as did the majority of accounting manuals which later appeared. If the reconciliation led to the discovery of differences, a re-examination of the accounting entries led to the dispatch of a new extract:

> We have received the letter ... in which you make various observations about the extract of your account remitted to you, enclosed you will find a revised one in which we have added and rectified all that we consider to be fair, as a result, on this new account you are indebted to us in the amount of 5 316. 7. 9 [livres, sols, deniers], would you be so kind as to examine it and sign it for its correctness if there are no further errors.[76]

For the intended receivers, the reading and interpretation of these extracts assumed a minimal level of competence. Nonetheless the graphic form and the vocabulary utilized would render it immediately intelligible to anyone who possessed the knowledge shared by merchants using double-entry systems. In effect, accounting served as an international language understood and shared within merchant networks extending across Europe and the Atlantic world. For each partner, the current account constituted a record or memory device of the relationship with the other party. If one adds to it the copy registers of active correspondence and the bundles of correspondence received, along with the various auxiliary books, one would be in the position to retrace the entire history of this relationship.

Preliminary Conclusions

Accounting information, and thereby the device that produces it, is almost always considered from a unilateral perspective, either that of the producer or that of the user. In terms of internal information for strategic decision making and operational control, producers and users are readily confounded – management accounting and control; information destined for investors and more generally, third parties, and respecting the set of norms intended to make the financial statements comparable across space and time – financial accounting. In the first case, one reasons in terms of pertinence; in the second, fidelity, transparency and perhaps pertinence yet still in terms of the individual decision maker.

Consequently the perspective that we bring to the history of accounting has been frequently guided and influenced by these same preoccupations, which has translated into much questioning into the emergence, diffusion and evolution of methods of cost calculation; or the evaluation, reliability and harmonization of financial information. All of these issues are important, and far be it for us (engaged in such endeavours) to debate their research interest. Nonetheless, another entire side of the production from routine accounting work is potentially overlooked; less noble and unremarkable it may be, yet also far removed from debates over cost calculations and fair value.

In a similar manner, despite the relative abundance of old account books, accounting historiography has tended to overlook these sources and studies that rely on their potential insights are rare. The archival documents of enterprises more frequently consulted are those which *describe* the systems used, offering on occasion a critical analysis, with frequent emphasis on their modification, adoption, decisions by boards of directors, regulations and internal memoranda. When account books are placed in the limelight, it is more often to study a specific operating category, for instance closing entries, or to focus on the use of a particular type of account. Our immersion *de longue durée* into the account books draws us into the practices themselves and allows us to envision the reality of the accounting work undertaken, something that is not possible from the study of accounting manuals alone.

Having at their disposal a significant administrative and accounting apparatus, in keeping with the variety, extensiveness and complexity of their business affairs, the Chaurand brothers did not wait on this system to furnish them with information about their profits. Only a few partial results appear in the accounting records, for example those from bottomry loans and active insurance contracts, where profits were earned immediately: the amount received or the amount paid! Moreover these figures are gross results, since we have no knowledge of the transaction costs of these operations. With respect to an inventory or the closing of accounts each year to provide a balance sheet and to calculate overall results, we are far from that possibility, not to mention the determination of a rate of return relative to the amount of invested capital. This case, among others, confirms that the essential contribution of double-entry bookkeeping to the emergence and expansion of merchant capitalism does not reside in this area.

Yet our analyses do permit us to speculate on what we consider to be the essential contribution of double-entry accounting that made the development of international commerce possible, in somewhat the same manner as maritime navigation and its instruments. Nonetheless we should not push the metaphor too far. If accounting assisted in taking stock of the situation, it did not necessarily indicate the direction to be taken!

Rather it was the role of this accounting object in relation to others that we underscore: the role played by the 'current account' object in the establishment of exchange relations between partners, in the institution of trust between these partners, in the extension and longevity of merchant networks. Other elements clearly intervened in the creation and functioning of networks of this nature, including social and family relations, matrimonial strategies, control and incentive mechanisms. However, the current account distinguishes itself as a necessary condition of such a network. It was indispensable in the construction of long-lasting commercial relations between two partners, once the latter had attained a certain volume and degree of complexity and/or had gone beyond the limits of immediate physical proximity. In the same manner, beyond a certain volume of business, the use of a set of open accounts for partners, as well as for operations and for assets, was indispensable for the exercise of commercial activity. Our conclusions are consistent with the general observation of Basu et al.[77] that records influence impersonal exchange and, as argued more eloquently by Jubé, in terms of the function of *rappel*.[78] While it is not possible to state precisely for the two cases when it took place, there is a point at which complexity could no longer be accommodated by more rudimentary accounting systems and double-entry techniques made these extensions possible. In terms of the double-entry discourse, our arguments align in certain ways with the views of Bryer[79] by underscoring the requisite nature of double-entry accounting once the scale and scope of operations reached a certain magnitude.

More generally, our approach is grounded in an anthropological approach to accounting which privileges the nature of accounting objects and their actual use, thus removed from a narrow theoretical vision that might be offered by accounting manuals or by accounting research lacking historical perspective. Along with the current account, which has been our present focus, we would need to add invoices, sales and profit accounts, *les comptes d'armement et désarmement*, etc. – all of these accounting objects that could not have been produced or used in a satisfactory manner without a minimum of administrative and accounting organization and which also contributed to the construction and the enduring nature of the co-operative commercial relations between their users.

2 WHY PROFIT AND LOSS DIDN'T MATTER: THE HISTORICIZED RATIONALITY OF EARLY MODERN MERCHANT ACCOUNTING

Pierre Gervais

Introduction

Account books from the eighteenth century are rarely presented as mysterious, opaque historical artefacts. They were ubiquitous; any archival repository in Europe or on the East Coast of the United States will hold dozens of more or less elaborate recording efforts, from the large volumes of an international merchant versed in the most arcane techniques of double-entry bookkeeping, down to the single daybook on which a rural market retailer would scribble her daily transactions. What was recorded seems equally unproblematic. In the standard economic approach, keeping accounts was a self-evident imperative in a world of rational economic agents trying to maximize their profit. Focusing on double-entry accounting, Hans Derks recently summarized this view by concluding that such recording would be kept 'to improve decision-making, to uncover gain/loss, to track the entity's [for which the accounts were kept] rights and obligations, and to achieve a greater control or surveillance of transactions internal and external'.[1] A detailed analysis of accounting textbooks from the early modern era by John R. Edwards, Graeme Dean and Frank Clarke Edwards, found six possible roles more or less explicitly given to private accounts: establishing one's financial position, measuring overall profitability and the resulting changes in capitalization, tracking the main components of the stock of goods traded, valuing them, computing the profit or loss on each of them and providing prospective information which would reduce uncertainty in decision-making.[2] Some textbooks were far less specific than others, and actual use of accounts was even further from the most advanced models. Accounting historians have long noted that systematic bookkeeping was still rare even in the eighteenth century, and that the techniques used for balancing books were often crude. Still, it is usually held that this was only a transitional stage in an overall process, through which progress in efficiency was constantly made, and each new development in control and recording merely prolonged and improved earlier efforts within an overall human drive towards ever more rationalizing and optimizing. While improvements in cost calculations mostly came from large agricultural and proto-industrial entrepreneurs, whose accounts form the basis of most of the research in accounting history (they were presumably prompted to be more careful because of their high level of fixed capital), financial reporting did include profit calculations as well, especially when the capital was 'socialized', that is, when it was shared by a plurality of actors, whether partners or stockholders.[3]

The present chapter will offer a dissenting view, based on the factual observation that when it came to trade, a sphere of economic activity which was central to economic development in the early modern era, merchant accounting, whether in textbooks or in practice, did not include the kind of profit calculations which would be expected within the framework of this standard, rather Whiggish history of bookkeeping. In other words, a much more systematic effort should be made to understand these sources on their own terms when it comes to what commercial actors at the time called 'profit'; in this respect, there was an 'Otherness' in early modern economic attitudes and practices which tends to be understressed in the historiography. An interesting symptom of this Otherness is the extent to which historians have remained unable to translate early modern commercial accounts into profit rates. One often comes across 'net profit' figures for individual 'adventures' in the slave trade and in the long-distance colonial trade, but these shipping accounts were not balance sheets for a whole 'firm', to use a partly anachronistic notion, whether for individual traders or for partnerships, and connecting these discrete accounts to a whole usually requires considerable approximations. Pierre Jeannin, arguably the most knowledgeable specialist on any area of European trade in the early modern era, tried only once to assess the profit of one of his traders, and concluded that the only valid result he could achieve was 'a very general idea of the volume of business treated yearly', and that any serious calculation of profit and cost was well beyond what was possible.[4] Balance sheets did occur from time to time, and more frequently among bigger traders, but they never seemed to provide the information needed to reach a reasonably complete profit and loss statement. Capital accumulation could be computed, in other words, as well as an implicit yearly rate of return, but the sources of profit or loss could not be accurately identified. Similarly, the Thirteen colonies gave rise to a considerable body of work on merchant practice, but again profit and loss calculations remained exceptional, indeed virtually non-existent, and even isolated rates of capital accumulation are seldom quoted.[5]

Why was that so? Part of the story is that profit calculations were not as useful for traders in the early modern era as they would be now. In an important article, Basil Yamey points out that while accounting textbooks advising traders to compute 'the particular gain or loss upon each article' had been around at least since the sixteenth century, as a practical matter the crushing majority of account books, not to say all of them, did not provide reliable cost and benefit data on specific products or ventures in a timely fashion, and consequently could not possibly be used as a basis for detailed cost–benefit calculations and strategic decision-making. As I have written elsewhere, in the absence of standardized production and enforceable norms of quality, each transaction was largely an act of faith on the part of the buyer, who was usually not expert enough to detect hidden faults and blemishes in quality, and had to rely on the supplier's good faith; and on the selling side, as soon as a trader was of some importance, it became necessary for them to use commission merchants or other agents and to trust them to sell the goods at their highest possible price, within a market which was basically unknown to the principal. In a world of highly segmented markets and very imperfect (and slow-moving) information, moreover, prices could fluctuate wildly, suddenly and unexpectedly, and defeat the efforts of even the best suppliers and the most committed selling agents. Thus forecasts were at best informed guesses, and the prices asked depended both on the specific quality of the good being priced and on the state of the market at the time of the transaction, two variables which never remained stable. Even granting that some textbooks developed the theoretical view that profit could be calculated in order to help decision-making and reduce uncertainty in trade (and we will see below that this is not as obvious a proposition as one would expect), the concrete conditions of commerce actually prevented such a use of accounts in most real-life cases.[6]

Good records could not really help forecasting; they were also not as necessary as they are today, since early modern traders did not have to deal either with demanding stockholders or with highly developed regulatory environments. Derk's third point, 'track[ing] the entity's rights and obligations', is based on the fact that both in British *Lex Mercatoria* as it had developed alongside Common Law, and in Statute law on the French side, well-kept books were supposed to be a key element in any evidence admissible in a court of law besides formal written contracts. However, the link sometimes made between this purported legal status and bookkeeping is misleading; lawful evidence could be derived from any single-entry chronological record, and the complex interweaving of accounts found in double-entry accounting was entirely unnecessary for this purpose. Moreover, in British Common Law at least, while any kinds of books could serve as evidence, there is no indication that they played an especially important role. In fact, a Jacobean statute from 1609 limited the use of such books for all 'men of Trades and Handicraftsmen' to within a year of the transaction in the case of debt proceedings, underlining that these craftsmen 'do demand Debts of their Customers' after they 'have inserted unto their said Shop-Books other Wares supposed to be delivered to the same Parties, or to their Use, which in

Truth never were delivered, and this of purpose to increase by such undue Means the said Debt'.[7] In France, the *Ordonnance du commerce* of 1673 did state that a compulsory balancing of accounts had to take place at least every year between parties to a contract (Title 1, Articles VII and VIII); and a whole, though rather short, chapter was devoted to the issue of books (Title 3, 'Des livres et registres des négocians, marchands et banquiers'). As in Great Britain, however, there was no mention of double-entry. What was required was a 'journal' or 'daybook', stamped on the first and last page by the proper authority, containing 'all their trade, their bills of exchange, the debts they owe and that are owed to them, and the money they used for their house expences', and written 'in continuity, ordered by date, with no white space left [between two transactions, to prevent fraud]'.[8] No calculation above and beyond this simple act of recording was needed.

I will not go into issues of internal control and surveillance here, since except for a handful of large international ventures such as the various East India Companies, such controls were irrelevant to early modern merchants, who operated through trusted partners and agents with at most a handful of salaried employees. What remains is the gain/loss calculation, which is indeed what Edwards and his co-authors deem central to the role of double-entry accounting as an engine of progress, with inventory tracking and valuation as a side benefit. Such calculations did take place, either over the whole invested capital, profit then being a 'ratio obtained by dividing some measure of profit (as a flow of income) by some measure of capital (as a stock of wealth)',[9] or for a specific merchandize or activity, for instance by balancing (closing) the account for a shipping venture or for a particular product. But what I want to argue here is that these calculations entailed economic and social assumptions very different from the ones which govern the notion of profit as we understand it, and that therefore the apparent semantic identity and continuity of the word itself should be questioned. Accounting historians today tend to argue that accounting methods and profit calculations in the past were designed to fulfill the needs of the people who used them, which is true as far as it goes. I have argued elsewhere that the core need of an eighteenth-century trader was to track closely the credit flows which underpinned every commercial activity at the time.[10] Thus the question becomes what consequences this focus on credit would have for profit calculations.

In standard economic theory, credit transactions are not different from any other monetarized transactions, but I hope to show in the following pages that this rather ahistorical approach misses important components of the historical record on profit in the early modern age. I will rely on the two main sources for profit calculations among eighteenth-century merchants, one theoretical, the other more empirical. On one hand, there are textbooks on accounting, a source often used by accounting historians, as we have seen; on the other hand, there are the quantified traces left by daily merchant activity in various archives, which consist mostly in account books. A sampling of both will be used in this essay, analysing several textbooks from Great Britain and France, as well as the account books of two large eighteenth-century traders, one in Bordeaux, the other in Philadelphia. Of course, any one of these sources could be unrepresentative, but the combination of all of them, pointing in the same specific direction, does constitute a good indication that we are dealing indeed with what was the standard attitude towards profit.

Evidence from Textbooks

Let us start with textbooks. While we should not confuse traffic laws with actual driving, still these books were sold to the public as training tools, and thus could not very well run counter to the basic assumptions held by this same public about the goals and structuration of this particular technique. There were customers out there who would test them in the process of training themselves; even though most young traders were apprenticed, either some of them felt the need for some written help, or there was a clientele of non-apprenticed merchant wannabees, otherwise there would not have been so many publications on the topic. Consequently, the narrative included in works on accounting was unlikely to depart very far from what young apprenticed merchants or would-be merchants would consider the common sense reasons for using accounting in the first place, and for expecting it to be a tool for success. Double-entry accounting in particular required much, much more work than a simple recording of transactions in chronological order. Special training was needed to apply this method, developed in the fourteenth century by an Italian monk, Luca Pacioli, and which required the writing down of two entries for each transaction. The first entry debited the account receiving whatever was exchanged, goods, cash, commercial paper, etc., for the value of what was received. The 'debtor' account thus 'owed' this value received, and became accountable for it, since it would eventually either have to show where it had gone, or give it back. The second entry credited the account which had provided this same value, and which therefore was not responsible for it anymore, its 'debit' being diminished in proportion.[11] Each transaction thus was translated into an increase of the value given to one account, which it would have to give back or account for when balancing the books, and a decrease in the value for which another account had been hitherto responsible, and which was diminished by the same value (note that in many cases only the value was recorded, not the specific list of goods traded; double-entry was rarely used as a tool for keeping track of inventories).

Such a system required both theoretical knowledge and practical skill, for the choice of which account to debit or credit for a given transaction was not always obvious, and went far beyond the requirements of mere recording. A whole universe of textbooks purported to instruct the young trader in the niceties of this art, but in most cases these textbooks used an approach by example which was undistinguishable from a few years of apprenticeship. And yet, in spite of these arduous prerequisites, double-entry had come to be widely in use among larger traders.[12] Was this tool applied to profit measurement? According to Edwards and his co-authors, out of forty-five textbooks on accounting published in Great Britain between 1547 and 1799, no less than twenty-six dealt explicitly with profit calculations. But what was meant by 'profit calculation'? I chose to concentrate on the most widely reprinted British and French textbooks from the eighteenth century, John Mair, William Gordon and William Webster in Great Britain, and Mathieu de la Porte and François Barrême in France. These were the few authors who had met with widespread approval to the point of achieving something close to classic status, as evidenced by a sometimes impressive number of reprints.[13]

Predictably, all three British authors are listed among Edwards and co-authors' profit-calculating textbooks. But a closer look at how profit was dealt with by them gives some surprising results. Let us start with John Mair, whose *Book-keeping Methodiz'd* went through at least nineteen editions (and was used by George Washington). As I have developed elsewhere,[14] according to Mair accounts were 'of three kinds, *viz. personal, real, and fictitious*. A *personal* Dr. or Cr. is a Person's Name; as *David Wilson* in the preceeding [*sic*] Post. A *real* Dr. or Cr. is a Thing; as *Cash, Sugar, Shalloon*, &c. A *fictitious* Dr. or Cr. is a Term made use of to supply the want or personal or real one; as *Profit and Loss, Voyage*, &c'.[15] These categories are still in use today, but the 'fictitious' accounts are called 'nominal' by twenty-first-century accountants, and are defined as temporary accounts, closed at the end of each accounting period and making up the income statement since they contain all revenues, expenses, gains and losses. For Mair, however, fictitious accounts received cases that 'cannot properly be divided into a Dr. Part and Cr. part, but consist of one of these parts only', the primary fictitious account being 'Profit and Loss'. He gave a series of examples of such cases, including an inheritance received by a friend, any gift of merchandise or money, gambling wins, as well as 'Shop-rent, Warehouse-rent, or other Things of the like nature'.[16] The common element in all these operations was simply that their outcome increased or decreased holdings without creating a transactional relationship with a third party. When a gift was received, no one would be credited since it was a gift; the owner decided to add its value to the capital, and the Profit and Loss account functioned as the tool to do so. Conversely, when a warehouse was rented or custom duties paid, there would not be any debitor, and the corresponding value was lost to the owner, who would subtract it from the capital, again through Profit and Loss.

Thus the main account recording profit was presented as a dustbin for 'incomplete' operations which had to be withdrawn from the normal flow of credits and debits. It could still theoretically be used as a primitive income statement at year's end, and in Mair's careful reconstruction of a Ledger it did play this role; the gains or losses on individual accounts were to be recorded one by one in the Profit and Loss account, he explained, and since expenses clearly associated with a given merchandise were recorded in the corresponding account rather than in Profit and Loss, the latter did provide a stylized picture of the profit on each account.[17] But the whole point is that Mair was primarily interested in ascertaining the 'true State of every part, and of the whole', of one's business. Once achieved, this true image could be used either to know one's own value, or to 'give a satisfactory Account ... to Persons concerned'.[18] The essentially descriptive status of accounting explains why neither prospective analysis not cost considerations played an important role in it. When he wrote, in a passage often quoted since, that a merchant ought to know 'what Goods he has purchased; what he has disposed of, with the Gain or Loss upon the Sale, and what he has yet on hand; what Goods or Money he has in the Hands of Factors; what ready Money he has by him; what his Stock was at first; what Alterations and Changes it has suffered since',[19] his primary goal in calculating profits either on a specific merchandise or overall was to make sure the assets of a merchant were correctly listed and valued. What counted was the end result, not the process whereby this result was achieved.

This explains why merchant profit was not individualized, but 'embedded' – in the sense of K. Polanyi[20] – within a larger set of activities, up to and including bets and card games, which seem to us very far from being part of a business. All these activities were lumped together in the Profit and Loss account, and even in some cases within particular accounts; such as in Mair's description of a merchant who 'takes a Piece of cloth, or any thing else from the Shop, to compliment his Friend, and omit to enter it in his Books; nothing is more certain, than that the *Cloth-accompt* in the *Ledger* would not shew how much of the Cloth were yet disposed of'.[21] The profit on the cloth was not at issue here, and Mair did not even think necessary to explain to which account this gift should be debited, since the problem was to determine the exact amount of cloth which remained on hand. Similarly, there was no reflexion on costs, because they appeared not in conjunction with profits, but only either as part of a specific merchandize or venture outside of which they did not make sense, or as inconvenient operations to be vacuumed out through the Profit and Loss account. The creation of subordinate 'Fictitious' accounts was explicitly left by Mair to the discretion of his readers, with a few possibilities offered (household expenses, insurance, interest charges, penalties incurred when a contract was not fulfilled and 'Charges of Merchandize'), but without any guiding principle of the kind Mair provided for real and personal accounts.[22] This was in complete contrast to Mair's treatment of shipping ventures; according to him, 'when a Merchant sends Goods to Sea ... there is no Dr.; for neither is any thing received in their stead, nor is the Factor to whom they are consigned, as yet chargeable'.[23] In other words, the shipped goods did not belong to inventory any more (they were outside of the physical control of the merchant), but were not yet under anybody else's responsibility. The seemingly obvious (for us) nature of these goods, as assets belonging to a real account, was thus not obvious at all for an eighteenth-century author, who gave theoretical priority to the kind of credit relationship embodied in an accounting transaction, over the tracking of profit by families of transaction. Since this was, again, a regal act of the owner, with no other party debited for the goods, it became logical to see such accounts as branches of the Profit and Loss account – from which they were extracted when they reached the factor. In practice, most merchants would sensibly take the view that adventures were real accounts; but Mair's more complex theory is worth noting.

The disconnect between profit calculations and accounting procedures is beautifully illustrated by another classic author of the period, William Gordon, in the second volume of his textbook on merchant arithmetic. Besides adopting the exact same classification and explanation of the 'Fictitious' account of Profit and Loss as a depository for 'defective' operations lacking a creditor or debtor, he adds a general discussion of profit which is particularly illuminating for our purpose. According to Gordon, profit calculations must positively not be used for prospective analysis: 'Commerce, like the course of exchange betwixt nations, is by nature variable and fluctuating: the branch which may have afforded considerable profit at one time, may scarce be worth embarking in at another, as the markets may be overstocked by a multitude of traders'. Consequently, what is needed above all is 'proper intelligence of the best markets, and a thorough judgment of the quality of goods' combined with 'a real certainty of an advantageous and ready sale ... The profit by trading does not arise so much from charging high, as [from] ready sales and quick returns'.[24] Within such a universe, profit could be measured ex post, but its quantification had no bearing on future profit. Information, networks, quality scales, credit flows and anticipations on the evolution of highly segmented markets were the key determinants of profit, and none of these elements were reflected in the accounts, which were thus largely useless in this respect.

Mair mostly left out a reflexion on profit, but his formulations were ambiguous enough to imply that such a reflexion could take place. Gordon dismisses it explicitly. Indeed, 'Loss and Gain' as a chapter heading does appear in his first volume, within an explanation of the way percentages could be used to compare profits on two operations of different value. Our author concludes his section with this fascinating paragraph:

> In selling on credit, merchants generally propose a certain profit, which they calculate upon the prime cost of the goods, added to the real and imaginary charges. – The real charges on goods are freight, insurance, lighterage, porterage, ware-room rent, &c. and the imaginary charges are risk of bad debts, dilatory payments, short insurance, possible accidents in the carriage, risk of having them long on hand, &c.; and where this calculation is made according to the profit they propose, the goods are marked on the cover with something characteristical of the price, which is known only to those concerned in the shop or ware-room. After all, merchants are frequently obliged to conform themselves to the market, selling under the rate they proposed, when there are few bidders, and as demands rise, taking the best price they can get.[25]

Again, Gordon is explicit: most of the components of the price-setting process were not drawn from the accounting record itself, with the exception of the cost of acquiring the goods, and of some charges – and even then since at least warehouse charges were explicitly listed in both Mair and Gordon as belonging to the 'Fictitious' account, a part of the price component could well end up coming from outside the account of the merchandise under consideration.

Together, Mair and Gordon present a very clear view of what accounting was supposed to achieve in relation to profit quantification. The latter was useful only within the framework of a general balancing of the account, carried out in order to determine precisely 'the true State of one's affairs', to use an eighteenth-century formula. Even partial balances on a specific venture for a specific merchandize were drawn with this overarching objective in mind, and certainly not to contribute to any kind of strategic reflexion on profit. The end result of accounting was indeed to determine how much had been gained and lost, but the goal was precision and exhaustivity rather than comprehension of the underlying sources of whatever profit was gained. This, then, was the view of the most widespread textbooks in Great Britain, including Webster, our third author, who did not add any significant element to the overall picture. He barely mentioned overall profitability, introduced the Profit and Loss account only in the framework of the closing of the accounts, and explained it very succinctly as follows: 'All such *Accompts*, as *House-Expences*, *Charges* on *Merchandizes*, *Refusals* of *Bargains*, &c. as they are only Particulars of irrecoverable Expences, or Disbursements which turn to no Account, so they are all ballanced by *Profit* and *Loss*'.[26] The reasoning is similar to Mair's and Gordon's, but this older author (the first edition dates back to 1719) stuck to the traditional teaching method by examples, and therefore did not feel obliged to try and outline general principles – his 'general rules' cover all of twelve pages in a pocket format. The practical examples he provided, though, are fully consistent with the general view outlined above.

The French authors do provide us with an even more direct expression of this view, however, thanks to what was already then (possibly as now) a French specialty: the grandiose methodological statement. One of the most edited French works in the eighteenth century was Mathieu De La Porte's *Science des négocians*, originally published in 1704.[27] In his opening sentences, De La Porte already drastically limited the role of accounting:

> The Science of Merchants is made up of two points: 1° To know all the qualities & circumstances of the goods they trade: 2° To know how to make the necessary entries to manage their trade in an exact order, which will give them a perfect knowledge of it at all times.
>
> The knowledge pertaining to the *first* point is acquired more through the practice of it among Merchants, than through the precepts one could provide about it.
>
> The Science pertaining to the *second* point, or to the Entries practiced in the counting-houses of Merchants, can be reduced with certainty to a set of principles or rules[28]

What is striking here is what was *excluded* from accounting, namely everything pertaining to the quality of the goods traded, and generally everything belonging to the material side of the transaction. Since quality was a key issue in any transaction, disconnecting bookkeeping from its study turned it into a tool of limited usefulness for profit analysis. But De La Porte was even more radical a few paragraphs later, writing that:

> It must nevertheless be agreed that a merchant who uses cash for all his purchases, who borrows neither merchandise nor money for his Commerce, & who lends nothing to anyone, could dispense with maintaining & keeping books, because he cannot fall into any of the cases described by the Ordonnance. He has neither active nor passive debts; as a consequence he fears neither failures nor bankruptcies, & he is in no danger of failing himself, nor of causing losses to his Creditors, because he has none. This case is not without example, and I have seen a Merchant (a retailer, in truth) who, during the more than sixty years that his shop was open, although he even had a fair amount of business, never borrowed nor loaned anything, & as a consequence he had no Book: However he conducted his business with much honor and probity, & without encountering any financial difficulties. But this is a very rare thing, & could not be the case of a Merchant with a somewhat considerable trade. It is therefore necessary for he who borrows and lends to keep his books very exactly, in order to see at all times the state of his Affairs. His Books will teach him which affairs and which negotiations have profited him or caused him losses, and he will know who are his debtors and creditors, in order to satisfy the latter and get himself paid by the former, & furthermore he will be in a condition to be able to account for his conduct, in the unfortunate event that his affairs began to suffer and he not have what he needs to satisfy his Creditors.[29]

Yes, accounts could tell a trader 'which negotiations have been profitable, and which have led to losses' and the 'state of one's affairs', but why were they useless in the case of cash transactions? The only possible explanation is that in a cash transaction the amount gained (or lost) was immediately clear, and that de La Porte, just as Mair and Gordon, was exclusively interested in measuring assets, and then again only once credit flows entered the picture. Accounting was useful only for tracking credit, and did not include issues of costs, supply and demand, or quality, which existed in a cash transaction, but did not deserve to be recorded since the change in assets was easy to track and its amount easy to calculate. Profit and loss became items to be recorded only insofar as the use of credit made it more difficult to compute them and keep track of them.

The same order of priorities is shown even more clearly in the work of another major French author, François Barrême, who proposed to create two accounts which, combined, corresponded exactly to Mair's Profit and Losses. The 'Capital' account received all exceptional gains or losses, such as '32000 *Livres* received as an inheritance from one of my Uncles', a sum which Barrême told his reader to credit to Capital since 'all these assets come to my profit [and] I will never be obliged to render an account of them to any of my correspondants'. This is exactly the same approach we found in Mair's work, but Barrême went further by crediting and debiting systematically all *ordinary* revenues and expenses to a second account, 'Profits and Losses', completely bypassing real and personal accounts. His example was the following entry: 'Cash owes to profits and losses 800 *Liv*[*res*] that I received as a payment for 6 months interest on 40000 £ State Securities'. Barrême argued that this way, the account containing these securities would contain only the value they represented, not an addition of this value and the income derived from them.[30] But the result of this was that neither charges not gains could be related to the original activity which generated them, since they were jumbled into the Profits and Losses account. For Barrême made no mention of ordering these gains and expenses according to their source, which confirms that his Profits and Losses account should not be read as a forerunner of the modern profit and loss statement. As with Mair, the point was *not* to analyse the sources of profits and of losses (an issue which again is not even raised in the passage), but to sift away revenues and expenses, in order to have a detailed picture of existing assets and liabilities.

And even this last formulation does not do full justice to the peculiarities of the early modern merchant mind. In a chapter entitled 'Reflexions on Various Accounts Established in the Ledger', Barrême noted that

> CAPITAL is the head account to which all the other accounts are subordinated, to which all the other accounts are forced to give accounts of their *income* & their *expense*. CASH is a Cashier to whom CAPITAL entrusted the use of his money. The State Securities account is a Clerk to whom CAPITAL has entrusted his State Notes. The Brandy account is a Clerk to whom CAPITAL has entrusted his Brandies[31]

The vocabulary here was not one of assets and liabilities, but of borrowing and loaning; the balance sheet was a list of loans. To build this general account, which described all that was owed to Capital (the primary 'Compte du Chef' in

French accounting parlance), and all that Capital owed, one had to extract from all other accounts all net revenues and expenses, as shown by the example of the revenue from State notes. Recording this revenue was thus not perceived as a possible tool to assess the profit from State notes in particular, and eventually to compare with each other the profits gained in various activities seen as competing parts of an interconnected whole, but as a necessary step in cleaning up each of these activities and reducing them to what they owed, or were owed to, from a credit point of view.

The French 'Comptes du Chef' and the British 'fictional accounts' were thus versions of the same underlying reality, that of credit flows, the tracking of which trumped any concern of profit measurement.[32] De La Porte, Barrême,and Gordon and Mair saw accounting as a tool for tracking credit flows, not a tool for analysing profits. What defined a transaction was not the activity which generated it, but its place in the credit structure the trader had built. The key differentiation was between transactions generated from outside this credit structure, entailing income or expense straight from or towards the trader's own capital, and transactions resulting from transfers of value between accounts belonging to this structure of credit. While profit calculations on discrete activities remained possible (discounting the issue of overhead), all authors considered such calculations as marginal at best. The key goal was the careful tracking of the value transferred between creditors and debitors, including inventory value. To reach this goal, 'fictional accounts' or 'Comptes du Chef' were set up in order to sift out incomes and expenses: in the minds of eighteenth-century accountants, they functioned as tools to charge and discharge capital stock, not as centres of cost and profit accounting.

Daily Merchant Usage: Two Case Studies

Theory is one thing; what of practice? The following section offers a short overview of the way two transatlantic traders of the second half of the eighteenth century managed their accounts. First considered is Abraham Gradis, whom we know thanks to one of the best kept merchant archives in France, that of the David Gradis & Sons house in Bordeaux, well-known and abundantly used by French Early Modernists such as Paul Butel.[33] According to Butel, the firm had outfitted 220 ships from 1718 to 1789, twice the average outfitting numbers of the most active firms in Bordeaux, making Gradis by far the biggest outfitter in Bordeaux. Most of this shipping activity was directed towards the Sugar Islands and Canada (Gradis was in business with François Bigot, the infamous *intendant du Canada* who ended up in the Bastille after 1760); a few slaving expeditions also took place. Concurrently, Gradis was dealing in Bordeaux wine, and in various agricultural produce, mostly within his region and in the West of

France. The Gradis journals available to us span most of the eighteenth century, and I have analysed the year 1755.[34]

Like most of his peers, Gradis completely ignored French law on regular statements of accounts; there is no trace of a general balancing of the book in Gradis's two journals, which covered eight years from 1751 to 1759. The lack of 'fictitious' accounts was also remarkable: both general and personal expenses were distributed over various accounts, insuring that no clear view of them could be gained. Thus the only profit Gradis could calculate was 'the gain or loss on a particular article', or on a particular venture. In practice, the account structure was overwhelmingly dominated by personal accounts (211 of them), to which should be added eleven partnership and factorage accounts, which in most cases included personal transactions along with those concerning the commissioned goods, and at the very least meant that a third party was involved. Moreover, some of the nine shipping accounts listed should be considered partnership accounts as well: while Gradis's accounts rarely specified whether a specific outfitting or cargo was the result of a joint investment by several traders, at least a few silent investors were almost always resorted to. Anyway, the choice of calculating returns on each shipment, rather than over specific goods or specific destinations, made profit calculations most likely useless beyond the usual, descriptive need to measure changes in assets, since each cargo mix was different. More generally, in all these cases, profit calculations concerned personal or credit relationships rather than product lines or defined markets: these accounts were individualized as possible profit and cost centres because of their position as source or destination of credit flows, with no obvious reference to the economic activity which underpinned Gradis's relation to the person or persons holding these accounts.

Thus, setting aside thirteen other accounts for Cash, commercial paper held by Gradis or his bankers, and some types of special contracts such as bottomry loans and freight fees advanced to customers (all these accounts bearing also on credit relationships anyway), unambiguously real accounts connected to merchandise rather than credit flows were limited to three accounts of cargoes entirely owned by Gradis (which Mair would still have seen as fictional accounts rather than real ones), and ten accounts of merchandises.[35] However, out of these ten accounts one, 'General Merchandise', was obviously not a specific product, and two others, 'Land in Talance' and 'Wines from Talance', were producer accounts, since Gradis had his own vineyard, and traced separately the wine he grew, thus bearing out the well-known link between producer status and cost accounting. Moreover, the 'Flour' account included flour sent to the King, whereas whatever flour Gradis bought and sold for his own account was recorded in 'General Merchandize',[36] so that it was impossible to calculate profit on 'flour' in general. Two sugar accounts ('Sugar our a/c' and 'Unrefined sugar our a/c') were virtually inactive throughout the year, with total sales of 143 £ tournois – though Gradis found a profit of almost 22,000 £ tournois when he closed them in September 1755, a hefty sum which had sat unrecorded for at least eight months. The same was true for the 'Campeche wood' account, which appears in 1755 only to be closed, and found to have been generating a profit of 2,000 £ tournois.[37]

Overall, only three accounts out of 259 ('Wine', 'Brandy' and 'Indigo our a/c'), can be seen as offering an opportunity to calculate 'the gain or loss on a particular article', rather than within the framework of a particular venture. Unfortunately, even then significant quantities of the good which could have been theoretically tracked were transferred to factors or cargoes in ships, with no attempt at keeping these subsets of merchandise identified in the accounts. Thus the fifteen casks of wine sent to Quebec as part of 'various ships', by having entailed unitemized 'costs' directly credited to Cash with all the other costs of the cargo, would eventually bring back an amount of money which would be listed within 'Merchandize sent to Quebec on our account', with no way to trace back what that wine brought in compared to other wine sent by other ships, or sold back home.[38] This confirms that the tracking of credit relationships was more important than the tracking of specific products; Gradis could have easily created a series of 'Wine' accounts ('Vins pour compte de la Société pour la cargaison N°7', 'Vins sur le navire Le Benjamin', 'Vins en commission'), which would have enabled him to calculate the expenses and profits associated to wine as a product line. And indeed he did precisely that for his 'Vin de Talance'; but this is because the wine in question was the one he produced himself on his own property in Talance. Because he was a producer of wine, he considered important to keep track of the revenues generated by that wine; because the King was a special customer, he created a special account for the King's flour; and because each shipping expedition was unique, he created an account for each. But the structure he set up made it impossible to track one particular barrel or crate of goods from its acquisition to its sale, so that buying price and selling price could be compared, and to this day no historian is in a position to come up with any such profit calculation, even though the Journal is perfectly well-kept. Whatever work Gradis devoted to selling high and buying cheap was done in a non-quantified, non-recorded fashion, while accounts focused almost exclusively on providing a clear view of the assets and liabilities at any one time, especially the credit position, in full agreement with the developments found in textbooks.

The adequation with textbook theory is especially clear if we consider that the Profit and Loss account had at most one subordinate account concerning incomes or expenses (a 'nominal' account in today's parlance), namely an 'Insurance Premiums' account – actually an ambiguous item, since an insurance premium was potentially both an expense and an asset, depending on the outcome of the insured shipping expedition. It did become a cost once the ships or goods had reached their final destination, and Gradis actually transferred the value of the insurance contract to the adventure which had been insured. But if the ship or goods were lost, the premium became an asset owed by the insurer. Opening a separate account for insurance premiums was thus necessary, but it was so because of the peculiar nature of the transaction, and it would probably be incorrect to analyse the presence of such an account as the result of an analysis of the components of charges and revenues. Thus we end up with only one account, 'Profit and Loss', accumulating day after day all the income received, or expenses incurred, from commissions, discounted bills, interests, closed personal or real accounts, adventures successful or not, as well as a host of hard-to-categorize operations, such as the rather obscure 'Profit and Loss Dr. to Jacob Mendes £ 237.5 for 4 tables he ordered from Holland', an expense which may be personal, or a gift to a third party (four tables for one person?), or perhaps part of a wider transaction.[39]

One finds also a long list of corrections to mistakes or omissions, sometimes several months old, and almost always made when 'settling', i. e. closing, a personal account, one more proof that Gradis was much more interested in keeping track of what he owed and was owed than in calculating balances and profits. In this category belongs the spectacular entry which follows: 'Profit and Loss Dr. to Wines on ½ Account with Baillet £ 1298.2.6 for 7 c(sks) 3 Bbls which he delivered heretofore to us pr our ½ debiting Profit and Loss considering that the Wines bought Account was Balanced without having been debited for this article'.[40] Gradis sold 1,298 £ worth of wine, left over from a previous venture, the proceeds and remaining inventory of which had been split with one Baillet, then, upon balancing his wine account, found that he had made a profit of 6,166 £ tournois, realized that this was too high a figure, and tracked the mistake down to the fact that he had forgotten to record the arrival of Baillet's wine in his stock – whereupon he debited directly Profit and Loss rather than correcting the final balance of the 'Wines bought' account. This proves, first, that Gradis did not track his inventory through his accounts (otherwise he would have realized sooner that the casks he was recording as sold were coming out of nowhere), and second that he was not interested in using his merchandise accounts as a basis for profit calculations, since he did not bother to calculate the correct profit for wine as he should have listed it, namely 4,868 £ tournois and not 6,166 £ tournois. Anyway, as we have seen above, the true profit on all this wine, which was most probably listed at buying prices, would only show (or rather, not show) after it was sold in Quebec or elsewhere, and would never make it back into the 'Wines bought' account.

Gradis was one of the largest French traders, and there is no reason to think his behaviour was eccentric. Moreover, it can be shown that the same behaviour was found in very different settings, thanks to Levi Hollingsworth, a large Quaker trader and importer in Philadelphia, who left behind archives as rich as the Gradis fund. In some ways, Gradis and Hollingsworth represented two basic elements of international, i. e. mostly colonial, trade. Our Bordeaux businessman imported into France colonial goods in exchange for finished goods and staples from Europe, towards which he redispatched his imports as well as his high-value Bordeaux wine. On the other side of the Ocean, the Philadelphian imported finished goods and some staples from Europe in a newly independent former colony at the periphery of the British Empire, and exported what agricultural goods he could, mostly flour, to the Caribbean plantations, as well as sugar back to Europe. Remarkably, both men used exactly the same double-entry accounting language, to the point where the two journals are basically identical, if one discounts the 'Laus Deo' with which Abraham Gradis, a Jew in a Catholic country, took care to start each of his pages. And above all, both men structured their accounts in much the same way. We find, again, the same crushing domination of personal accounts, the same role of credit categories as key determinants of various accounts, the same paucity of nominal accounts, whether for expenses or incomes, basically replaced by one large Profit and Loss account filtering away the results of the various other accounts.

Personal accounts were even more pervasive in Hollingsworth's case; the 686 accounts I found are only part of a larger whole, since it should be added to this total an unknown number of commission accounts opened in two separate books lost for the year I studied, 1788, a 'Flour journal' and a 'Sales book' – only the latter was included in the yearly balance, with no itemization, but for a total amount of over 7,000 £Pa (Pennsylvania pounds). On the whole, there is good reason to think that Hollingsworth kept open over a thousand accounts at any time, which made him look a lot like a regional bank. Otherwise, the categories I found fitting for Gradis can be reapplied to Hollingsworth with virtually no modification. Contrary to what one could be led to believe, a number of accounts which look to us like expense accounts ('Hauling', 'Weighing', 'Cooperage', 'Inspecting', 'Storage', etc.) were nothing of the sort; each of these accounts listed fees incurred by Hollingsworth as commmissioner for others, while the same fees, when paid on account of his own goods, were often (but not always) debited to 'Charges of Merchandize', or to individual merchandise accounts. Similarly, 'Shallop's Disbursements', 'Freight' and 'Outstanding Freight' were accounts belonging to a partnership Hollingsworth had entered into with two other traders, and which owned a flotilla of coastal ships. The Philadelphian recorded the expenses incurred for these ships, as well as the income he had received from them ('Freight', which was thus not an expense account at all but an account listing income from an asset held in partnership), then closed each side to the credit and debit of the partnership. He recorded separately, in the 'Outstanding Freight' account, the share his partners owed him on that part of the proceeds of the partnership which had come into their hands. All in all partnership, commission or loan agreements accounted for no less than thirty-five accounts. There were also twenty 'Adventure' accounts, some of them probably in partnership as well. Conversely, the Profit and Loss account was barely more developed than in Gradis's books thirty years earlier. Insurance premiums were as usual accounted for separately. The listing of household expenses, or of cash and goods Hollingsworth withdrew for himself, was merely a continuation of the medieval tradition of keeping track of one's expenses. In terms of the structure of the accounts, cost analysis, such as it was, was limited to the creation of the catch-all 'Charges of Merchandize' account, and to the appearance of a separate account for Hollingworth's horses.

Some differences do appear, partly as a function of time and space. Means of payment in the newly created United States were more diversified, so that 'State Money' and 'Soldiers' certificates' appeared alongside 'Cash'. There were also banks, and bank-related accounts (two: one for stock, one for deposits), again leading to a diversification of the means of payment. On the other hand, the dearth of currency was such in Philadelphia in 1786 that Hollingsworth did not even bother to keep his Bills receivable account separate from his main Cash one; by all appearances, his 'cash' box contained only commercial paper, and virtually no metallic currency.[41] Also noticeable is the limited range of credit contracts individualized in the accounts, with no signs of bottomry loans or notarized sales contracts, for instance. Compared to Gradis, our American trader was living in something of a backwater, and while he may have entered into these more complex forms of credit relationships, his daily activity was confined to simpler forms. But, quite strikingly, there was the same relaxed treatment of mistakes, with a 'Suspense Sales' account which listed a set of sales so badly recorded that Hollingsworth could not determine to whom the proceeds belonged. On 31 January 1788, this account included the sale of a barrel of coffee, the owner of which was unclear, for the significant sum of 106 £Pa; the same sale was already listed in the preceding inventory of January 1787, and one must wonder how many years it took Hollingsworth to decide that the rightful beneficiary would never show up.[42] An identical account, 'Suspense sales of Flour', could be found in the 1786 Flour Book, listing no less than seventeen barrels of Flour, worth 36 £Pa, described as 'so much Flour to be accounted for when claim'd, sold as follows'.[43] This rather carefree recording hardly fits with the careful tracking of inventory and precise calculations of profit figures double-entry accounting was supposed to make possible.

Hollingsworth's system is more original in its use of the Profit and Loss account. A 'Profit and Loss running account' was active year round, as with Gradis, and received all expenses, costs and incomes that Hollingsworth felt convenient to write off. On top of this however, our trader made a general balance of his books each year, around the end of January or February (the year in the British colony still started on 1 March). He started by closing all personal accounts into a final balance. As a second step, he opened a new Profit and Loss account, in his Journal rather than in his Ledger. Then he closed into this final, 'Journal Balance' Profit and Loss account the 'Profit and Loss' running account he had used all year, and also all the active accounts, mostly merchandise, partnership and commission accounts, which he had not yet closed into his other balances or into the original 'Profit and Loss running account'. He did so by transferring the value of what merchandise was left, and of whatever had not yet been paid or received and remained due by or to him, into a new account, in turn closed into the general balances, and crediting or debiting the remaining value, in other words the net result of that particular account, to the same general Profit and Loss account he had just opened. This is why some accounts, like 'Bar iron', appeared twice; once as a closed account, with a net profit debited to Profit and Loss, and once as a real account containing Hollingsworth's stock in Bar iron and a few unpaid debts linked to that particular activity, and listed as an asset in the final balances. Once all the accounts had been cleaned up in this fashion, Hollingsworth drew up his general balance, calculating the value of his assets and liabilities, including the balance of Profit and Loss, and producing a 'Nett worth' figure which translated efficiently the state of his wealth, and could be compared from year to year.

It could be argued that Hollingsworth's accounting was significantly more sophisticated than Gradis's. He did follow the contemporary practice of listing part of his expenses in asset accounts, thus inflating the value of his landed properties, for instance: every time he paid a fee on these landholding, he added this expense to their value. But he also created a depreciation account for the two boats he owned in full, reducing their value at every settlement, and his two Profit and Loss accounts, along with a few subordinate accounts such as House expenses, could form the basis of at least the beginnings of an income statement, admittedly not a complete one, but one clearly separated from assets when the balances were drawn. But the way these Profit and Loss accounts were generated is actually a perfect illustration of the theoretical approach used in textbooks. They were primarily, and consciously, used as a filter which would clean up, so to speak, all revenues and expenses, and leave the net value of assets and liabilities. Because very few subordinate expense accounts were created, and because the Profit and Loss account remained open throughout the year (and in 1788 at least, took up no less than four different pages of the Ledger), various sources of revenues and expenses were jumbled together, and no analysis of the sources of profit and loss was easily achievable. Indeed revenues and expenses recorded during the year did not reappear in any way in the final process whereby the Profit and Loss account was closed, since only the balance of the 'running' Profit and Loss account was transferred into the 'final' one, losing all details on this particular result. Moreover, numerous costs, fees and expenses were recorded within the merchandise accounts, over the whole year, which means that they did not appear in the Profit and Loss account at all. And of course Hollingsworth followed contemporary practice when shipping goods, and transferred the goods shipped to the adventure account, so that the 357 £Pa 15s 4p listed in 1788 as the profit on the flour stocked and sold in his shop remained entirely disconnected from the profit realized on 'Flour taken up in the Jerseys', or within the framework of any other adventure.

Conclusion

On the whole, what we can gather from the activity of these two large traders buttresses the vision we derived from textbooks: double-entry accounting was undoubtedly used in the context of tracking credit flows as precisely as possible, but had little to do if at all with the measurement of profit and loss. This is quite logical, since trade in the eighteenth century rested first and foremost on the forbearance of creditors, whose advances enabled one to go on with one's business. When one adds to this element the necessity to use outside expertise for the goods one bought, it becomes obvious that one of the keys to success was the ability to rely on other traders, on a circle of allies. This was far more important than any bottom line in any discrete transaction, or even in a series of transactions. Double-entry accounting thus kept track of the quantitative, revolving part of a larger credit, that granted to a trader by other traders. There was a difficult balancing act to maintain on this score alone, making sure that enough cash was on hand to satisfy punctual demands for payment, and weeding out as much as possible potential defaulters from the ranks of those to whom a trader granted credit, with temporalities playing a key role in the whole process. Again, this was not a simple issue of bottom-line, since the other part of the equation, the necessity to have agents, had to be taken into account. When Gradis committed his wine to Jonathan Morgan in Cork, Ireland, he relied on Morgan's agency, both legally and materially, to fetch a good price and a profit. If Morgan delivered, then cutting him loose because of a late payment meant forsaking this particular source of income, at least for a time; another agent would have to be found and tested, and there was no telling what would come of it, nor whether the terms of payments one would obtain would not end up being worse for the change.

On the whole, each personal account should be read as a partial record of a more complex story, that of a relationship built over the years between two or more people around a specific market, product or place. There was not much interest in calculating a profit, even at this basic level, since the judgement on a relationship would entail a host of other parameters, most of them qualitative. But such a calculation became utterly pointless as soon as one tried to combine several such accounts; apple and pears could not be added. To take, again, Gradis's wine, each shipment was contextual, and Morgan's performance in Ireland was not to be compared with the results of a shipping venture to Quebec with the backing of the local *Intendant*. Conversely, the relationship with a supplier was centred on whether the quality level one was promised would actually be delivered, at what point in time and at what price – all pieces of information among many. Again, the overall judgement could not have much to do with accounting, or even with prices; whether the price of a wine was right was eminently a qualitative judgement, and was much more important in assessing a supplier than whether the price was low.

This is not to say that nothing should be recorded; when one had to deal with several hundred accounts exchanging their values on a daily basis, it became interesting, and even necessary, to track these flows as precisely as possible, all the more since making too many mistakes could well damage one's reputation, and lead to a loss of credit – a far, far worse risk than a mere loss of assets in this credit-dominated age. And it did not mean either that traders could not calculate the overall change in their assets, only that not too much should be read into their doing so. Observing an increase in assets was always gratifying, but did not have any practical impact on profit-making, since whatever lesson the past held for the future was not contained in the numbers of an account, but in the intangibles which underpinned the relationship it represented. And even when it came to overall performance, relying on accounting may not have been such a good idea. The distribution of one's wealth, as reflected in a general balance if one chose to draw it up, was bound to be transient, since the primary imperative was flexibility and the search for opportunity. For this particular quest, the hard numbers of early modern commercial accounting were much too static a source to be of much help, which means other tools were used, in ways the rest of this volume explores.

Acknowledgements

The present paper has benefitted from funding from the French ANR project MARPROF, and From CNRS UMR 8533 IDHE. I thank Dominique Margairaz, Yannick Lemarchand, and Robert DuPlessis for their helpful guidance and advice.

3 TERMS OF PAYMENT IN RETAILING: A TOOL FOR FOSTERING CUSTOMER LOYALTY OR A FORM OF MANAGERIAL CONSTRAINT? A FEW OBSERVATIONS BASED ON ACCOUNTING FROM LORRAINE IN THE EIGHTEENTH CENTURY

Julien Villain

Introduction

As discussed in Chapters 1 and 2, Basil Yamey has pointed out that merchants in the early modern period rarely tried to precisely calculate their profits.[1] This may be explained in his view by practical reasons – among shopkeepers, by the haphazard character of debtors' payments. Indeed, calculating profit during a given period implied that one take into account immobilization: debts which had not been recovered after several months represented a loss of income for the merchant, since the amount, if it had been paid back quickly, might have been reinvested. Since the vast majority of sales were made on credit, and payments were often made in the form of installments rather than in a lump sum, calculating the cost of immobilization on every sales operation was very difficult. Merchants, however, still tried to assess their profits and control their credit flows.

Credit relations are generally studied from the point of view of social history.[2] Very few studies, however, have focused on the role played by credit in merchants' businesses, or in the management practices it induced. Researchers have often been stumped by this question, deemed unsolvable or too difficult to treat given the current state of the record, or else they remained content with a few passing remarks aimed at showing the global level of sales on credit.[3] This gap complicates our knowledge of how a shop functioned during the early modern period. Whether negotiated or imposed, credit to consumers actually represented a strong constraint on commercial businesses: merchant bankruptcy was often caused by the passing insolvency of shopkeepers, temporarily unable to satisfy their creditors' demands.[4] As F. Braudel has pointed out, retail merchants were at the interface of two different systems of credit: one, developed among merchants, enforced a rapid rhythm of payment, while consumer credit was characterized by much longer delays.[5] Using the collected papers of three retailers from Lorraine from the first half of the eighteenth century, I propose to study the credit relations of shopkeepers with their creditors and debtors and to reflect on the constraint these relations represented for the merchants, and on the means they used to limit its effect.

The collected papers of several retail tradesmen can be found in the archives of the *Juridiction Consulaire* (Merchant court) from Lorraine and Barrois. The chapter examines the accounts of Jean-François Leléal,[6] active in Nancy from the end of the seventeenth century to 1722, of his son Dominique, a merchant in the same town from 1722 to the 1760s,[7] and of Germain Empereur, a merchant-clothier in Pont-à-Mousson from the 1720s to 1756.[8] In all three cases, the people studied were retail merchants specialized in the sale of cloth, thread, silk and accessories for clothing. As they were all three among the reputable merchants of their different cities, they sold mid- to upper-level quality merchandise to customers from all levels of society, but among which the prominent citizens of the town and of the local countryside were nonetheless overly represented. The operations carried out by these merchants were fairly similar: cloth sales and no money-lending, except a few hundred livres per year by Germain Empereur.[9]

Except in the case of Leléal the younger, who for the few months studied kept double-entry accounts, we are dealing with single-entry accounting. The documentation used is based on the day-books which recorded the sales made. The way in which the accounting documents were kept raises difficulties for the historian attempting to interpret them. Actually, shopkeepers in the early modern period often made do with a simple crossing out of the various parties involved when the debt was paid off by the customer, a practice which makes it impossible to study the length of consumer credit.[10] Luckily, the merchants studied here opened accounts for a large part of their customers, and recorded the instalments in their 'Sales' ledgers, a recording practice which gives us an idea of the terms of payment.[11] I analysed several months of entries in the day-books and sales ledgers of these three merchants, from January to December 1707 for Leléal the elder, from January to December 1722 for his son and from October 1752 to March 1753 for Empereur.

Behind the great variety of terms of payment several regular features appear. The 'good customers' – frequent buyers – benefitted from more generous terms of payment than occasional customers. Yet because merchants could not afford to structurally lose money, they necessarily had to compensate for the length of these stretched-out terms of payment. How did they do it though? No mention of any interest can be found in the accounts. However, it is possible that those who had promised to pay with the longest delay, or those who were judged by the merchant to present a greater risk, would have their merchandise sold to them at a higher price than the others: this is a hypothesis of price discrimination, the solidity of which I will try to assess. It is also possible that the extent and generalization of credit practices forced merchants to sell their products with large enough margins to compensate for outstanding debts or payment delays.

Terms of Payment in the Retail Business: How Extensive Were They?

A Large Amount of Outstanding Debt

One of the first constraints for retailers was the risk of default on the part of their customers. The accounts of Dominique Leléal and those of his father allow us to measure the general level of outstanding debt. However, I was not able to base this research on documents of the same time frame: the account books of the former only cover a period of three years, against twelve years for his fathers' papers. In both cases, nonetheless, the figures are telling.

Uncollected debt represented a considerable burden on these merchants' business, on the order of around 10%. For Jean-François Leléal, out of a total of 45,046 *livres lorraines* (£L) 19 *sous* (s.) of sales in 1707, 4,530 £L 11 s. were never recovered, which comes to 10.1% of sales. His son's accounting leads one to hypothesize a loss of the same order: three years after the sale, there were again 17.2% of the 28,101 £L 7 s. of sales in 1723, exactly 4,824 £L 6 s., both in wholesale and retail, which were outstanding. Indeed if one considers retail sales only, the amount of outstanding debt after three years reached 23.2%.

These rates seem very high: the only calculated comparison that I have been able to find until now concerns retail businesses in Tuscany in the fourteenth century, where outstanding debt amounted to 3 to 5% of total sales[12] – yet, it must be said, with considerable delays of recovery, on the order of several years. Was this very high degree of loss a structural characteristic of the retail business in the eighteenth century? Were such loses a result of bad markets faced by merchants at the time? Or were they related to errors of judgement on their part when it came to the solvency of their customers? The first hypothesis is the most plausible: Jean-François Leléal was bolder than his son in his extension of credit to consumers, but Leléal the younger nonetheless experienced his first bankruptcy in 1726. Thus, a rate of 10% of outstanding debt after twelve years did not keep a merchant from prospering.

Were customers of certain social categories worse at paying back than others?[13] The breakdown by social and professional category of Leléal the younger's clientele shows that in his retail business, all categories of the population had nearly comparable rates of outstanding debt at the end of three years, of around

10 to 15% – with the exception of the 'better sort' (commoners) and clergymen, who accumulated 50% of outstanding debt, and of professionals (*capacités*) and servants, held down to rates of respectively 0 and 5% in default. In his father's business, the only social category clearly above average in outstanding debt were also the higher ranks of the commoners, with an 18% default rate for an average of 10.1% of outstanding debt. Once again, *capacités*, crafstmen and nobles were among those who were good at paying up. Clergymen were also good debtors at the time. In both cases, it was thus rather the town bourgeois who were bad payers, the nobles having a tendency to pay off their debts in a satisfactory manner.[14] The study of the terms of payment, however, will bring to light some more noticeable social profiles.

Customers' Terms of Payment, a Major Constraint

The various kinds of accounting used allow us to find out the terms of payment commonly used in our merchants' businesses. For reasons pointed out in the introduction, we are in a position to know what all of Dominique Leléal's terms of payment for sales were in 1722. In the case of his father, I will only deal with those customers having a current account, i. e. 252 customers out of 408 (61.2%). The terms of payment have been studied in a very basic way, by comparing for every account the overall accumulated amounts of purchases and of payments.[15] These terms, computed here in weeks, thus correspond to the period of time separating the conclusion of the sale from the payment of the amount by the customer. I will study both the terms of clear payments settling the balance of a transaction and the terms for the payment of the first installment after a sale. In most cases, if truth be told, these two operations were conflated – i. e. there was only a one-time payment.

Cash sales – a settlement the same day or the day after – represented but a small part of operations. For Dominique Leléal, out of 20,807 £L of retail sales, only 3,461 £L of merchandise was paid for on the same day or the day after – that is 16.6% of all sales. If one makes this calculation including only the transactions actually paid off at the end of three years, the proportion increases to 21.7%, still a very small share. Two thirds of the amounts in cash were paid out in the month of January 1723 – this was a way no doubt for the young merchant to build up a sufficient preliminary financial reserve, at a time when he was just beginning his activities, a move which also proves that it was a common and natural practice in the retail business to extend credit.

The terms granted to customers extended over several months, or even several years: in the case of Dominique Leléal, six months after the sale, one third of the amounts due had not begun to be paid back. If one includes only the amount which had indeed been paid, two thirds of the amounts owed to Dominique Leléal would remain outstanding for over two months before being entirely paid off; one fourth remained due from two and six months; one fifth from six months to a year; and another fifth for one to three years. The figures are even more impressive for Jean-François Leléal's account holders: out of 26,642 £L 5 s. of sales paid for which we have indications on the terms of payment, 86.5% of the amounts due were still entirely outstanding six months after the sale, 70.7% one year later. As for clear payments, they took place only seven years or more after the sale for nearly 42% of the amount due! After six months, our merchant had obtained clear payments on only 747 £L 16 s. – barely 3% of his sales! The terms consented to by Empereur, while less spectacular, were of a similar nature overall.

These figures seem very high compared to other situations. For East Anglia in the 1650s, Craig Muldrew has shown that only 42% of plaintiffs waited more than six months after the conclusion of a deal to begin legal proceedings for default against their debtors, and 21% more than two years. Almost 60% of proceedings thus concerned claims on which sums had been owed for over one hundred days to a year, and even 18% were started over debts due for less than one hundred days.[16] This would tend to show that the customary terms of payment were rather short. One and a half centuries later, the Widow Colombo from Nice granted her customers very tight terms of payment: 'after 15 days or a month, the right-hand page of the register shows that the debtor has freed himself of his obligation'.[17] For his part Daniel Thorp, who studied merchant inn-keepers in North Carolina for the years 1750 and 1760, computes for current account holders an average interval of fourteen months between the last sale and the final payment of the debt.[18]

Perhaps in these three cases the outcome should be linked to the very small amount of money actually involved? Since the debts from which the customers needed to be freed were small, paying them was easy. The Lorraine merchants, on the other hand, made sales amounting to tens or even hundreds of £L, large amounts which were thus difficult even for wealthy patrons to pay off immediately or all at once. Thus, terms of payment ought to be distinguished according to the kinds of businesses and according to the size of the transactions carried out. Shops making sales worth large amounts (especially luxury or semi-luxury items) probably had the same type of terms as our Lorraine merchants: at Aubourg's, a Parisian jeweller studied by Natacha Coquery for the 1770s, the biggest buyers paid off what they had bought only after several years.[19]

Another Constraint: Credit between Merchants

These terms of payment were often in contradiction with those practised within the merchant sphere. In their relations with suppliers, retailers often had to pay off their debts within a mere few months. The Sales ledger of Germain Empereur allows us to give a few estimates for the period from 1720 to 1750: I have selected several personal accounts of suppliers with whom business relations extended over ten years or so and which are representative of his overall channels of supply.

Empereur generally paid his suppliers within a year, and the majority of payments were even made within six months. Indeed very often payments were made in cash within a few weeks. Out of twenty-seven purchases he made between 1724 and 1730 from the Passavant and sons merchant house in Frankfurt, amounting to a total of 19,960 Imperial florins, only eight were paid off after more than six months, for a total amount of 8,427 florins (42.2%) – and all of these were paid off within a year. Nine sales were paid for within less than three months, for a total of 2,436 florins. A similar distribution is found for the Jewish merchant from Frankfurt, Isaac, who around the same dates supplied 6,379 rixdales worth of merchandise: ten out of nineteen sales were paid for within less than six months, for 57% of the total amounts due, and the rest of the debts was cleared in less than a year. The terms were just as tight in the case of Bellile from Amiens, who sold Empereur more than 12,300 livres tournois (£t) worth of merchandise from 1730 to 1739: 73.3% of this amount was paid off within six months, 21.8% within from six months to a year, the remaining 4.9% after fifteen months at most. Concerning the 27,543 £t 18 s. due on sales by Guiraud of Lyon from 1732 to 1740, 44% was paid off in six months or less, 32.4% within from six months to a year, and 8% in less than sixteen months. One purchase worth 4,207 £t, made in December 1740, took four-and-a-half years to be paid off, but this was the beginning of Germain Empereur's shortage of funds, which would prompt him to ask for an extension in 1742. As it turns out, the bi-annual or annual rhythm of payments was related to the fairs of Frankfurt or Champagne, where Empereur, like many other Lorraine merchants importing goods, met with his suppliers once or twice a year. But the terms he received from his creditors in Lorraine were similar: out of 33.404 £L 15 s. worth of goods purchased by Empereur from the Coster brothers of Nancy between 1736 and 1742, 48.5% were paid in six months or less, and 34.5% in six months to a year. The only three claims paid with terms of over a year again reflected purchases made in the 1740s, out of which an amount of 4,046 £L was paid within twenty four months. Similar sales terms can be found in our shop-keepers' own records: the few wholesale and retail wholesale sales made by Empereur and Dominique Leléal were characterized by optimum rates of recovery. In the case of Leléal, such sales amounted to 7294 £L 2 s. in 1723, or 25.9% of his total sales. Of this amount, 52% was already collected after six months, and 46% in six months to a year.[20]

Why was there such a difference in terms of payment between credit to consumers and the realm of regional or inter-regional credit? The correspondence exchanged among merchants is in fact full of more or less sincere complaints about how slim profit margins were. If one were to believe the suppliers of the

Widow Navière, a wholesaler in Nancy, they earned little more than the rate of interest on money – 6% in Old Regime France. The firm Dollfuss brothers, Vetter et Cie. of Dornach near Mulhouse thus wrote on 28 April 1757:

> We were very surprised upon opening your honored of the 21st instant to see that you find our ribbons to be more expensive than those that you say you get from Basel. We cannot conceive why it is so since *we quote prices at the lowest rate possible and we only earn the interest of our money.*

The letter of J. Proust from Nogent-le-Rotrou, on 26 April 1758, follows the same line of argument: 'I find the profit here so limited that it would be more advantageous to offer my money on the market'.[21] Such reduced earnings in large-scale trade meant that rapid payment on the part of customers was indispensable. Given the stability of the supply channels of Lorraine merchants in the eighteenth century and the relatively low number of suppliers, it was no doubt impossible for them to default on payment to one of them without risking their credit with the others. That was in all likelihood a motivation to pay one's creditors quickly.

On the whole, after four or five years, merchants were able to recover nine tenths of the amount of their sales for one year: payment for the sales of the preceding years thus covered more or less the expenses of the current year. It is possible, however, that these terms were mostly in use in the luxury and semi-luxury trade, and that they were tighter in more modest shops – but even in these, the balance of the cash-flow probably would have been irregular. Still, terms of payment were not totally random and corresponded to well-established practices of relations with the clientele.

Differentiated Forms of Credit to Customers

Retailers did not offer the same conditions of credit to all the patrons of their shops. 'Good customers', who bought large quantities of merchandise, thus paid with very long terms, which was not the case for occasional customers. This point will be elaborated here through an analysis of Germain Empereur's accounts.

Differentiated Lengths of Credit

In Empereur's shop, terms of payment were differentiated according to the kinds of customers. A certain clientele, which paid on very generous terms – with most of its members having a current account – should be distinguished from the customers who paid their debts quickly – and who frequently purchased items only once, or only occasionally.

The study of the terms of payment for customers without an account is possible thanks to the inventory established by Empereur on 15 March 1753. While completing it, our merchant actually opened a special chapter for unpaid active debts contained in the 'new journal' – precisely the one from which I have drawn my information. Thus I could take note of the amount of every sale made between 1 October 1752 and 15 March 1753, and check to see if the debt contracted by the client was still outstanding at the time when the inventory was made. While this method does not allow us to find out how much time it took for each debt to be paid off, one can evaluate on a weekly basis the share of debts contracted since 1 October 1752 which was actually settled by 15 March 1753. This gives us an estimate of the speed with which debts were cleared. The table below shows in the first column the amount of sales for every week from 1 October 1752 to 15 March 1753 ('W-24' refers to the twenty-fourth week before the inventory was created, thus the week of 1 October 1752: for every week, the last column shows the percentage of debts recovered by 15 March 1753).

Table 3.1: Debt recovery from customers of Germain Empereur not holding current accounts, October 1752–March 1753.

	Sales	Still due as of 03/15/1753	Recovered as of 03/15/1753	Recovery rate
W-24	331.25	171.25	160	48.3
W-23	481.3	79.2	402.1	83.5
W-22	169.45	0	169.45	100.0
W-21	30.1	16.8	13.3	44.2
W-20	156.8	23.2	133.6	85.2
W-19	381.2	52.7	328.5	86.2
W-18	736.55	83.8	652.75	88.6
W-17	568.75	127.65	441.1	77.6
W-16	8.3	0	8.3	100.0
W-15	799.25	127.2	672.05	84.1
W-14	193.2	100.55	92.65	48.0
W-13	956.75	37.8	918.95	96.0
W-12	203.85	0	203.85	100.0
W-11	458.35	0	458.35	100.0
W-10	608	207.15	400.85	65.9
W-9	168.95	39.6	129.35	76.6
W-8	1065.25	564.9	500.35	47.0
W-7	153.25	29.95	123.3	80.5
W-6	85.8	79.8	6	7.0
W-5	618.3	406.3	212	34.3
W-4	523.3	76.9	446.4	85.3
W-3	273.35	268.3	5.05	1.8
W-2	356.05	214	142.05	39.9
W-1	397.1	397.1	0	0.0

Overall, the debt recovery rate sharply decreased only ten weeks before the date at which inventory had been made. On the whole, recovery rates reached 85% for sales made before this date – this level incidentally would have been much higher without two sales made during the weeks 'W-24' and 'W-14' to a very bad payer, one Sheldon, an English aristocrat lost in Lorraine. On the date of the inventory, 37.2% of the sales made during the month preceding its making (W-5 to W-1), the total amount of which was 2,168.1 £L, had been paid for, and of those made in the previous two months previously (W-10 to W-6), for a total of 2,081.25 £L, 55.7% were paid for. Only the sales of the preceding week had not brought in any payment at all. In other words, while no payment was made within a week, a third of the amounts owed was collected by the end of one month, more than half by the end of two months, and almost 80% by the end of three months. Thus one can conclude to a certain regularity in the terms of payment, which were not totally random: debts were paid off within one to three months.[22]

The terms of payment were much longer for account holders, however. Out of 160 sales made to customers holding accounts between 1 October 1752 and 15 March 1753, only three purchases had been paid by the time the inventory was made. For the remaining 157 transactions, there were several scenarios:

(1) In ninety-four cases, the sale was paid in full at the time of a later global payment for several successive sales.

(2) In twenty-six cases, the payment was made in several instalments, partial payments being made especially at the time of new purchases.

(3) In twenty-two cases, Empereur had not been paid at the time of the closing of the book: one must thus compute a *minimum* term of payment, by comparing the date of the last purchase and the date of the last payment.

(4) In eight cases, one can determine only a *maximum* term of payment, by comparing the columns 'debitor' and 'creditor' when the postings on the 'creditor' side are not precisely dated.

(5) The seven other cases correspond to specific situations, in which clients had signed promissory notes to Empereur, with no mention of actual payment being made.

Payment transactions of the first kind are easiest to treat and to analyse. By comparing the purchases made, recorded in the 'debtor' column, with the payments which were made for these goods, recorded in the 'creditor' column, the clearance time of each debt can be determined, expressed in months.

Table 3.2: Debt recovery from customers of Germain Empereur holding current accounts, October 1752–March 1753.

	2 months	2 to 6 months	6 months to a 1 year	1 to 2 years	over 2 years	Total
Number of sales	1	14	19	37	23	94
Percentage	1.1	14.9	20.2	39.4	24.5	100.0
Amounts of sales	51	499.3	473.55	1,651	856.15	3,531
percentage	1.4	14.1	13.4	46.8	24.2	

Sales paid for within the period considered normal for customers without accounts were clearly the exception here. Only one sale paid for in less than two months can be found here, and fifteen paid for in less than six months, and for only 15% of the amounts involved. For a majority of payments, Empereur had to wait from twelve to twenty-four months; at the end of two years, he had only been able to collect three-quarters of the amount of his sales. The study of the payments for the other sub-categories confirms these observations: in category (3) cases, it is certain in eighteen cases out of twenty-two that the term of payment was longer than six months (these eighteen cases amounting to 710 £L worth of sales, or 71.3% of the total amount of sales in that category), and in thirteen sales payment certainly took over a year. The study of payments in several instalments, i. e. category (2), is more difficult. Still it is possible to calculate that out of twenty-six cases (the total amount of sales being 1918 £L 5 s.), the first instalments were paid six months after the sale only in seven cases; the initial sums thus recovered by Empereur totalled 221 £L, out of 608 £L 1 s. due to him by these same seven customers. In other words, he had recovered a little over a third of the claims he had on barely a third of his total sales in this category. The period within which the first instalment was paid equal to longer than one year in twelve cases, worth 883 £L 1 s. of sales. As for final payments, they point to truly unbelievable terms of payment: the claim most rapidly paid off took already nine months to be settled. After a year, six of these claims were paid, but twelve others had not been cleared two years after the original sale. When all is said and done, it is no exaggeration to consider that for debts owed by account holders, it took two years to reach recovery rates of three-quarters, while this same rate of recovery was achieved in a mere three months for debts of customers not holding accounts.

These differentiated rhythms of payment are consistent with what has been observed for the English merchant Abraham Dent, active in Cumberland in the 1760s: occasional clients generally paid their debts within ten days, whereas regular customers were granted six months' credit.[23] While these figures are not applicable here – all the more so because they are not provided with any degree of precision in the original study – it cannot be denied that credit practices among these merchants varied according to the degree of loyalty and reliability of the clientele.

Opening Accounts with Merchants

Such a marked difference in the terms of payment may be explained in several other ways: one might think customers holding accounts did not have the same social origins as non-account-holders, that there were more nobles or prominent citizens among holders of accounts, and that the aristocratic practice of not honouring one's debts on time influenced the rate of payment. One cannot rule out either, and this is the second possibility to be considered, that Germain Empereur was fairly strict with the customers he did not know, demanding tight terms of payment, whereas he was much more generous with regular customers, especially if he knew them to be solvent. The study of the social breakdown of his clientele corroborates the latter hypothesis.

Table 3.3: Social circumstances of Germain Empereur's account-holding customers, 1752–3.

Account	Individuals		Sales		
holders	num.	%	amt.	%	Average sale
DAY	0	0.0	0	0.0	0.0
CRAFT	19	19.6	496.3	7.2	26.1
MERCH	2	2.1	367	5.3	183.5
STAT	3	3.1	71.15	1.0	23.7
BETT	21	21.6	1,566.2	22.6	74.6
PROF	7	7.2	438.65	6.3	62.7
ADM	3	3.1	339.4	4.9	113.1
NOB	16	16.5	2,129.3	30.7	133.1
CLERG	11	11.3	1,153.8	16.7	104.9
NSPEC	15	15.5	363.85	5.3	24.3
	97	100.0	6,925.65	100.0	71.4

See note 13 for categories in the Notes section on pp. 13–14.

Table 3.4: Social circumstances of Germain Empereur's non-account-holding customers, 1752–3.

Customers	Individuals		Sales		
not holding an account	num.	%	amt.	%	Average sale
DAY	1	0.7	13.1	0.1	13.1
CRAFT	22	15.9	562.45	6.4	25.6
MERCH	9	6.5	244.05	2.8	27.1
STAT	7	5.1	539.55	6.1	77.1
BETT	41	29.7	2,358.85	26.7	57.5
PROF	17	12.3	889.35	10.1	52.3
ADM	10	7.2	1,235.75	14.0	123.6
NOB	10	7.2	1,743.6	19.8	174.4
CLERG	9	6.5	829.85	9.4	92.2
NSPEC	12	8.7	409	4.6	34.1
	138	100.0	8,825.55	100.0	64.0

The size of the purchases of these account-holders, from tens to hundreds of livres, excluded large segments of the population. Indeed, Empereur's account-holders were mostly from among the elite of the city and its region, with the percentage of nobles, administrators and clergymen reaching 30.9%, as opposed to around 21% among non- account-holders. Nobles bought around one third of the merchandise sold to account-holders; adding clergymen and administrators, the elite group accounted for half of all sales. This being said, while the social origins of account-holders were undoubtedly more aristocratic than those of non-account-holders, this fact cannot explain in and of itself such long terms of payment, since nobles also owed over one-fifth of the total amount of debts due by non-account-holders – the two groups were not so different in this respect. Moreover, bourgeois clients from the city and the countryside, as well as other commoners, were responsible on their own for at least 45% of all sales to account-holders. While the aristocratic *ethos* may have driven noble customers to pay late, it must be observed once more that they had no exclusive claims on long terms of payment.

Table 3.5: Social circumstances of customers being granted an account at Empereur's, October 1752–March 1753.

Customers obtaining an account	Individuals		Sales		Average sale
	num.	%	amt.	%	
DAY	0	0.0	0	0.0	0.0
CRAFT	0	0.0	0	0.0	0.0
MERCH	2	10.5	291.7	10.2	145.9
STAT	0	0.0	0	0.0	0.0
BETT	6	31.6	292.4	10.2	48.7
PROF	3	15.8	673.8	23.5	224.6
ADM	2	10.5	927.2	32.4	463.6
NOB	3	15.8	377.5	13.2	125.8
CLERG	2	10.5	294.9	10.3	147.5
NSPEC	1	5.3	4	0.1	4.0
	19	100.0	2,861.5	100.0	150.6

The opening of an account at Empereur's was closely linked to the frequency of purchases: from the second purchase an account was generally opened for clients. The cases observed are too few to allow us to draw conclusions about their breakdown into social categories. The average amount of sales per customer becoming an account-holder over the six months observed came to 150 £L, that is, more than double the average sales to account-holders. The admittance into the category 'customer with an account', it thus seems, may be explained by functional criteria: from the time a customer made repeated and large purchases, Empereur opened an account for this person. Given the average level of purchases made by these customers, and their sociological background, one may gather that these were people deemed solvent and commanding a sufficient amount of credit. Empereur would thus not have been very demanding with them concerning terms of payment, because he knew them, had already 'tested' them and knew that they would end up paying. Trust in these customers, or at least a wager on their solvency, seemed to outweigh the desire for a rapid completion of payments.

Terms of Payment and Negotiation

In Lorraine as in the kingdom of France, the only two ways to make possible the attachment of a writ of execution to a debt was to bring customers to sign a promissory note, or to settle their accounts with them. Both of these procedures were recognized in the jurisprudence, and made it possible to force the recalcitrant debtor to pay up on his debts by force of law. Explaining this in his famous *Parfait Négociant*,[24] Jacques Savary seems to deplore that these instruments were so little used by merchants. Indeed, we meet cases of accounts being settled as recommended by Savary only a few times throughout Leléal the Elder's dealings, who on these occasions at least had customers sign a promissory note for the amounts outstanding. However, this practice only involved a few large customers who were late in settling their accounts, and from whom our merchant demanded a clear commitment to pay up. Most of these notes were 'payable on order', without any mention of a set date. Was all this just hot air? Germain Empereur's practice was different from that of Leléal the elder's, since he demanded promissory notes only from those customers he did not know, generally customers of a lower social level than his usual patrons, and in whom he had apparently little confidence – a practice he records in his Sales ledgers as 'signed accounts'. Thus on 20 November 1752 he sold 13 £L 2 s. worth of cloth from the North and of printed calico to Nicolas Portier, an unskilled worker from Pont-à-Mousson, but on the condition that he would be 'paying at the next Easter festival'. Empereur even forced him to find two cautions, François Laîné and Jean Blanchetête, who signed next to his mark.[25] In any case, it seems that it was very rare for the merchants examined here to seek guarantees for payment.

Were they any different from their colleagues in this respect? Bankruptcy inventories made between 1715 and 1730 for retail merchants in the province unfortunately do not indicate systematically whether a given active debt had brought about the drawing up of a note:[26] The inventories generally include all of the debts within the same category without distinguishing whether they are promissory or simply mentioned in the account books. However, for eight merchants for whom this distinction was made, the proportion of promissory notes was high, often around half the amount owed by the customers,[27] and as often over 60% of this amount:[28] we are far from a merely sporadic use of promissory notes on the part of our shopkeepers.

However, nothing indicates that the obligations created by these notes had to be met within the stipulated term of payment. In 1752, Empereur held twenty-nine promissory notes signed directly onto his journal, for a total amount of 871 £L 13 s. – which is less than 5% of the total sales for the year. Of this amount, 30 £L 19 s. were never paid, and a sale worth 27 £L was rapidly returned. A large sale worth 167 £L 16 s., having given rise to a promissory note payable in one year, was indeed paid by the theoretical due date, with a second promissory note, with no term specified, and concerning which nothing indicates that it was ever settled. Of the twenty-two remaining promissory notes, amounting to a total of 626 £L, ten were payable 'on order': except for one, which was paid after seven months, the others were settled, for half of them, from one to two years later, and for the other half, after two to three years. For the twelve other promissory notes, in which a date or time of year had been mentioned ('by next Christmas', 'at the next grape harvest'), the terms were respected only in two cases – and even anticipated in one of them. For all other cases, the delays were once again very long, on the order of three years. Thus the terms of payment in the case of promissory notes were in fact extremely lengthy, and delays to the agreed upon dates almost systematic.

What the shopkeepers sought to obtain above all from those owing outstanding debt were commitments to pay.[29] This was achieved through various arrangements of which Germain Empereur's account books give us a glimpse: M. Danglard, from Crincourt, had been paying Empereur since 1751 by having sent directly to the latter his pension of 400 £t, which he received as a veteran soldier from the French Royal Treasury;[30] on 14 March 1753, M. de Mercy from Nomeny, who wanted to clear his debts, signed to the order of Empereur an obligation for 1,400 £L 'payable in two years'.[31] One can even find a very curious case, in which Empereur put the English aristocrat Sheldon up as a lodger in his own home for two years. This may have been a way to control the amount of his spending and to demand regular payments from him.[32] The analysis of the bankruptcy inventories of Lorraine retail merchants between 1715 and 1730 shows that these various arrangements, called 'contracts', could amount to up to one-fifth of a retailer's active debts.[33]

Judicial proceedings for debt were not necessarily meant to obtain the immediate payment of amounts due, but were part of a context in the negotiations between a creditor and his debtor: they were used to speed up the conclusion of an arrangement.[34] They were resorted to only infrequently: in the active debts of bankrupt merchants, the amounts due 'by judgement' were comparatively of minor importance, representing around 5 to 10% of the total amount outstanding.[35] While it is not possible to consider our limited survey on this point as conclusive evidence, it does not seem that merchants went very often before mid-level or low-level jurisdictions such as *bailliages* or *prévôtés* to obtain payment of debts owed to them. Out of 209 investigations conducted in 1752 by the court of the *prévôté* and *bailliage* of Nancy, forty-six involved persons related to craft or to commerce, of which only seventeen were over issues of payment,[36] – and since the description of these cases in the trial notes was very brief, it is not even certain that all these trials had been brought about by sales which had not been paid for. But in any case this figure sounds quite low. This reluctance to use judicial means, especially to obtain the seizure of debtors' property, perhaps explains the very high number of 'rotten' or 'lost' debts among bankrupt merchants. In the bankruptcy inventories studied, good debts amounted generally to between 50 and 60% of all outstanding claims, the rest being considered 'rotten', 'dubious', 'bad' or 'lost'.[37] Even among those bankrupts whose situation was not as dire, between 15 and 25% of all debts were deemed difficult or impossible to recover.[38] For the merchants to demand their due, but not with so much insistence as to risk their reputation in the communities where they resided, was certainly a tricky proposition. The club-like and interlinked relationships through which members of the Pont-à-Mousson local elite were acquainted, and in which Empereur took part as councillor of City Hall, in all likelihood made it dangerous for the latter to present excessively pressing demands for payment: once offended, wouldn't his patrons go to the competition?[39] Beyond private arrangements with their debtors, shop-keepers thus either couldn't or wouldn't use the legal tools to enforce the payment of overdue debts.

Long terms of payment corresponded to deeply rooted practices, whether these were imposed by clients or integrated by merchants into their commercial strategies. Because of this practice, they were faced with long delayed repayments over a large part of amounts owed to them, and even in some cases with substantial loss. How then did they manage to even out their incomes and outlays?

How to Break Even: The Issue of Sales Prices

Merchants compensated for the immobilization of their funds by setting high sales prices, implicitly including the annual interest rate on capital – 6% in the French market in the eighteenth century – in the price sticker of the goods they sold.[40] Depending on the social position of the customers, particularly whether or not they were going to be able to quickly repay them, merchants may also have practiced some form of price discrimination.

Gross Margins

Let us now attempt to build some gross margin percentages. I used Germain Empereur's journals for 1752, and noted the recorded prices of purchase and sale of cloth for the most representative among his various product lines. Since prices varied both when purchasing and when selling, I have calculated the range of possible gross margins for each product studied. I calculated the exchange for foreign currency (Imperial florins or Livre tournois) at par: 129 ⅙% for French currency, and 163% for Imperial currency. By carrying the study out over a single year, I hoped to reduce the bias that inflation might have introduced in the price level measurements.

Table 3.6: Germain Empereur's gross margin rates on merchandise purchased in Frankfurt, 1752

Merchandise (place of purchase)	Unit purchase price (in £L per Paris *aune*)		Unit sales price in Lorraine (in £L per Paris *aune*)		Gross margins	
	Minimum	Maximum	Minimum	Maximum	Minimum	Maximum
Ordinary Calico (Frankfurt)	34 s. 11 d.	37 s. 6 d.	42 s.	45 s.	12%	29%
Calico for furniture (Frankfurt)	35 s. 6 d.	38 s. 1 d.	44 s.		15%	24%
Ordinary *Calancas* (Frankfurt)	77 s. 6 d.	90 s. 6 d.	4 liv.		−11%	3%
Fine *Calancas* (Frankfurt)	5 liv. 16 s.		6 liv. 5 s.		8%	
Ordinary Flannel (Frankfurt)	46 s. 6 d.	47 s. 10 d.	50 s.	3 liv.	5%	29%
Ordinary North Cloth (Frankfurt)	7 liv. l. 4 s.		8 liv. 10 s.	9 liv. 10 s.	18%	32%
Semi-fine North Cloth (Frankfurt)	9 liv. l. 6 s.		10 liv.	11 liv.	7.5%	18%
Ordinary English Druggets (Frankfurt)	2 liv. l. 16 s.		3 liv. 3 s.	3 liv. 10 s.	18%	25%
Twilled English Druggets (Frankfurt)	4 liv. l. 8 s.		3 liv. 5 s.	3 liv. 15 s.	13%	25%

North Cloth = 'Drap du Nord', Twilled English Drugget = 'Droguets d'Angleterre croisés'.

Table 3.7: Germain Empereur's gross margin rates on merchandise purchased in France, 1752.

Merchandise (place of purchase)	Unit purchase price (in £L per Paris *aune*)		Unit sales price in Lorraine (in £L per Paris *aune*)		Gross margins	
	Minimum	Maximum	Minimum	Maximum	Minimum	Maximum
Ordinary Buckram (Champagne)	11 s. 7 d.		24 s.		107%	
Ras de St Maur (Champagne)	8 liv. 8 s.		10 liv. 3 s.		21%	
Ras de St Cyr (Champagne)	5 liv. 9 s. 9 d.		8 liv. 5 s.	8 liv. 12 s.	50%	57%
Ras de St Lô (Champagne)	6 liv. 15 s. 7 d.		7 liv.	7 liv. 10 s.	3%	11%
Cadiz (Champagne)	1 liv. 5 s. 9 d.		1 liv. 10 s.		16%	
Black Segovia Fine (Champagne)	4 liv. 15 s. 7 d.		5 liv.	5 liv. 10 s.	5%	15%
Dauphine (Champagne)	1 liv. 14 s. 9 d.	1 liv. 16 s. 3 d.	1 liv. 16 s.	1 liv. 18 s.	–1%	9%
Elbeuf Cloth (Champagne)	18 liv. 14 s. 9 d.		19 liv.	20 liv.	2%	7%
Striped Muslin (Champagne)	2 liv. 7 s. 9 d.		2 liv. 10 s.		5%	
Muslin *mi-bouchon* (Champagne)	2 liv. 7 s. 9 d.		3 liv. 10 s.		29%	
Imperial (Champagne)	5 liv. 16 s. 3 d.		7 liv.		20%	
Scarlet plush (Champagne)	6 liv. 9 s. 3 d.		8 liv. 10 s.		32%	
Serge of Mandres (Champagne)	1 liv. 11 s.		2 liv.	2 liv. 6 s.	29%	48%
Laval Linen (Champagne)	2 liv. 1 s. 5 d.	2 liv. 19 s. 5 d.	2 liv. 6 s.	3 liv. 5 s.	–23%	9%
Marville Drugget (Lorraine)	1 liv. 10 s.		2 liv. 6 s.		53%	

Buckram = 'Bougrand', Cadiz = 'Cadis', Black Segovia Fine = 'Prime Ségovie Noire', Elbeuf Cloth = 'Drap d'Elbeuf', Striped Muslin = 'Etamine rayée', Muslin *mi-bouchon* = 'Etamine mi-bouchon', Imperial = 'Impérial', Scarlet Plush = 'Pluche écarlate', Mandres Serge = 'Serge de Mandres', Laval Linene = 'Toile de Laval', Marville Drugget = 'Droguet de Marville'.

Despite their high level of differentiation, Empereur's gross margin rates were frequently of more than 15%, even reaching quite often 20 or 25%, and in a few cases going up to 30 or 40% or even more. Still, our merchant must have incurred losses on some products such as *calancas*, *dauphines* or Laval linens;

these goods were not very profitable, but they were popular with customers, so that they doubtless fulfilled a function of loss leader. On the whole, what stands out is that Empereur apparently achieved a global gross margin of 20%. This allowed him to make a decent living off his business, provided that:

(a) the amount of unrecovered debts did not exceed 10% of the total amount of sales;

(b) the quantity of unsold goods remained limited – unfortunately, it is impossible to estimate it, since one cannot trace a given good in the accounts; given a limited amount of unsold products, around 5% of the value of the total inventory, Empereur's commercial position was tenable as long as other expenses and shop management costs were kept reasonable;

(c) in the same vein, Empereur did not not employ sales-clerks, the transportation costs on the fabrics kept being small (at most, they were on the order of 1 to 2% of the price at which fabrics were purchased),[41] and he could buy cheaply the commercial paper he needed in order to make the necessary remittances to his creditors.[42]

Still, it must not be forgotten that Empereur had made the choice of reaching outside of the province he lived in to get his own assortment (and the same was true for the Leléals), and that he did so almost entirely without having recourse to the wholesale merchants in Nancy. For this reason, his margins were no doubt larger than those of retailers who had to rely on these large local traders in order to build up their stock on hand. Had they used similar credit practices, retailers without outside suppliers would have found it much more difficult to keep their heads above water than the solidly established shop-keepers studied here. Other local merchants thus may not have granted credit quite as liberally as Empereur or the Leléals, and the latters' commercial practices may have been a luxury that could be afforded only by a few large retailers with outside supply sources.

Price Discrimination?

Were there special prices for 'bad payers'? In which case, the price of a good would take into account the 'quality' of the customer, and would include an implicit interest rate according to an agreed-upon or hoped-for date of payment. I have attempted a comparative study, here only in rough draft form, of the price levels and effective terms of payment for Germain Empereur, using the sales recorded in his journal between 1 October 1752 and 15 March 1753. Given the extreme variety of the merchandise, I have only retained for this analysis goods which were traded in at least ten transactions; to avoid any bias which might have been introduced by the quality of the products, I have distinguished the products within the groups of merchandise by their degree of fineness and by their colour when it was significant.

Table 3.8: Germain Empereur's sales prices for various types of fabrics, October 1752–March 1753.

	Number of occurrences	Average price per *aune* (*sous*) (1)	Standard deviation (in *sous*) (2)	Coefficient of variation (2)/(1)
Cadiz	59	30.3	1.5	5
English Drugget	10	69.65	1.95	2.8
Mulsinettes	20	84.4	5	5.9
Flannel	34	50.5	5.5	10.9
Calico	11	43.3	1.2	2.8
Flannelettes	15	80.5	4.0	5.0
Plushes	36	77.1	5.8	7.6

Cadiz = 'Cadis', Muslinettes = 'Etamettes', Flannelettes = 'Molletons', Plushes = 'Pluches'.

Despite the absence of a set price for merchandise, the variations were limited: generally around 5 to 6% of the average price, and not much more than 10% in extreme cases. But how can we account for this lack of a set price? Admittedly a narrow sample has been used here, but I still tried to test the hypothesis of a calibration of prices on the agreed upon terms of payment: a customer who was a 'bad payer' or who did not inspire confidence would receive a slightly higher bill than other customers for his goods, within a range of 5 to 10%. I was able to identify sixteen sales of grey plushes ('pluches'), for an average price of 77 s., slightly lower than the average price for all of the coloured plushes. Prices varied from 70 to 80 s. per *aune*. The five customers who paid the most – 80 s. – were all account-holders for whom the terms of payment were from ten to thirty-seven months. Of the five who paid the least, between 70 to 75 s. per *aune*, four were not account-holders, and all of them paid what they owed within four months. The fifteen sales of flanelettes ('molletons') were made for amounts between 77 s. 6 d. and 90 s. Of the five buyers paying the most, at least three took more than five months to pay up; indeed the widow Plaît had yet to pay for her purchases three years after the sale. Conversely, of the five who paid the least, 77 s. 6 d., four had paid their debt within four months. This rough correlation between the price and the length the term of payment support the theory that a differentiated billing of goods was calculated according to customers' payment habits or according to an agreement at the time of purchase. The modulation of prices remained moderate: Germain Empereur was not the only merchant in Pont-à-Mousson doing the same business and local competition set sharp limits to the extent to which he could raise his prices.

This explanation is but a rough outline and calls for further elaboration. Information on the actual quality of the products may well have been missing from the Sales ledger, or limited, whenever it was mentioned at all, to remarks about the colour or fineness of the cloth: since production was not at all standardized at the time, and thus any fabric was in a way a unique artefact, it might be that within a single general category (for example 'ordinary') there could be several degrees of fineness of a product that would explain slight price differences. Indications about the general state of the fabric are perhaps also missing: an old piece or one that is somewhat faded would be sold for less than a completely new piece. Thus might price differences, apparently here on the order of 5 to 10%, not be better explained by quality variations that cannot be captured from our sources? Or perhaps such variations should be linked to the nuanced differences between merchants' personal relationships with customers, which to a large degree escape our observation? This is no doubt the most plausible explanation: in Jean-François Leléal's sales records, members of the ducal court benefited from special prices, with an explicitely listed 'profit at 2 *sous* per Livre', that is a margin of 10% above the purchase price, even though these customers were not characterized by the speed with which they paid, indeed rather the reverse![43] Thus at this point the hypothesis that there was price discrimination proportional to terms of payment is not based on strong enough empirical evidence to be either disproved or confirmed. While cases were found of price discrimination for 'bad payers', it does not seem to have been a systematic practice: moreover, it remains to be seen whether 'bad payers', recognized as such, *always* paid more.

Conclusion

Careful study of the sales and clientele of these three shop-keepers from Nancy and Pont-à-Mousson, purveyors, notably, of local high society, reveals that the retail trade was a fairly risky activity, because of the difficulty of mastering cash flows. This difficulty was due to the terms of payment the merchants had to accept, especially from their regular customers. It is possible however that the cases observed here exaggerate features otherwise common to all shopkeepers. Our merchants were also importers, a fact which allowed them to do without the mediation of wholesalers in order to build up their stocks. For this reason, their gross margins were fairly high, and they were therefore able to offer long-term credit to their clientèle and to incur without too much difficulty up to 10% of their balances remaining outstanding. Still, there is no doubt that these particular merchants granted credit too liberally; this would explain the bankruptcies of Leléal the younger in 1726 and of Empereur in 1756. Their colleagues at the same level of business, but also more modest merchants from the small towns and the countryside, certainly had less generous – and less risky – credit practices.

What can be learnt from this exploration of the way shops worked within the framework of a study of merchant profit? First of all, even though retail traders did indeed care about profit, as can be seen in their correspondence, they did not equip themselves with the instruments which would have allowed them to measure it. Credit practices admittedly made it tricky to calculate profit satisfactorily, but these retailers did not even calculate their costs: in the accounting used here, expenses for the transportation of goods, shop-related costs, or even the cost of procuring commercial paper, were not even mentioned. This confirms that accounting had as its primary function the tracking of the flow of credit.

Actually, profit estimates must have been based to a large degree upon conjecture and extrapolation: our merchants knew roughly what margin they realized on every operation, and were thereby able to estimate their global profit. Moreover, the moderate rise in the price of fabric in the eighteenth century probably contributed to the relative stability of their margins – and to their predictability.[44] In parallel, the operating costs of the shop, which were undistinguishable from those of the household, were subject to few uncertainties, as were those for the transportation of products, which remained stable throughout the century and were quite marginal in the fabric trade. Finally, the state of the coffers was a good indication of the level of payments made by the customers. In any common year, barring economic difficulties hindering the timely payment of amounts due by customers, profit could be roughly estimated and predicted.[45]

The credit practices of our merchants, especially their refusal to have outstanding debt systematically attached at law in order to obtain rapid payment, suggests that they were not necessarily always seeking to maximize their profit from their retail operations. Frequent recourse to the courts would no doubt have damaged their credit and their respectability in the community in which where they operated, saddling them with a reputation as litigious overreachers. Indeed our merchants were rather perhaps in search of the 'fair' profit described by Jean-Yves Grenier: profit obtained in an honourable fashion, allowing them to repay whatever others advanced them, and to maintain a lifestyle in conformity with the exigencies of their station.[46] In which case we could interpret the credit practices presented here as the reflection of a broader economic system in which the agents were motivated less by wealth than by social recognition and respectability.

4 THE WINGS OF A BUTTERFLY: PRIVATE CREDITOR STRATEGIES IN THE 'CHINESE DEBTS' CRISIS OF 1779–80

Frederic Grant, Jr

A debt crisis exploded on the China coast in the late 1770s. Groups of private creditors, notably British and French citizens, sought to collect over $5 million which they claimed was owed to them by Chinese hong merchants. This chapter examines these claims, the creditor groups and the strategies that were employed to recover monies advanced to Chinese citizens. French and other foreign creditors received nothing. British creditors collected a fraction of their claims, which was paid without interest over ten years. This episode caused the Chinese government to modify the rules governing the Canton System leading to their final or mature form.

The issues involved in this crisis, and the regulatory response to claims of foreign creditors seeking the payment of principal and interest alike, are all familiar today. As with the flap of the wings of an imagined butterfly, consequences of the demands for payment in full of 1779–80 were felt across the globe. One idea produced by this debt crisis, carried from China to the United States, evolved and transported across the globe, is now a fundamental of banking regulation worldwide.

Introduction

The crisis of 1779–80 arose from loans that had been made by private European lenders to Chinese merchants over approximately the fifteen preceding years. The crisis arose in Canton, the locus of a burgeoning trade that was both confined to that port and closely regulated by the Qing government. The centres of power – political and economic, in Europe and in China – were far away. The crisis broke at a vortex of monopolies, yet it had nothing to do with monopoly. The borrower hong merchants were licensed by the Chinese government to conduct maritime foreign trade on a monopoly basis. The lenders, private parties or their agents, all had some connection with the European East Asia Companies. The era of these behemoths was not yet over, but their influence was waning. In this crisis, the great companies had no direct connection with the loans that had been made, and depended on the Chinese debtors in order to carry on foreign trade. For the most part, they viewed the private foreigners who lent and did other business in their shadow as an irritant. Yet the future would be seized by the private traders. The loans themselves were doubly illegal under Chinese law, which had prohibited lending to hong merchants since 1760, and also barred collection of any interest in excess of the principal amount advanced. From a Western viewpoint, this conflict had little to do with standard conceptions of profit, as in the context of the fruits of the land or even of industrial investment. It arose in part due to a bottleneck in the then novel business of the repatriation of capital to Europe by means of credit bills issued by the East India Companies.

The events which are the subject of this essay thus occurred at the margins, at a time of transition. The issues framed in this crisis and their resolution anticipate a new financial world that was then coming into being. The crisis was forward-looking, not only because it anticipated the Opium War of 1839–42. That later conflict also had as one of its main causes problems collecting defaulted hong merchant debts that were supposed to have been paid under a guaranty. Those debts totalled $3 million in 1839 (as opposed to $6 million claimed for the opium seized by Commissioner Lin Zexu that year). Collection of this debt was a key British war aim. To the extent that the earlier crisis (1779–80) also involved private lenders looking to a national government to make good on guaranteed debt, after default by the debtors and the guarantor body, these struggles on the Chinese coast foreshadow much of the storm and stress swirling about contemporary state-sponsored bank guaranty programmes.

The Funds Lent

The cry of British creditors was that the funds lent to hong merchants were the proceeds of fortunes they had made in India. This is largely true.[1] The claims of other foreign creditors probably also largely represented gains made in Asia. One exception is the claims of French creditors, which include monies which had been sent from France to China on the solicitation of French East India Company employees to be lent to hong merchants.[2] Lending in Canton of funds sent from France, by private French agents, sought to accomplish the same ultimate objective as the lending in Canton of funds sent from British India, by private British agents – that is, hastening the day when the expatriate agents themselves would have built up a fortune sufficient for them to retire and return to Europe.[3]

According to the British creditors, their funds had been trapped in Canton as the result of a bottleneck in the usual repatriation of capital through the British East India Company (EIC). The first step in this process, which occurred in India, was the investment of funds in a cargo bound for China. In Canton, that cargo was sold for cash, presumably yielding some profit. These funds were next to be delivered to the British EIC in Canton, to purchase bills payable in London. This secure mode of repatriation of capital had annual limits, and was subject to the company's own needs. In the difficult year 1774, the Canton treasury of the British EIC was closed on orders from the Court of Directors, and private parties were barred from acquiring bills on London.[4]

As these remittances helped fund its tea trade, the British EIC sometimes directly encouraged transfers. This was accomplished by means including a favourable exchange rate (British Pound to Spanish Dollar) or by offering freight-free shipping on Company ships bound for China.[5] Repatriation was also available through the treasuries of other European companies. They too sometimes encouraged remittances with a favourable exchange rate. George Stratton, a long-time British EIC employee, later complained that his funds became trapped in Canton because he obeyed Company orders and remitted via Canton, refusing better offers made to him by the French at Pondicherry.[6]

The funds that arrived in Canton may be identified as 'profit'. The British monies were fruits of what Jessica Hanser calls 'post-Plassey plunder ... the process by which many Company servants (the most notorious being Robert Clive) personally enriched themselves through plunder, "gifts" and private contracts with local Indian leaders'.[7] Given their somewhat suspect origin, perhaps these funds are best placed under the *Encyclopédie*'s general heading, 'Profit, Gain, Lucre, Emolument, Bénéfice'.

The foreign funds that arrived in Canton were at risk. No banking facility existed in Canton, and there was no easy way to hold cash safe and secure. The act of holding a significant sum of specie carried with it the inherent risk of *dépérissement* or wasting away. While in today's very low interest rate environment some banks charge fees just to hold large amounts of money, in late eighteenth-century Canton, funds wasted in a different fashion. Security costs, for the rental of a safe storage space, and perhaps to pay one or more armed guards, represented a constant expense to be charged against idle funds. One alternative was to advance funds to a trusted party to be held secure for a time period, as the European companies sometimes did between trading seasons. That approach was not risk free. The British EIC thus learned in October 1794 that Gonqua (Shi Zhonghe) had dipped into ninety-four sealed chests containing $470,000 it had entrusted to his care, triggering the collapse of his Eryi hong.[8] There were also risks of robbery, of piracy and even of shrinkage (the disappearance of coins from a repository). In Canton, as in many places in the world in the 1770s, holding money meant losing money.

The Attractions of Hong Merchant Lending

The hong merchants enjoyed the advantage of a state-conferred monopoly of China's maritime trade with the West. Unfortunately, with but few exceptions, they were chronically short of the capital they needed to do business. This problem grew worse as the volume of foreign trade grew, contributing to the weakness of the loosely organized hong guild in its dealings with the powerful European East India Companies. The hong merchants were in constant need of short- and long-term credit. These loans were attractive to the hong merchants, as they facilitated trade, and to certain Chinese officials as well, because foreign credit supported an enormous commerce upon which much of Southern China had become dependent. There was an exuberance in the trade from Canton; an official thus complained in 1815, 'the people of Guangdong rush towards profits like ducks'.[9] Loans to hong merchants attracted foreign lenders because they seemed safe, and offered an above-average return. In the view of George Smith (of Canton), who served as agent for many of the British lenders, the Cohong 'had been appointed by imperial order to carry on all transactions with Europeans of every nation'. The Europeans therefore had 'undoubted' security because each guild member was 'responsible for the other, and the guardian of the whole'.[10]

Starting no later than the 1760s, many hong merchants borrowed large sums from private Western lenders.[11] The loans made in the 1760s and 1770s were at high interest, with rates ranging from 16 to 20 to 24% per annum, and some at interest rates as high as 40 per cent. More loans were made in the difficult season 1773–4, putting to use foreign capital that was held up in Canton as the result of the closure of British EIC credit facilities that year.[12] The rates foreign lenders charged on hong merchant loans were objectively high, considerably above interest rates charged on comparable loans in India during the same period (perhaps 9% to 12%).[13]

These high rates attracted foreign capital. The loans were typically managed in Canton by private Europeans, who acted as agents for absent individuals who supplied the money that was lent. When the loans matured, some were indeed paid on the due date, but a pattern is evident – early on – in which maturing loans were rolled over rather than paid in cash.[14] Renewal was often a matter of necessity for cash-strapped hong debtors, and seems to have been regularly agreed to by the Canton agents of their foreign lenders, at least until 1775. The ledger balance of principal plus ever accruing interest presumably pleased the lenders, as did the fairly good payment history of hong merchant debtors.[15] Losses on past extensions of credit to hong merchants had been minimal. The debts of the Ziyuan hong merchant Beau Khequa (Li Guanghu) had been fully paid, albeit as the result of government pressure, after his death in 1758.[16]

As the credit mechanism gradually stalled, in the 1770s, more hongs failed. A pivotal moment occurred in 1777, when an imperial edict issued in the matter of attempts (since 1772) to collect the relatively small sum of 11,725.75 taels ($16,286) owed by Wayqua (Ni Hongwen of the Fengjin hang) to the British EIC. The Emperor sharply criticized local officials for their failure to 'show benevolence' to the foreigners. Relatives had in the meantime come forward with 6,000 taels ($8,333), which left a 5,725.75 tael ($7,952) balance due. Canton officials, from the provincial level down to the county level, were ordered to pay the remainder out of their salaries (the sum was recouped from the hong merchants). This forceful resolution, albeit in a small matter, encouraged other private foreign creditors to seek official redress.[17]

The Risks of Loans to Hong Merchants

Extensions of credit to hong merchants were not risk free. For the European lenders, they involved substantial advances of their funds into a country into which they themselves were barred entry. The loans were also unsecured. No assets could be pledged to pay the loans in case of default, as mortgages of hong property to secure foreign loans had been banned since 1760. While a local legal process existed through which debts could be collected from hong merchants, it was idiosyncratic. This process, and the Chinese law applicable to debt collection, was poorly understood by the lenders and their agents. For the hong merchants, borrowing risk lay primarily in the dreadful consequences of default, including judicial beatings, collection pressures on family members and colleagues, and potential banishment to Ili in distant Xinjiang. For the Chinese state, risks arose from conditions of dual dependence, first on large extensions of foreign credit to facilitate a trade on which the nation had grown dependent, and second the risks posed to the regional economy if the credit-driven foreign trade failed to maintain pace, or was halted entirely.

The greatest risks to foreign lenders arose from Chinese law. Loans to hong merchants were banned under trade regulations promulgated in Canton in 1760,[18] and the collection of interest in excess of the amount of principal advanced was prohibited under the Qing statutes.[19] When the debt crisis broke, the foreigners claimed ignorance of regulations that barred extensions of credit to hong merchants, on pain of forfeiture of the loan by the foreign lender and banishment to Ili to the hong borrower. The Europeans seem to have been well aware that interest could not be collected in excess of principal, under Chinese law. From this rule arose the practice of entirely rewriting every hong merchant loan at the time of renewal. The former loan (including high rate interest accrued through maturity) was thereby transformed into the principal balance of a new loan. The 'new' loan thereafter 'began' to accrue interest, with the statutory interest cap thereby evaded (or so the Europeans hoped).[20]

It was only after hong merchant loans began to go heavily into default, in the years after 1775, that foreigners began to examine seriously legal and other risk factors which might best have been studied when the loans were made. Sadly, this error can still be observed in credit risk control. Problems are too often evaluated post-default rather than in the halcyon days when credit is extended.

The Hong Merchant Defaults

As credit tightened in Canton in the early 1770s, hong failures soon followed. The Zhufeng hong of Sy Anqua (Seunqua II) was determined to be insolvent early in 1775. In debt proceedings, its business was found viable. Seunqua II was ordered to continue trading for the benefit of creditors and to pay 192,018 taels ($266,692) in foreign claims over ten years without interest. The foreign loans were not ordered forfeited, nor were the foreign lenders otherwise punished by the Chinese officials.[21]

The Seunqua II default had the effect of frightening the foreign lenders. They refused to lend or to extend the maturity of existing hong merchant loans, and tried to collect amounts due. The debtors found themselves trapped. They could not pay old debts, could not make new or refinancing loans, and found it increasingly difficult to pay even basic operating expenses. This deadlock was patently dangerous for the Canton trade and all parties involved. Writing in 1936, Earl Pritchard presciently described the situation in 1779–80 as 'reminiscent of that produced by the cessation of American loans to Germany after 1929'.[22] According to an EIC investigation in Canton in 1779, the total debt claimed by private British lenders stood at $4,347,300.[23] These claims were evidenced by 248 bonds (promissory notes). Having reviewed the best information it could gather, the British EIC concluded that of the total claimed 'the Chinese never received in money or goods more than $1,078,976'.[24] With French claims, estimated at $600,000± (and no less inflated),[25] the total face value of foreign claims against hong merchants stood at about $5 million as the crisis broke.

All of the hong merchants were involved in the 1779 debt crisis. The primary debtors were Yngshaw (Yan Shiying of the Taihe hong), Coqua (Guangshun hong), Seunqua III (Cai Zhaofu of the Yifeng hong), and Kewshaw (Zhang Tianqiu of the Yuyuan hong). Their debts to creditors were: $1,502,407 (Yngshaw) ($1,387,310 owed to British and $115,097 to French creditors); $1,428,128 (Coqua) ($1,156,342 owed to British and $271,786 to French creditors); $634,784± (Seunqua III) (indebted to British creditors only); and $448,016 (Kewshaw) ($339,463 owed to British and $48,553 to French creditors).[26] The Seunqua III debt was largely the original principal amount plus interest accrued since the 1775 failure of his father Seunqua II's Zhufeng hong. The senior hong merchant Puankhequa I (Pan Zhencheng of the Tongwen Hong) paid off his $75,672 debt on 28 February 1780.[27]

Creditor Interests and Strategies

As between the claims of the British and the French, the British lender claims were larger in total. The British claimants also seem to have had better political connections. As summarized by Jessica Hanser, the private traders and British EIC employees who lent or acted as lender agents in Canton in turn

> financially represented well over fifty Company servants and their wives including: Madras, St. Helena, Surat and Bombay council members and servants; Company surgeons, including the Surgeon-General of Madras; Company ship-captains; a Madras chaplain; the Governors of Madras and Bombay; the Lieutenant-Governor of St. Helena; three members of the Company Court of Directors; and last but not least, three Members of Parliament. According to an informant of Warren Hastings, 'almost all of the European inhabitants of any long standing have large debts due them in China'.[28]

This last observation refers to the French lenders, and also to other lenders of Danish, Dutch and Swedish nationality, about whom less is known.[29]

The framing and the execution of strategy in the debt crisis was complicated by issues of representation, distance and conflict of interest. Residents of Canton who had lent their own funds to hong merchants could easily represent themselves in Chinese debt proceedings. The actions of Canton agents who acted for nonresident lenders (who had advanced most of the money) were complicated by the length of time it took to communicate by sea with their distant clients, by problems gathering the proof required to establish claims in Chinese debt proceedings, and by the scope of their legal authority. The scope of authority was problematic for private parties who did business on their own and apart from their nation's East India Company. Chinese officials tended to view the senior representatives of a nation as both responsible for and legally able to bind other citizens of that nation present in Canton. This attitude not only confounded officials of the British EIC, who often had to disassociate the company from the activities of solitary British (such as the remarkable Abraham Leslie),[30] but seems to have played a role in the final outcome of the Chinese Debts crisis of 1779–80.

Direct conflicts of interest among constituents, at least among the British, were particularly harmful. Types of conflict were noted by the Council of Supercargoes of the British EIC in its Canton records.

> Some bonds [i.e. promissory notes] were outstanding for more than three times the amount of the original principal; on some the principal had been paid off and only interest was left. Some bonds were for goods delivered where no interest had yet been

> paid. They noted with particular concern that 'most of [the] bonds if not all, appear (on the face of them) to be of the same kind, that is to say each bond stands for a sum of money, with the date of the year, in which it was last renewed, without specifying, what is principle or interest; or when it was lent.' Many of the older debts had been turned into new bonds, which mixed principal and interest, so that the two were indistinguishable.[31]

An entry made on 15 January 1781 concluded that this chaos could never be set perfectly right. 'The bonds of money lent have been so often renewed, and blended with principal and interest, likewise bonds for large sums in one name divided into smaller, in the names of two or three persons, that it is impossible to be quite right'.[32]

The strategies that were employed in the crisis by these national groups, or subgroups, are known more by outcome than by explicit design. Many of the European lenders seem to have either ignored or to have failed to timely prove their claims in the pre-1779 Chinese debt proceedings. This is evidenced both by the magnitude of their stated claims in 1779 (French) and by the Chinese position that legal rights as creditors had been waived by a failure to timely assert claims (British). One prominent group of British creditors opted for firm action, causing a warship to be twice sent from Madras to coerce debt payment, but the results of that effort forcefully disprove the adage that fortune favours the bold. Other British creditors fumbled the presentation of proof of their claims in the Chinese debt proceedings in 1779–80, with negative consequences.

The Debt Crisis of 1779–80

Some of the British creditors in Madras favoured strong action, believing that pressure from their government and from the British EIC would result in the payment of their claims. Four of the principal Madras creditors accordingly sent a representation to London on 17 December 1777, complaining of unpaid 'Chinese Debts' and seeking the active assistance of the British EIC. They warned of a danger of general bankruptcy among the hong merchants, and stated that the French were also seeking governmental assistance in collecting Chinese debts. On 23 December 1778, the Court of Directors of the British EIC in London sent instructions to their Supercargoes in Canton to do all in their power, consistent with company interests, to help collect these private debts.[33]

In July of 1779, the Madras creditors next turned to Rear Admiral Sir Edward Vernon, commander-in-chief of the British fleet in India, for assistance. As an incentive, they promised 10% of the amount of debt collected through his efforts. The Madras creditors took heart from the Emperor's forceful resolution of the Wayqua case in 1777 and also from a 1779 letter from Jean-Baptiste-Joseph de Grammont, a Jesuit missionary in Beijing, to a missionary in Macao which stated that if the Emperor knew of the debts to Europeans he would see that they were paid at once. Admiral Vernon dispatched the frigate *Sea Horse* under Captain John Alexander Panton, which reached Canton on 23 September 1779. His arrival dismayed the British EIC. The Supercargoes of Canton warned Captain Panton that his intervention would result in the bankruptcy and banishment of several hong merchants, as well as the restoration of the formal Cohong (which had been dissolved in 1771), but Panton insisted that he would persist. Concerned about damage to their trade, the Supercargoes presented Panton with a formal protest on 19 October 1779 warning him that the British EIC would hold him personally responsible 'for all losses of Goods, Monies, demorrage [demurrage] for detention of Ships, and every ill consequence that may (and we think will) attend the present premature representation to the Viceroy of Canton for Debts owing to private Persons from the Chinese Merchants'. The hong merchants sought negotiations and offered Panton $40,000 to withhold his letter and remonstrance, without success.[34]

On 24 October 1779, Captain Panton appeared before Governor Li Zhiying and Hoppo Tu-ming-a, with representatives of the major European East Asia Companies. Governor Li was somewhat bewildered by the vague petition that had been presented to him by Captain Panton, which failed to identify the debtors, their creditors, or even the amounts sought to be recovered. Evidently John Crichton, who was to have prepared a detailed statement of the hong debts, had 'suddenly became so desponding that he could not give any assistance towards forwarding a plan which he had projected', and Captain Panton ended up sailing for Canton without a specific statement of the claims he sought to have paid.[35] At this first session, or at a meeting soon thereafter with representatives of the British EIC, the Chinese insisted that an accounting of the foreign debts must be provided, distinguishing loans made before and after the 1760 edict. The British offered to send a boat to Madras, to 'investigate the names of the people involved and the amounts of silver owed'. They were told to do so quickly.[36]

In response to Captain Panton's claims, the chiefs of the European East Asia Companies presented a written petition asking that their business not be harmed by Panton's conduct. In his record of the initial audience in October 1779, the American Samuel Shaw states that 'all the chiefs of the trading companies' had been summoned to attend in person. All attended, except the representatives of the French East India Company. Addressing the Europeans, Governor Li Zhiying

> demanded if they had any claims, in behalf of their respective companies, against the estates of the bankrupt merchants; to which they replied in the negative. To the further question, whether, individually, any of them had a claim for himself or friend, the answer was also in the negative. It was necessary that they should give such an answer, for an acknowledgment that they were creditors of the Chinese would have been a virtual admission that they had acted contrary to their engagements with their own

> companies. But in this instance, the English had the advantage of all the others, as that nation alone allows its subjects in India to carry on a trade with China, independently of the company. Accordingly, the English gentlemen observed, that, though, for the company, or for themselves individually, they had no claims, yet, as agents for British subjects who had, they begged justice from the viceroy in their behalf, and hoped that he would be pleased to take some measures for the relief of such persons, who, with their families, had suffered greatly by the said bankruptcies.

British EIC records corroborate Shaw's account. They state that the company chiefs 'all declared [that] no private debts were owing from the Chinese merchants to individuals of their respective nations', and that these representations were untrue, as 'the servants of the Dutch, Danish and Swedish Companies are greatly involved [in hong lending]'. Only the British EIC admitted that British citizens had claims against the insolvent hong merchants.[37] Addressing the naval officer from Madras,

> His Excellency assured Captain Panton that proper inquiries would be made; and likewise told him, that the emperor, in 1760, having been informed of the distresses occasioned to the merchants, in consequence of borrowing money from the Europeans at a high premium, had issued an edict, forbidding such loans upon any conditions, under penalty to the European of a forfeiture of his money, and of banishment to the Chinese, – a circumstance well known to all the Europeans and Chinese in Canton, the edict having been published in the usual manner, and translated into several European languages. He added, that, notwithstanding this flagrant violation of the emperor's edict, his Majesty should be made acquainted with the present application, and Captain Panton might come back for his answer the succeeding year.[38]

On 6 November 1779, Captain Panton received the formal reply of the Governor and Hoppo, stating that 'Justice [will] be done agreeable to Imperial Laws'. He departed for Madras on 8 November 1779, empty-handed. Before departure, the Captain issued a proclamation, forbidding the lending of money to the Chinese by British subjects.[39]

On 29 February 1780, three months after Captain Panton returned to Madras, the Governor and Hoppo issued a joint communication:

> The Select Committee were 'reminded' of the Imperial Decree of the 25th year of Kienlung [Qianlong] (1760), by which the taking of loans at interest by Chinese from Europeans, or by Europeans from Chinese, was strictly prohibited under penalty of banishment (transportation) to Ili for the Chinese, and forfeiture of the loan for the Europeans; they were also 'reminded' of the provision of Chinese law that accumulated interest should not be allowed to exceed the original principal of a loan, i.e. that no loan should be more than doubled by interest. A statement was to be drawn up, distinguishing between money lent before and money lent after the twenty-fifth year; and efforts were to be made to effect a settlement.[40]

All of the Europeans claimed ignorance of the decree prohibiting foreign loans.[41] An accounting of foreign debt, distinguishing between loans made before and after the date of the 1760 edict, was again requested, and an accounting was provided in about March 1780. At a meeting of the Hoppo and British EIC representatives, held on 22 March 1780, the Hoppo expressed surprise 'at the largeness of the Sum; which he observed greatly exceeded' the estimates of the hong debtors. Negotiations then ensued, but the private British creditors, emboldened by armed naval support from Madras, rejected the Chinese proposals.[42] The creditors' account of a final May 1780 meeting with the Nanhai magistrate states that the official 'behaved rudely, and in an overbearing manner. He was certainly not well pleased for he went away without taking any notice of anybody and to show his authority, called out in the middle of the factory, to the linguists, to see that those people meaning the Bondholders, went to Macao immediately'.[43]

The Consequences of the Debt Crisis

As was correctly anticipated by the Council of Supercargoes of the British EIC, the intervention of Captain Panton resulted in insolvency proceedings against several hong merchants. The debts of Yngshaw, Kewshaw and Munqua (Cai Shiwen of the Fengyuan hong) came before the local magistrates in 1780, in proceedings believed to have been instigated by Puankhequa after the debt settlement negotiations stalled. Puankhequa is reported to have paid 30,000 taels ($41,667) to local officials to speed the Yngshaw and Kewshaw cases, seeking to acquire their properties cheaply at a distress sale. Munqua avoided bankruptcy by entering into and performing a plan under which his British creditors agreed to accept payment of their $141,112 in claims over three years with 5% interest. Munqua later assaulted Puankhequa, trying to kill him 'with a dagger to the chest', but without success.[44]

The spectacular failures of 1780 left six surviving hong merchant firms, only four of which had appreciable business – those of Puankhequa, Chowqua, Shy Kinqua and Munqua. The Canton officials put intense pressure on these merchants to agree to resolve the massive debts of their failed colleagues. Hoppo Tu-ming-a ordered them to come to his office, daily, waiting from morning to night, but never received by him, a ruinous diversion from active business. The Hoppo's deputy, the *weiyuan*, questioned the merchants over and over about paying the old debts. The merchants adamantly refused to do so. Their responsibility as licensed hong merchants was limited. They had a legal obligation to pay customs duties left unpaid by guild colleagues, only, but not all of the debts incurred by the other hong merchants. The *weiyuan*, increasingly exasperated, said he would disgrace the merchants by putting chains upon their necks unless they signed an agreement to assume these liabilities. The four merchants replied by offering to surrender their licenses and withdraw from foreign trade. The surviving records offer no further detail as to the persuasive force that was put to bear on the hong merchants in these 'negotiations', but they were pressed hard. If they did not agree, their lives would be made miserable. The four hong merchants ultimately gave in and signed a written agreement assuming collective liability for foreign debts.[45]

The resolution did not represent total surrender, but rather reflected negotiation with the Canton officials. The hong merchants agreed to accept liability for the foreign debts of failed colleagues, as demanded. For their part, the officials agreed to impose a new tax on the trade that would be used to support a newly created guaranty fund, to be maintained by the hong merchant body under state supervision. The fund was supposed to cover repayment of the debts of hong merchants on a current basis and in the future. The hope was that the burden on the guild would be minimal, and that the repayment expense would be passed on to foreign customers through the new tax. In theory, the collective guarantee of foreign debt accomplished a Confucian ideal. Were a debt problem to arise, payment made under the guaranty would solve it. Any occasion for dispute and legal process would be obviated, and harmony would be maintained among the Chinese and foreign trading communities. Unfortunately, the results of the actual practice of collective liability for debt did not conform with Confucian theory.

The fund that was established in 1780 to pay the Yngshaw and Kewshaw debt, and other common obligations, was known as the Consoo Fund. It took its name from the guild hall of the hong merchant body, where it was initially kept in specie in a chest or chests. Its purpose was to pay charges sought by the government from the hong merchants. Each hong merchant was required to make an initial 6,000 tael ($8,333) contribution to establish the fund, which was thereafter to receive the income from a set of surcharges on traded goods. This tax became known as the *hangyong*. A few years later, Hoppo Li Zhiying authorized an increase in the number of goods subject to the tax to sixty-nine. The list of import and export items surcharged for the benefit of the Consoo Fund was unchanged through to the end of the Canton System in 1842.[46]

The claims of foreign creditors were determined in the Chinese debt process, in accordance with Chinese law. European claims against Coqua were disallowed, on the basis that they had been waived by not being asserted when he was petitioned against as insolvent in 1778.[47] Foreign claims for accumulated interest were slashed, by application of the statutory rule of *yi ben yi li*, capping interest at the original principal amount of the loan. The amount of British creditor claims ordered repaid was about 20% of the face amount of those claims. This decision was reported in a 15 May 1780 joint memorial to the Emperor by Governor Li Zhiying and the Hoppo. After referral to and upon the joint recommendation of the Li Bu (Civil Office) and Xing Bu (Justice Office) in Beijing, the memorial was approved in an Edict of the Qianlong Emperor dated 7 July 1780.

The Imperial Edict required that the hong merchants were to fix uniform prices, and that they were to be put under direct official supervision. They would henceforth meet at a stated place under the direction of the *weiyuan*. The Hoppo's representative would have a say in prices, levies and perquisites voted at meetings, as well as access to the books of individual guild members. While this was not a technical restoration of the unified Cohong (dissolved in 1771), it accomplished much the same result. Higher prices soon followed, in tandem with the introduction of the *hangyong* surcharges on traded goods, to the considerable dismay of the Western traders. Unfortunately, the inside knowledge of hong affairs provided to the Canton authorities soon undercut whatever incremental improvement in profitability the hong merchants may have enjoyed after 1780. Current business information facilitated exactions, timed 'as they [the officials] found the trade able to bear'. Heavy draw from the hong merchants by the Canton officials, for local, national and venal purposes, became a severe problem in the 1790s and in the first decades of the nineteenth century.[48]

Approximately 600,000 taels ($833,333) in the debts of Yngshaw and Kewshaw was thereafter paid from the Consoo Fund to British creditors in ten annual installments, without interest, completed in 1790.[49] As the Governor and Hoppo had warned Captain Panton in November 1779, justice was done in accordance with Imperial laws.

Conclusion

In August 1780, before the Imperial edict had reached Canton, Captain Panton and the *Sea Horse* returned. This time the Captain had been sent by Admiral Sir Edward Hughes, successor to Admiral Vernon, directed to press the Governor-General for 'a statement of his intentions regarding the debts "justly due His Majesty's subjects"'. The second voyage was made over the objection of the Governor and Council of Fort St George (Madras). In Canton, Captain Panton was received in audience by the Governor-General, and Admiral Hughes's letter was presented, but no assurances were provided by the Chinese authorities. The matter was soon thereafter resolved with the arrival of the Imperial Edict of 7 July 1780, which approved decisions previously made by the local officials. Earl Pritchard, a historian of the British EIC, succinctly described the results of the Madras-initiated collection strategy:

> Thanks to the Private creditors' usurious demands backed up by gun-boat diplomacy, of the $4,400,222 claimed by them not over $1,198,189, slightly more than the total principal, was ever required to be paid them. Had they not called in the aid of the Navy and had they accepted the supercargoes' advice in 1779, over twice this amount might have been realized, Yngshaw and Kewshaw saved from bankruptcy, and the establishment of the Co-hong and the Consoo fund prevented.

The British EIC subsequently refused to cooperate in further efforts to collect private debts from the hong merchants.[50]

One sad lesson of the 'Chinese Debts' crisis of 1779–80 is that all creditors, including the British, fared worse for their efforts. Danish, Dutch, French and Swedish creditors came out worst of all. They recovered nothing. The traditional explanation is that they could not assert claims because the representatives of their national companies denied that such claims existed when questioned by Governor Li Zhiying on 24 October 1779. Were these private parties bound by admissions made by the representatives of various East India Companies? Perhaps not. Yet none of these parties are known to have stepped forward to seek payment of their claims (either from the Chinese or from their own nationals who waived them). The creditors, and their Canton agents, stood silent. French citizens alone held $600,000 in claims; one would think this to be sufficient reason for a creditor or local creditor agent to have taken some risk and to have tried to seek justice through the available Chinese process. Perhaps internal conflicts, the long distances involved and the time required for collective decision-making and assembling of proof, proved an insurmountable obstacle. On this theory, creditor agents stood silent due to conflicts of financial interest among their clients or a lack of duly authorized direction. Perhaps the foreign creditors believed they had been legally bound by their company chiefs. Perhaps the foreign creditors were effectively gagged because the loans they made violated their terms of employment. In lending to merchants who did business with their EIC employers, Samuel Shaw flatly states that they had 'acted contrary to their engagements with their own companies'. It is also possible that some of the company chiefs also served as the Canton agents of private foreign lenders. In other words, their reply to Governor Li gagged them personally. Each of the foregoing theories has its appeal, and perhaps with time and research this conundrum will be resolved. For the moment, all that is known with certainty is that the Danish, Dutch, French and Swedish creditors recovered nothing on account of their claims. Whatever collection strategy they employed, availed them not.

Recounting this debacle, Earl Pritchard confidently states that British creditors would have collected over twice as much, had they only accepted a compromise offer extended to them by the hong merchants in 1779. Is this correct? Perhaps, but only if the payments (over time) were duly made. Pritchard's cheerful alternative requires the assumption that a last and best offer made by the hong merchants in 1779 would have been performed. Sadly, promises are sometimes not performed – even promises made with the very best of intentions. As discussed above, hong merchant finances were in a shambles as of 1779. Guild members remained inadequately capitalized, stressed by and in need of credit for the trade they were conducting. To have saddled these merchants in that year with a collective repayment obligation exceeding $2 million (on top of the current costs of credit needed simply to do business), without the adoption of any trade reforms, reads more like a deferral of conditions of default than a true solution of the debt problems plaguing the hongs.

At its heart, the debt crisis of 1779–80 was about law and accounting. Since the adoption of trade regulations in Canton in 1760, it had been illegal to make loans to hong merchants (it was also illegal to trade in opium). Such loans were nonetheless made, and in large amounts. The Canton System had come to depend on foreign credit, and despite the stated ban the Chinese government never penalized a foreign lender during the entire period of the Canton System, 1760–1842 (in contrast to trading in opium). The foreigners claimed ignorance of the loan prohibition, but functionally it was a dead letter. Though officially illegal, these loans were nonetheless made and uniformly enforced by the Canton officials – in accordance with Chinese law.

In contrast to the hollow loan ban, foreign lenders always understood that the statutory prohibition on the collection of interest in excess of the amount of principal (the rule of *yi ben yi li*) was a serious risk factor under local law. This risk could be controlled, as for example by requiring regular payments from hong debtors, by not permitting accrued interest to exceed principal, or by refusing to renew a loan when the amount of interest was equal to the amount of principal. Such a loan, if illegal under the trade regulations of 1760, was enforceable under Chinese law in Canton.

Problems arose when interest on an advanced loan began to exceed the amount of principal. This situation had its enticements, as the prevailing interest rate on hong loans was significantly better than was available in comparable markets. Rollover can also be a means of avoiding loss recognition, hence the adage, 'a rolling loan gathers no loss'. The challenge to the lenders was to make a renewal programme work, i.e., to see that the loan would be paid and, if unpaid, that repayment would be enforceable. The strategy that was employed, by many of the foreign lenders, required the frequent renewal of aging loans by the execution of new bonds (promissory notes). As described above, the 'principal' amount of the 'new' loan would be the sum of the principal and all interest that had accrued under the 'old' loan. Employing this evasion strategy, large numbers of loans were written and written again over many years.

The principal problem with the renewal (treating accrued interest as principal) system lay in its complexity. Any effective system must be understood by the parties involved, and they must know how to operate it. On the Chinese side, the debtors do not seem to have understood (respected) the niceties of the scheme. They knew the amount they had been lent, kept track of the interest that accrued and were of course aware of the interest cap under Chinese law. In debt proceedings in a local Chinese tribunal, before a local magistrate, the Chinese language accounts of the hong debtors would be received in evidence and understood. On the European side, the complexity of a renewal programme that had gone on over many years got ahead of the Canton agents and the Madras lenders also. When the crisis erupted, British creditors alone held 248 bonds (promissory notes). In Madras, home of the principal creditors, John Crichton was assigned the task of preparing an accounting of claimants and amounts due prior to the first voyage of Captain Panton, but he seems to have then suffered a nervous breakdown.[51] The task may have seemed impossible, or perhaps he saw an elaborate scheme unravelling, with large losses looming. What Crichton thought, we do not know. When the notes were challenged under the rule of *yi ben yi li*, no one in Canton knew how to disentangle the accrued interest from the principal that had been advanced to the hong debtors. It is possible that this complexity was intentional, that somehow it was hoped that by creating an utter mess the creditors could collect bottom line totals they could not fully explain. Whatever the strategy, its execution was a failure. Seeking to collect debts from the deck of his warship, Captain Panton found himself unable to explain basic elements of the claims of the Madras lenders to a bewildered Governor Li Zhiying. The British EIC had to scramble a boat to Madras to get better information, which reached Canton in a confused state, to defend claims for payment that British nationals had raised with the Canton authorities. In the end, the claims against the hong merchants were allowed in a reduced amount in accordance with the well-known statutory cap, and directed to be paid accordingly. An elaborate avoidance programme that involved rolling old interest into new principal collapsed both because the creditors failed to prove and explain it to the Chinese authorities, and because relatively simple accounting (from the books of the hong debtors and also on the face of the lenders' belated submissions) showed that the great bulk of the lenders' claims were for interest in excess of the statutory cap.

Was this long financial struggle now over? As an accounting matter, the amount of allowed claims had been determined in Chinese insolvency proceedings. Nothing had been received in hand, however. These sums were ordered to be paid over time, without interest. Some book entries certainly recorded a loss in or about 1780, as a bad debt or with some other expletive. There remained a gap between the book entries and the availability of the physical cash that the entries represented. This discontinuity had existed since the day the funds arrived in Canton. Some of this money was 'hot money' on arrival, drawn by the high interest rates prevailing on hong merchant loans. One can regret the outcome of the loans that were made, as the lenders doubtless did. In retrospect the high interest rates seem to have screamed out a warning. Some contemporaries thought that the lenders were avaricious fools. Lord George Macartney, British Ambassador to the Court of the Qianlong Emperor, lampooned them in a long pseudonymous entry in the travel journal he kept during his 1792 embassy to China:

> However what everyone, not absolutely blinded by cupidity, might expect soon happened. The borrowers were ruined by this exorbitant rate of interest, and became absolutely incapable to fulfill their engagements. The lenders then cry out in all the fury of disappointed voracity and loudly reprobate as fraud the insolvency, of which they themselves were the authors. As indefatigable, as insatiable, they pursue their object, without remission, and without any consideration whatsoever before them but the recover [*sic*] of their losses[52]

The lenders may have been avaricious, and even foolish, but their actions responded in part to a money management dilemma rarely encountered today except in war zones. The foreign money that came into their hands as agents in Canton in the 1770s was subject to waste, by security expenses if nothing else, unless it was invested. At this place and time, loans to hong merchants were believed to be a prudent way to hold, protect and grow liquid money.

Written twelve years after the conclusion of the 'Chinese Debts' crisis, Lord Macartney's present tense commentary reads strangely. Should it not be an epitaph? The hong loans had been made almost twenty years earlier. The loan losses occurred in 1780. The payment of allowed claims from the Consoo Fund was ordered in 1780, and payments were completed on schedule in 1790. Yet in 1792 Macartney refers to the British lenders as 'indefatigable, as insatiable, they pursue their object, without remission, and without any consideration whatsoever before them but the recover[y] of their losses'. A politician, Lord Macartney described reality. In the years after the 'Chinese Debts' crisis of 1780, British lenders pressed hard on the home front for aid collecting the (very large) part of their claims which were not paid after the resolution of the Canton debt cases under the Imperial Edict of 7 July 1780. To these creditors, their claims against the hong merchants lived on although they had been pronounced to be dead, like zombies in an especially long-running feature film.

As an accounting matter, the final parts of this story, acted out in Great Britain, stand as reminders both that book entries are inherently subjective and that they can reflect arbitrary points in time. Entries are subjective in that different but even closely allied parties may record events differently. The circumstances giving rise to loss recognition remain controversial today. The Chinese authorities and the British EIC felt that the unproven debts had been lost as of 1780, but this was not the view of all creditor agents, or of all the British creditors themselves, some of whom were politically powerful and outraged. Entries made at a particular point in time can also be arbitrary. In the modern economy, as in Canton in the late 1700s, little truly halts. 'Profit' measured at a moment can be something like an entry recording a moment in an unfolding experiment in a chemistry laboratory. The process continues regardless of the notation, in chemistry as with the economy. The observed 'profit' of the moment may thereafter increase, decrease, vanish or be utterly transformed. The contents of a bottle of wine exemplify this process. Writers about wine typically focus on wine captured some optimal number of years after bottling. Writers of history, too, often focus on 'profit' seen at a pinnacle moment. In economic history, as with wine, nothing is eternal.

George Smith (of Canton) was a substantial lender to the hong merchants (his personal claim stood at $763,111) and also the Canton agent for many of the Madras lenders. After he was forced to return to London by the British EIC in 1781, he found himself quickly forced into bankruptcy. Smith remained mired in bankruptcy from 1782 through to 1794.[53] During this period he did everything he could to realize value from his Chinese claims. Smith and his allies became involved in efforts to promote a British embassy to China, which they hoped might improve trading conditions, and result in the payment of the residual pre-1780 claims.[54] For Smith, now in England, the threat of debtor's prison and other indignities of late nineteenth-century British penury surely spurred his efforts. It is likely that his motivations were mixed. Perhaps he hoped to recoup enough money to be restored to gentry status. Perhaps, as an agent and promoter of a lending programme that ended very badly, he was driven (as some debtors are) by the fundamentally non-economic goal of demonstrating that his investment judgement had been sound in the first place.

The late efforts of Smith and his allies in Britain to recover value from his hong claims were unavailing (witness the acid critique of Ambassador Macartney). They represent a final closing of creditor accounts that had run forward from the 'Chinese Debts' crisis of 1780. Just as many hong merchants had failed when their loans were called, many of their British lenders thereafter failed as well. The two George Smiths ('of Canton' and 'of Madras', the latter a client of the former, both having long traded in Canton), each of whom had lent to hong merchants, ended up bankrupt in England.[55] In Madras, two of the principal country trade firms of the era – Crighton and Smith and Hutton and Gordon – were crippled by losses on hong loans, and thereafter ceased doing business in China.[56]

In Canton, the problem of hong merchant insolvencies stood unresolved. After a period of relative calm in the 1780s, insolvencies spiked in the 1790s and then remained a serious problem thereafter through the demise of the Canton System in 1842. In 1790, British EIC records state that a country trade captain from Bombay was considering 'seizing the property of the merchants (as is the custom among the Chinese) and keeping it in my possession, until indemnified by the Cohong hong merchants'.[57] While debt and payment problems continued to plague the hong guild, the era of this type of 'self-help' collection efforts by private foreigners was over.

From 1780 onwards, the collective guaranty payment system implemented in the form of the Consoo Fund, crude and in some respects unfair as it was, had the effect of encouraging foreigners to trade with and extend credit to hong merchants (it is known to have encouraged business with the weakest firms, because the frail often offered the best terms, a pure example of moral hazard).[58] Foreigners continued to trade, and also continued to extend credit, which with time again crept up to amounts due in the millions of dollars as was exposed by major hong failures in 1795, 1810, 1828 and 1837.[59] In this new era, debt exposure was cushioned by the existence of a state-sanctioned guaranty fund that operated under official supervision. The Consoo Fund paid losses – albeit over time and without interest – when a hong merchant defaulted on foreign debt. There was some irritation with the system in its early years, with the Dutch, Danish, French and Swedish all annoyed that the ten-year repayment of British creditors was funded with a tax on the entire trade including their business.[60] Trade went on, and increased. While the cost of insurance (the guaranty fund) represented a small general increase on the total cost of trade (which was passed through to Western consumers), all of the foreign traders stood to benefit equally in theory from this insurance in case of loss. From 1780, though, European creditors were careful to avoid allowing interest on their claims to exceed the amount of principal advanced to a hong debtor.

Epilogue: The Wings of a Butterfly

It has been postulated that the movement of wind created by a flap of the wings of a butterfly, set out across the world, can end up causing the formation of a hurricane in a distant location. It is true that actions have effects, and that effects can move across the globe and across time. History offers many examples.

The 1779 voyage of the *Sea Horse* and arrival of Captain John Alexander Panton, was a flap of the wings of a butterfly. The resort by British creditors to government assistance in debt collection, in the form of a warship sent twice to Canton in 1779–80, resulted in the creation by the Chinese state in 1780 of a guaranty fund to pay future foreign creditor claims against hong merchants. That private guaranty fund, the Consoo Fund, was supported by a tax (variously 3–7%) on the Canton trade. Maintained from 1780 through to 1842, the fund failed as the result of a crisis of confidence brought on by the international depression of 1837 and the 1834 withdrawal of the British EIC from the China trade. Creditors, foreign and domestic, rightly doubted the ability of either the Consoo Fund or the hong merchants who stood behind it to pay $3 million in claims without the reliable long-term British EIC tea contracts, now ended. In that later debt crisis, as in 1779–80, British creditors once again began to look to the Chinese state to pay the defaulted debts of its citizens. Charles Elliot, British Superintendent of Trade in Canton, stated that the Chinese government had in effect guaranteed payment of the hong merchant foreign debts as the *quid pro quo* for privations the foreigners suffered in abiding by the restrictive rules of the

Canton System.[61] When war broke out, the collection of unpaid hong debts ($3 million) was a principal objective, as was compensation for the opium seized in 1839 by Commissioner Lin Zexu ($6 million). Each objective was achieved.

In 1829, the American State of New York took the Consoo Fund as inspiration for its Safety Fund statute, the first ever bank deposit insurance statute and the ancestor of all bank deposit insurance programmes in existence today. That guaranty fund operated from 1829 through to 1866. The Consoo Fund was irrecoverably damaged during the depression of 1837. The Safety Fund of the State of New York, like the Consoo Fund, had a short life but long influence. It inspired the creation of bank guaranty funds in a series of American states over the following century, none of which were individually successful, but which collectively led to a belief that bank deposit insurance might succeed if it was taken nationwide.[62]

Its hour came with the banking crisis brought on by the depression of 1929. Bank deposit insurance was enacted on a national basis in the United States under the Banking Act of 1933. It has remained in effect since, with gradually increasing insurance coverage levels, the introduction in the 1950s of a 'no depositor loss' objective, and over more recent years the development of the too big to fail policy. Judged a success, bank deposit insurance, after the American example, has since been implemented in over one hundred nations worldwide.[63]

If one views the voyage of the *Sea Horse* as a flap of the wings of a butterfly, it has had considerable effects across time and continents. Bank deposit insurance and other programmes of unlimited financial guaranty are effects which have remote origins in the 1779 efforts of angry British creditors in Madras. The future course of modern financial guaranty programmes is neither certain nor free of controversy. Like an entry in a ledger, we know them only as they exist today.

5 THE TRANSATLANTIC FLOW OF PRICE INFORMATION IN THE SPANISH COLONIAL TRADE, 1680–1820

Xabier Lamikiz

Introduction

The eighteenth century witnessed a significant growth in the commercial exchanges between the European metropolises and their American dominions. One crucial feature that helped trade to expand was the increasing flow of commercial information across the Atlantic. However, this development has been studied primarily in the context of the British Atlantic, where the commercial press played a major role, as John McCusker and others have shown in great detail.[1] In stark contrast, the flow of information that made Spain's trade with its American colonies possible remains for the most part shrouded in mystery.[2] There are three main reasons for this: first, a Spanish commercial press did not appear until very late in the century, and even then it offered very little information on prices; second, very few early modern private business records have survived in Spain and Spanish America; and, third, historians working on the Spanish colonial trade do not seem to have shown much interest in studying the mechanisms of underlying price formation and information flow.

By using a cache of confiscated letters and documents belonging to Spanish merchant ships intercepted by the British navy in the eighteenth century, this chapter tries to answer important questions about the flow of commercial information across the Spanish Atlantic, such as: how much did Spanish merchants trading with America know about prices in the colonies? And vice versa: how much did the Americans know about the ups and downs of prices in European markets? And how much were their business decisions affected by price information? The creation of prices and then the flow of information about them were intimately linked both to the structure of transatlantic trade (including the formation of merchant networks, frequency of exchanges, goods traded, and the use of credit) and the market structure. This essay attempts to explain how changes in trade and market structures had major implications in moulding the type of commercial information that crossed the Atlantic during the long eighteenth century.

A basic rule of trade states that the price at which a product is sold determines the profit or loss a merchant will make. It is therefore safe to say that early modern merchants cared about prices. However, price information was not always readily available, particularly when the destination market was thousands of miles away. This was a problem that Spanish merchants involved in colonial trade faced for over three centuries. It was only in the eighteenth century that attempts were made to attenuate its damaging effects.

As I have demonstrated elsewhere, over the course of the eighteenth century the frequency and quality of the transoceanic flow of information improved significantly in the Spanish Atlantic.[3] Merchants went from having serious difficulties in maintaining regular communication with their agents and correspondents from across the Atlantic (a persistent feature since the very days of the discovery of the New World), to getting mail delivered more frequently and reliably (with the exception of periods of war). Even though it is hardly an accident that this improvement coincided with a century of commercial expansion, historians of the Spanish colonial trade have tended not to consider the availability of information. Instead they have concentrated on both the implementation of the so-called Bourbon reforms and the quantitative effects of those reforms.[4] On the rare occasions when they deal with the importance of commercial information, the discussion tends to end rather abruptly with Spain's failure to establish business gazettes or newspapers until the final years of the century. Even when the first newspaper of this kind was published in October 1792 (a government initiative), merchants all over Spain complained that the data it supplied was inaccurate.[5]

Spanish policymakers such as José del Campillo y Cosío (minister for the navy, war and the Indies to Felipe V, the first Bourbon) knew only too well that information was a cornerstone of commercial success. In 1743, the year of his death, Campillo stressed that it would be very useful if the king ordered the governors of Spanish America 'to submit monthly [to Spain] the current prices of European goods in their respective jurisdictions, making distinction between the different types [of goods], and noting the abundance or scarcity of each one'.[6] Campillo also recommended that customs houses officials in Spain should report on ships setting sail for America, their cargoes and destination ports. All that information, including prices in America and ships and cargoes leaving for America, should be published in a monthly gazette. Although unpublished until 1789, Campillo's economic postulates were gradually adopted by Spain in the second half of the eighteenth century, breaking with the idea that the tonnage of goods for America should be fixed and dispatched from only one Spanish port. However, the creation of a business press containing information from both sides of the Atlantic was not undertaken until as late as the 1790s. It may seem remarkable that Spanish merchants trading with the colonies showed no interest in tackling this problem by themselves, without having to wait for governmental initiatives. Their stance raises several questions about the transatlantic flow of price information. Why did Spanish merchants care so little about setting up a business press? Did they not require a public means of information to carry out their dealings? And, ultimately, was it necessary to have information about prices from across the Atlantic in order to make business decisions?

There can be no doubt that market information mattered to any merchant involved in colonial trade, but perhaps having access to current prices was less important than we might think. The conditions under which merchants had to operate need to be analysed when making any reference to price formation in the Spanish Atlantic. These conditions were not only determined by a peculiar system of colonial trade based on annual fleets (and the demise of that system, which will be explained below) but by changing patterns of trade that emerged out of merchants' daily practice. For a new pattern of trade was the result of confronting new challenges with new strategies. Many features of the Spanish colonial trade can be better understood if looked at from this angle. The functioning of merchant networks is one example; the role played by price information another. Among the numerous questions worth asking about the expanding trade between Spain and its American domains throughout the eighteenth century, this chapter addresses quite an important one: did the flow of price information contribute to the expansion of Spanish colonial trade? And if so, when and how did this happen?

The period studied here is broadly defined by two moments in time. In June 1683 the Spanish *flota* to New Spain (the merchant fleet that linked Spain with Colonial Mexico once every one, two or three years) arrived at the port of Veracruz carrying a large cargo of European merchandise. A few weeks later, following a customary procedure, the representatives of the Mexico City merchants met their Spanish counterparts in Veracruz in order to discuss the prices at which the merchandise brought by the fleet should be sold.[7] More than a century later, in 1792, the prices of American commodities would be published twice weekly in the first Spanish commercial newspaper that provided such information, the *Correo mercantil de España y sus Indias*. This chapter will identify and explore the transformations that took place between those two moments. If improvements in transatlantic mail were accompanied by an increasing flow of price information, then the transition from price negotiations at the American fairs (Veracruz/Jalapa for the trade with colonial Mexico, Portobelo for the trade with Peru) to the publication in Spain of American commodity prices should speak volumes about merchants' ability to adapt their practices and strategies to new challenges.

One reason for historians' scant interest in exploring the flow of commercial information across the Spanish Atlantic is the lack of private records. As mentioned above, for this study I have used a cache of confiscated documents and letters belonging to Spanish merchant ships intercepted by the British navy in the eighteenth century and at the beginning of the nineteenth century.[8] This was correspondence sent by merchants in America to their contacts in Spain. It includes not only letters but also envelopes, accounts, bills of exchange, company contracts, invoices, notarial documents, promissory notes, textile swatches and, crucially for this work, lists of prices. All these documents are held in the archive of the British High Court of Admiralty (HCA), held at the National Archives, London.

Along with the HCA sources I have also used some private records held in the Archivo General de Indias (Seville) and the Archivo General de la Nación (Lima), as well as the Spanish and Mexican business press from the 1790s and 1800s.

Prices and the Spanish American Fairs

In 1675, the Frenchman Jacques Savary wrote in his *Le Parfait Négociant* that

> All the benefits of [the Spanish colonial] trade come from knowing two things: the first, if the number of goods that the fleet has brought to Portobelo is greater or less than the gold bars, silver bars, pieces of eight, or other goods that the *Peruleros* [merchants of Peru] bring to the [Portobelo] fair ... The second thing is to know what kind of merchandise is more in demand and needed in the Indies.[9]

In other words, under the fleet system, merchants in Spain made their business decisions based on gold and silver production and colonial demand; prices would only be known when the merchants were actually presented with American precious metals and European merchandise on colonial soil.

It seems that price negotiations between the merchant communities of Spain and Spanish America were an integral part of the double fleet system that supplied New Spain and Peru (the two main colonial viceroyalties) with European goods from the 1560s up to the eighteenth century. Theoretically the fleets followed a schedule in which the *flota* would set sail for New Spain in May, and a second fleet, made up of *galeones*, would depart for the north coast of South America (calling at Cartagena de Indias) and the isthmus of Panama (calling at Portobelo) in August. Both fleets would winter in the Indies, then rendezvous at Havana and return together to Spain in March. However, by the second half of the seventeenth century this schedule was only rarely adhered to, with fleets generally departing only every two or three years.

On both trading routes, exchanges took place at fairs: the Portobelo fair in the case of the *galeones* and the Mexico City, Veracruz or Jalapa fairs in the case of the *flota*. The former was more important during the sixteenth and seventeenth centuries (hence Savary's emphasis on Portobelo) while the Mexican fairs became more prominent in the eighteenth century. The setting up of fairs responded to a tacit agreement between the two major American merchant communities (those of Lima and Mexico City) on the one hand, and the merchant community of Seville (the monopoly port of colonial trade until it was transferred to Cádiz in 1717) on the other. It was understood that neither the Sevillians nor the Americans would go beyond Portobelo or Veracruz.

Obviously this double system of fleets and fairs gave rise to enormous problems of coordination, since the preparations necessary in order to mobilize tens of vessels, hundreds of merchants, millions of pesos in gold and silver, and thousands of tons of merchandise were very costly and took many months. In addition, merchants (through their respective guild or *consulado*) used all sorts of delaying tactics as a means of generating conditions of scarcity, although scarcity became harder to achieve as foreign contraband trade began to grow significantly after the mid-seventeenth century. The unsurprising result of all these problems was the gradual decline of the fleet system. And as the system languished, the negotiations aimed at agreeing prices at the fairs became more acrimonious.

This portrayal of the organization of trade between Spain and its American domains is indeed somewhat simplistic, but before going any further to explain its intricacies in more detail, it is useful to pay careful attention to the functioning and purpose of price negotiations. Speaking of the Portobelo fair, historian Allyn Loosley states that the prices of commodities entering Portobelo were fixed at the opening of each fair. 'Before the commodities were unloaded and placed on sale', writes Loosley, 'the representatives of the Spanish and Peruvian merchants, together with the royal officials, met on board the ... admiral's flagship ... [where] the prices of various classes of merchandise were fixed'.[10] Once prices were agreed they were publicly announced and merchants attending the fair were expected always to conform to them. But on what basis were the prices fixed? Perhaps surprisingly, this is not a question with a straightforward answer. According to Loosley, the customary procedure was to multiply by two the price which the merchant had paid for the goods back in Spain. 'This, after allowing for the cost of transportation, deterioration, customs duties, and other expenses involved, apparently was designed to leave about fifty per cent profit to the merchant'.[11]

Naturally, as noted by Savary in 1675, another important factor to take into account was the amount of precious metals arriving at the fair, which was often a source of serious disagreement when negotiating prices. For instance, in October 1731 the merchants in Lima held a meeting at which they maintained that

> it has never been possible to make a fixed rule which could balance the amount of money taken [to the Portobelo fair] from Lima against the merchandise brought from Spain, and the latter has always been the greater. This imbalance has been due primarily to the mistaken idea which the Spanish merchants have about the inexhaustible supply of gold and silver from this Kingdom.[12]

Fixing prices before the opening of the fair, however, does not seem to fit with the individual nature of the transactions. In fact, there are fundamental flaws in the assertion that prices were fixed in order to leave a predetermined profit to the merchant. Despite its monopolistic nature (only Spaniards could participate and, until 1765, only one Iberian port was allowed to send ships to the colonies), the Spanish colonial trade was not carried out by a chartered company but by hundreds of merchants and companies working for their own individual benefit. This means that exchanges at the fairs had to leave some room for competition. An identical profit for everyone implies that every Spanish merchant had bought his goods at the same price back in Spain. Carlos Álvarez Nogal has identified this fundamental flaw, stating that such information was hardly verifiable by anybody, even the Seville/Cádiz merchant guild itself, because merchants were extremely secretive about their businesses. Besides, any regulation regarding prices would have been to the detriment of the buyers (the American merchants who would resell the goods to colonial consumers), who would certainly have preferred to buy as cheaply as possible at the fair.[13]

Having discussed the theoretical organization of the American fairs, we can now concentrate on merchants' actual experience and practice. Price negotiations at the Veracruz fair in July 1683 provide a good opportunity to see the functioning and real purpose of such deliberations. In January that year a mailboat had been sent to Veracruz with instructions for the viceroy of New Spain, the Count of Paredes, to summon the merchants of Mexico City to Veracruz, where a fair would take place upon the *flota*'s arrival in June or July. The *flota* arrived in mid-June, and on 10 July four representatives of the merchants of Mexico City and four of their Sevillian counterparts met to discuss the prices of the merchandise brought from Spain. The talks were presided over by the commander of the fleet, Diego Fernández de Zaldíbar, and were held in the local governor's house. The negotiations were intended to open up the fair by making, as Zaldíbar himself put it, 'a purchase of up to 100,000 pesos in order to set an example for the entire kingdom'.[14] Had it followed the official schedule, this fleet would have left Spain in May 1682. As the negotiations carried on, commander Zalbíbar was anxious to see merchants agree as quickly as possible so that the fleet could return to Spain carrying millions of pesos in colonial commodities and silver. If no agreement was reached, then the so-called *flotistas* (Spanish merchants travelling in the *flota*) were likely to go inland as far as Mexico City and other colonial towns to dispose of their goods. This, Zaldíbar feared, could delay the return leg to Spain for many months. On 11 July the Sevillians presented the Mexicans with a four-page list of 175 goods with their asking prices written in the margins. Two days later the Mexicans sent back the list with the prices they were willing to pay. To Zaldíbar's dismay there was a gulf between the two sets of prices. The list went back and forth three more times in the next two weeks until both sides acknowledged that an agreement was unlikely to be reached. After four rounds of offers and counteroffers the gap between their positions remained quite wide. Table 5.1 shows the progression of the negotiations and the final deadlock, taking as examples two popular European goods: *ruán florete* (a printed cotton cloth from Rouen, Normandy) and *morlés angosto* (a narrow linen cloth from Morlaix, Brittany).

Table 5.1: Price negotiations between the Spanish and Mexican merchant communities before the opening of the Veracruz fair, 10–25 July 1683 (in reales).

round	a piece of *ruán florete*		a piece of *morlés angosto*	
	asking price	offer	asking price	offer
1st	9	4.75	8	4
2nd	8.5	5	7	4
3rd	8	5.20	6	4
4th	7	5.25	5.5	4.5

Source: 'Testimonio de las diligencias hechas en Veracruz sobre ajuste de precios de una feria,' Archivo General de Indias, Seville, Consulados 87, no. 15.

The Mexicans' total first offer for the 175 goods was 48% below the Spaniards' total asking price. By the fourth round the difference was 33% – still very significant. At this point it was clear that the fair would be a failure and that most Spaniards would enter the viceroyalty.[15] But this is as far as institutional and governmental documents can take us. From then on it was up to the merchant himself to do whatever was best for him. The trouble is that there are very few records to shed light on what that 'best' may have been.

A unique opportunity to explore merchants' experience of trading in New Spain under the fleet system is provided by a cache of confiscated letters belonging to the *flotista* Pedro de Munárriz, held in the archive of the HCA.[16] Munárriz arrived in Veracruz on board the *Santo Cristo de San Román*, one of the twenty-two vessels of the *flota* commanded by general Velasco, in October 1699, and was to spend over two-and-a-half years on American soil. On the return leg, due to the break-out of the War of Spanish Succession (1702–13), the fleet changed its customary route and entered the Bay of Vigo, in north-west Spain, where it was attacked by English and Dutch ships on 23 October 1702. The English were able to confiscate many papers and documents, and from Munárriz they took a set of 236 letters covering most of the thirty-three months he had spent in New Spain. These provide valuable information on both how he managed to sell his merchandise, and what the market prices (*precios corrientes*) were in comparisson to the official prices at the fair (*precios de feria*). They also demonstrate the frequency and quality of his communication with Spain during his stay in the colony.

Munárriz resided in Puebla de los Ángeles, half way between Veracruz and Mexico City. From there he exchanged information on prices and markets with

44 correspondents located in the main cities and towns of New Spain (Mexico City, Veracruz, Oaxaca, Campeche, San Luis Potosí, Pachuca and Guatemala). Apart from Puebla, his attention was mainly focused on Veracruz (the gateway to Europe) and Mexico City (by far the largest colonial market). Of the 236 letters, twenty were copies of letters sent by Munárriz himself. However, of the entire set, only six letters had come from Spain and another two were copies of letters sent by Munárriz to his principal in Seville. Such a low number of transatlantic letters may have been caused by problems of communication with Spain due to the upcoming war, but the content of those few letters clearly indicate that the quality of commercial information crossing the Atlantic was rather poor. In fact, Munárriz included no information on prices and said very little about how sales were going. Such information only seems to have circulated within the colony. Figure 5.1 shows a set of current prices in Mexico City inserted in a letter sent by *flotista* Francisco Ferrari to Munárriz in August 1700. The goods listed are mainly European textiles brought by the *flota*.

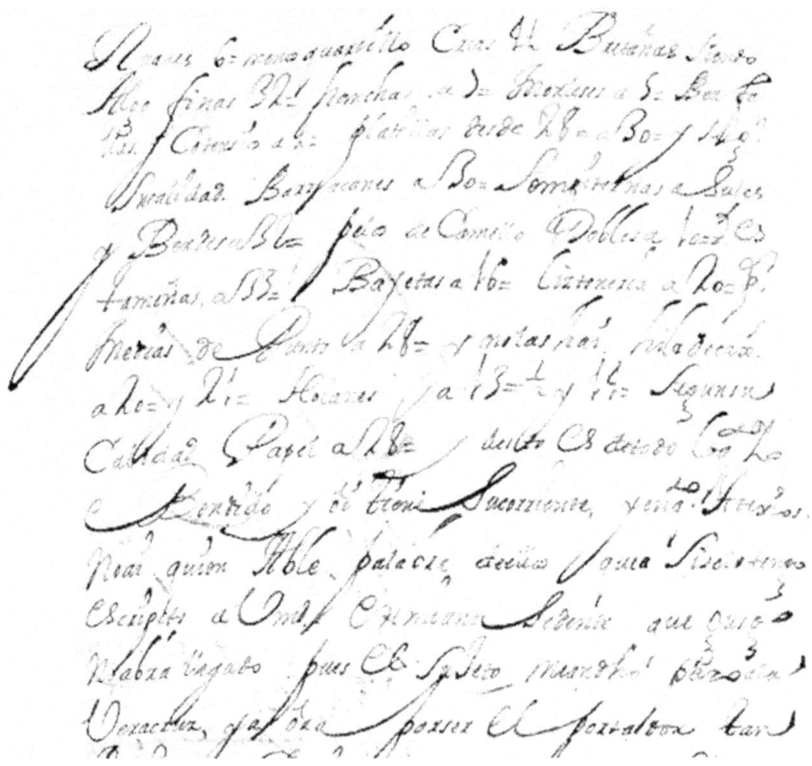

Figure 5.1: Prices of European merchandise (textiles such as *ruanes*, *bretañas* and *morleses*) in Mexico City, included in a letter sent by Francisco Ferrari (Mexico City) to Pedro de Munárriz (Puebla de los Ángeles, Mexico), 2 August 1700. National Archives, London, High Court of Admiralty 30/230.

But what about the Veracruz fair? The Munárriz correspondence shows that *flotistas* preferred either to go straight to urban areas such as Mexico City and Puebla, or to disperse around the viceroyalty in search of customers. It seems that fairs took place in Mexico City and other towns, even in Veracruz, before the return of the *flota*. From Veracruz his brother-in-law, Vicente Ros de Ysava, asked Munárriz to keep him informed on the 'state of the [Puebla] fair'.[17] The prices at the Mexico City fair were of particular interest to merchants: were there price negotiations before the opening of these fairs? Although the correspondence says nothing about negotiations, Munárriz's contacts make reference to the prices at the fair and say they should be avoided at any cost. For instance, Munárriz ordered Ysava to buy a few sacks of cochineal for him in Veracruz. A few days later Ysava replied that 'nobody accepts 90 or 96 pesos per *zurrón* [sack] of cochineal, they would not even sell at the fair price'.[18] From Mexico City a horrified *flotista* called Francisco de Preen y Castro wrote that some of his colleagues had already started to sell their merchandise *a precios de feria* (at fair prices), something that, in his opinion, would ruin them all.[19]

The obvious question arises of what the point of fixing/negotiating prices was if merchants did not comply with them. The prices at the fair can be seen as a reference point, as a benchmark that helped merchants to make a broad appraisal of the market and to gauge the net profit or loss they could expect to make for a particular good. Thereafter it was up to them to use their commercial acumen and find customers willing to pay more. Equally important, price negotiations also had a transatlantic purpose. Information regarding the prices at the fair was useful for principals back in Spain, since many merchants, especially the wealthier ones, did not travel to America but entrusted their goods to employees or other colleagues, usually younger and less affluent than them, who would act as commission agents. For the Seville principal, the American fair prices, which were conveyed to Spain by representatives of the Seville merchant guild, would serve the dual purpose of reducing information costs and monitoring his agents' efficiency and honesty once they returned from the colonies. Hence the transatlantic flow of price information under the fleet system was not intended to encourage or discourage supply, but to assess the outcome of the exchanges.

Price Information under the System of Register Ships, 1739–83

In truth, one should not expect to find much information about prices crossing the Atlantic under the fleet system. Such information would have been of limited use for one simple reason: prices in the colonies changed, often dramatically, as each new fleet arrived with thousands of tons of merchandise. No doubt merchants in Spain tried their best to foresee the state of the colonial market by discovering what other merchants shipped to America, but that information was virtually impossible to get. Cargoes were packed in bales wrapped in sacking, and only the owners knew the contents (which was also, of course, a major problem when it came to taxation). Nevertheless the fleet system was enormously attractive to merchants: it made uncertainty more manageable by shrinking time and space. In other words, the exchanges took place during a few months and competition occurred within the colonies, not across the Atlantic. That is why merchants were never going to ask for significant reforms – not even in the first decades of the eighteenth century when it became increasingly apparent that foreign interlopers were glutting and distorting the colonial market with their cheaper prices.[20] To the Spaniards' dismay, reforms came by way of a new war against Britain.

In October 1739 Britain declared war on Spain (the so-called War of Jenkins' Ear, followed by the War of Austrian Succession until 1748), and on 21 November the British admiral Edward Vernon destroyed the fortifications of Portobelo, thereby disrupting commercial exchanges between the Spaniards and the Peruvians. It did not take long before the Spanish monarchy decided to cancel the system of fleets (their movements being too predictable when faced with a powerful enemy such as the British), and resolved to send *registros sueltos* (single 'registered' ships) to the colonies instead. This new, improvised system gave the trade more frequency and regularity. There had been fleets to New Spain in 1706, 1708, 1711, 1712, 1720, 1723, 1725, 1729, 1732 and 1735 (ten in forty years), and the fleet to Portobelo had crossed the Atlantic only in 1706, 1721, 1723, 1730 and 1737 (five in forty years). In contrast, under the single-ships system transatlantic exchanges were carried out several times every year. The cancellation of the fleet system had major ramifications – above all the transformation of the nature of risk and competition.

Prior to 1739, risk had been associated primarily with how well the system of fleets and fairs was functioning, which was affected by foreign contraband and the ever-present problems of coordination. After 1739, the risks associated with agency and competition became more important. For the merchant in Spain it was no longer a matter of sending merchandise to Portobelo or Veracruz every four or five years, or financing merchants who attended the fairs. Sales were now made with no official fixed prices and under much more competitive conditions. Moreover, prior to 1739, merchants had spent a few months on American soil, which led them to sell their goods in bulk for full payment so that they could catch the returning fleet in time. With the new system and the growing competition it brought about, sales began to be made increasingly on credit. This compelled Spanish agents to remain in the colonies for longer periods. In short, merchants on both sides of the Atlantic became concerned not only about the increased frequency of the exchanges but also about the resulting volatility of prices.[21]

With the increased frequency of exchanges and the unscheduled nature of the shipments, did information on prices begin to play a new role in the Atlantic basin? It must be remembered that it was precisely in 1743 that Minister José del Campillo y Cosío stressed the need for current American prices to be sent to Spain for publication in a monthly gazette. We know that his proposal was not acted upon until the 1790s. But what about merchants and their private means of communication, did they send lists of current prices to the other side of the Atlantic? The intercepted mail held in the HCA archive sheds light on this, showing that as soon as the supply of European goods became more frequent and regular, price information began to cross the Atlantic on a regular basis. Between 1740 and 1744 some 120 ships (many of them French, for France was Spain's ally) set sail from Cádiz for the Spanish American colonies.[22] Most of them went to New Spain and the Caribbean, and a good number would be captured by the British on the return leg. Rather revealingly, the mail sent from Veracruz, Havana and Cartagena to Cádiz in the mid-1740s included the prices of a considerable number of commodities[23] – and comments made by some merchants in their letters reveal the purpose of these prices. From Havana, Diego Morphy [*sic*] posted the Veracruz prices to his Cádiz principal and fellow Irishman Jacinto Butler, adding 'in case you want to send something there'.[24] From Veracruz, Francisco Vizcay did something similar, indicating to Lorenzo del Arco that 'the following list, which a reliable friend has just sent me from Mexico City, will inform you about the current prices of the articles from Europe in that city'.[25] All this information was intended to make sure that merchants in Cádiz did not, as an agent writing from Cartagena de Indias put it, 'act blindly'.[26]

Lists of current prices also crossed the Atlantic in printed form, although there is no telling what was the duration or frequency of these periodicals. Printed in French, a *Prix courans des Mzes. à la Vera-cruz*, sent to Cádiz, listed the prices of fifty-six European commodities (a wide range of textiles, paper, cinnamon, saffron, wax, and so on) around August 1746. As can be seen in Figure 5.2, the document, a rare surviving example of commercial ephemera, was printed on one side of the page and, apart from the fifty-six commodities and their prices, it also contained eleven 'articles quí manquent totalement' (goods in demand) and eight 'articles sans demand' (goods with no demand). As historian John McCusker has noted, the history of this type of commercial list remains obscure because many of them, containing merely names and numbers, have been studied only cursorily.[27] Nevertheless, these single-sheet serial publications deserve to be recognized as newspapers. McCusker and Cora Gravesteijn found a list similar to that of Veracruz (this one smaller in size and printed on both sides) in the Archive de la Chambre et l'Industrie at Marseilles: it is entitled *Prix courans au Mexique le 30 May 1745* and listed seventy-seven European commodities.[28] They argue, understandably, that the fact that it listed only European goods, was written in French and had its prices denominated in Spanish currencies (pesos and reales) is a strong argument for it having been published in Cádiz. However, the Veracruz list, from a ship intercepted on the way from Veracruz itself, proves that both were actually printed in New Spain. These printed lists testify to the preponderance of the Cádiz-based French merchants in the Spanish colonial trade in the 1740s. They also seem to have been the first 'price currents' printed on American soil, since none were printed in the British North American colonies until after independence.[29]

✠

Prix courans des Mzes. à la Vera-Cruz.

	Ps.	Rs.
Bretagnes Larges piece.	9.	
Ditto etroites piece.	8.	
Platilles piece.	5.	6.
Eſtopillas piece.	10.	
Sangalettes piece, ...	8.	4.
Roüens. . . / Crees larges. / Morlaix. . . } vara.		7.
Brabant fleuret vara.	1.	4.
Ditto ceru vara.		6½.
Preſſilles vara.		5½.
Fil de Salo la lib.	2.	2.
Rubans de fil ordinaire la doucene.	1.	6.
Ditto idem fin la libre.	1.	6.
Drap anglois primere ſorte vara.	7.	
Ditto ſecunde vara.	5.	
Ditto dabbeville & elbeuf vara.	6.	
Ditto d'Holande vara.	5.	4.
Ditto de Carcaſſonne ordinaire vara.	2.	4.
Ecarlatre d'Hollande vara.	7.	
Camelot poil & Soye vara.	5.	
Ditto Soye, & Laine vara.	1.	4.
Ditto de lille vara. , ...		5½.
Etamine glacée vara.		4½.
Ditto dumans aſſortie vara.	1.	
Ditto pour moines melangees piece de 28. vs.	26.	
Anaſcots blanc piece de 28. vs..	26.	
Sempiternes piece.	21.	4.
Bavettes vara.	2.	6.
Chapeaux de Caſtor blanc, & noir.	[illegible]	
Velour noir vara.	10.	
Rubans de Soye de Naples N. 10. 15. & 20. la lib.	21.	
Ditto de Genes batus N. 10. à 40. Maſſe. . .	18.	
Bas de Soye de Genes pour femme vnis paire.	2.	2.
Ditto à la turqueique.	2.	4.
Ditto de tournay a fourchette blanche la dne.	6.	
Egalles No. 1. à 7. le millier.	1.	1.
Razades noir fins la maſſe.	2.	2.
Fer le quint.	18.	
Huille l'arrobe.	11.	
Canelle la libre.	4.	2.
Saffran la libre.	9.	4.
Cire en marquettes la rove.	40.	
Papier la Rame.	3.	6.
Lau de vie le barril.	75.	
Amandes le quint.	120.	
Raiſin ſec la libre.		2½.

Articles qui manquent totalement.

Toilles batiſtes de toute qualité.
Haut brins.
Toilles de Chollet.
Toille rayée a matelas.
Toille Coity.
Dentelles de Flandres fines, & ſuperfines.
Soye platte de Calabre.
Coral.
Couteaux.
Perles fauſſes.
Dez à Coudre.

Articles ſans demande.

Dentelles entrefines, & ordinaries de Flandres.
Ditto de Puy.
Ditto de Larraine.
Ditto de Ayamunte.
Ditto de Barſelone.
Tiſſus brocards, & offes, & galons or, & argent.
Anaſcots noir.
Soye retorte.

Figure 5.2: 'Prix courans des Mzes. à la Vera-Cruz' (Current prices of merchandise in Veracruz, Mexico), recto only; sent from Veracruz to Cádiz by an anonymous merchant, undated, mid-1740s. National Archives, London, High Court of Admiralty 30/250.

Both the Veracruz and Mexico price currents were most likely short-lived. Once peace arrived and the trade returned to normal, French ships and merchants were not allowed to travel to Spanish America. Besides, the Spaniards do not seem to have been particularly interested in undertaking and developing the publication of price currents in the 1750s. Even if they had been, they would not have had much time to do so because the moment peace treaties were signed, merchant guilds began asking the government to resume the old system of fleets. As was to be expected, the majority of Spanish and American merchants took a dim view of the permanent adoption of the system of register ships. Even the foreign nations established in Cádiz, who traded with Spanish America through Spanish front men (*prestanombres*), preferred the pre-1739 situation. Writing to a London merchant early in 1752, the Cádiz-based Irishman James Comerford declared that 'this commerce is overdone, with woollens of all kinds especially, and will not retrieve its pristine vigour until the American navigation is reestablished with Galleons and flotas, and the registers and single ships debarred'.[30] For the government this was a difficult decision to make, because *registros sueltos* on a large scale had generated more treasury income than the far less frequent fleets.[31] Yet merchants' unwillingness to participate in a more frequent and unscheduled trade over such long distances was too great. As a result of their stubborn determination, the fleet system was partially resumed in 1754: New Spain would be supplied by means of *flotas* (the first fleet would not set sail for Veracruz until 1757) and the Jalapa fairs, whereas the *galeones* and the Portobelo fair were both abandoned.[32] In the following years there would be *flotas* to New Spain in 1757, 1760, 1765, 1768, 1772 and 1776 (six in twenty years), until the system was finally terminated in 1778.[33] It is fair to assume that price information in this period played a similar role in the pre-1739 era. It was in the trade with Peru, with register ships regularly crossing the Atlantic and entering the Pacific after the 1740s, that the transoceanic flow of price information would take a new turn.

The first register ships arriving in the Pacific via Cape Horn carried a diverse cargo but knew nothing either about prices or real demand. The sixth register ship departing from Cádiz to the Pacific in the 1740s, *El Henrique*, arrived in Concepción (Chile) in April 1744. Immediately upon arrival the local merchants began to prepare inventories of goods they wished to purchase. The merchants travelling in *El Henrique* received a list of goods on 26 May. As with the price negotiations at Portobelo, the Spaniards put each article's price in the margin of the document and then sent it back to the Chileans. But the Chileans were reluctant to buy anything because they were, as a certain Pedro Hernández Dávila put it, 'terrified of the ships arriving at Buenos Aires ... and the uncertainty of more ships coming from the Cape'.[34] Seeing that they would not do any significant business in Concepción, Hernández and his colleagues decided to go to Lima. But before heading north some of them posted lists of European commodity prices to Spain. A merchant named Juan de Sobrevilla sent the prices of forty-six commodities on 'the coast of Lima and Concepción' to his Cádiz principal, the Frenchman Jean Behic. The list of current prices and the letter that accompanied it were posted to Spain via the Caribbean. In Havana they were put on the merchant ship *San José y Nuestra Señora de la Granada*, which would subsequently be captured by a British privateer near the Bermudas in April 1745. These current prices were not intended to encourage Behic to ship more goods to Peru, because, as Sobrevilla warned, 'you should not trust [the list] much for [goods] are coming to this port via Brazil and via Portobelo when least expected'.[35]

It seems that in the 1750s and 1760s merchants in Lima kept sending lists of prices to Cádiz, as shown by merchant Juan Cranisbro's 1758–9 letter-book, though yet again this information was intended to discourage rather than encourage trade. In March 1759 Cranisbro (a *jenízaro*, or Spaniard of foreign parentage) sent a letter to the Cádiz merchant Thomás Núñez (or Nugent). Towards the end of the text he wrote: 'If I have the time I will include [along with this letter] a list of current prices, but only to let you know what the situation is like, and not to encourage you to ship [merchandise] here because I fear it will not be sold'.[36] No firm conclusion can be drawn from Cranisbro's example, for the evidence is too patchy. Much more convincing, however, is the evidence from a set of correspondence intercepted by the British in the 1770s.

On 9 October 1779 two British privateers, the *Sprightly* and the *Shark*, encountered a Peruvian merchant ship near the Azores. The ship, *La Perla*, had set sail from Callao on 12 May, that is, five months before. War between Spain and Britain had broken out while *La Perla* was crossing the Atlantic en route to Cádiz, so the Spaniards were taken by surprise. *La Perla* and both its cargo and crew were sent to Falmouth. There, when asked about the mail and the ship's papers, its captain declared that none had been destroyed or thrown overboard. Indeed, several bags containing 1,931 envelopes (franked and not franked) of correspondence were seized by the British. There were 540 principal senders (envelopes included letters by other people as well) and 926 main addresses (those whose names appeared on the franked envelope); about a third of them were merchants. The mail included 2,269 letters and numerous accounts, bills of lading, contracts and inventories, but not a single list of prices.[37]

Very few merchants writing from Lima in 1779 made references to lists of current prices, and none was actually posted. José Joaquín de Azcona, for instance, wrote to Juan Martín de Aguirre that on this occasion he was not sending the current prices of European goods in Lima, because the passengers and the mail travelling to Spain would tell him enough.[38] From what the correspondence suggests, it seems unlikely that merchants in Cádiz shipped merchandise to Peru based on what they knew about prices there. Following his Lima correspondent's reports, the merchant in Cádiz would ship goods (usually textiles and clothing) to Lima along with an invoice (*factura*) of the buying prices in Cádiz and the costs involved in duties and transportation. For a commission he would ask his Lima correspondent, who would act as an agent, to sell the merchandise at the highest price possible, taking care to sell above the prices noted in the invoice. When (and if) the sale was completed, the Lima correspondent would inform the principal about the selling prices and the profit made. For example, José Antonio Lavalle sold some merchandise belonging to a Cádiz merchant, making a 21.3% profit. He then went on to explain what good business this had been, because he had sold at prices well above what other importers were asking – but he included no information on current prices in the mail.[39]

What about trade in the opposite direction: were the Lima merchants interested in the prices of American staples in Spain? They were indeed, although very few of them solicited that information. One exception was Joaquín de Tajonar, who asked the Cádiz merchant Juan Francisco de Vea Murguía to let him know 'the current prices of Vicuña wool, lead, tin, copper, cinchona bark and cocoa [in Cádiz]; and also whether lead and tin are exported to France'.[40]

The reason why most merchants trading on the Cádiz–Lima route did not require current prices from the other side of the Atlantic is open to speculation. One possible explanation lies in the five-month navigation that separated the two cities: the great distance, combined with the contraband arriving by land from Buenos Aires and by sea from the isthmus of Panama, might have reduced the reliability and utility of current prices. A second possible reason is related to the structure of trade. Most register ships rounding Cape Horn after 1742 were vessels of over 500 tons, were in general larger and carried richer cargoes than those bound for the Atlantic coast, and there were only three to six of them a year in either direction.[41] The cargoes coming from Spain were made up of relatively expensive merchandise such as textiles. Similarly ships bound for the metropole carried high value cargoes made of precious metals; Peruvian and Chilean staples such as chichona bark, cocoa and copper were shipped along with the precious metals, but their low relative value meant they played a secondary role and did not encourage further shipments. Hence the merchant who found ship space for his staples knew he had a decent chance of selling them at good prices in Spain. Finally, there is another possible reason why the flow of price information was of limited use, and it is also related to the structure of trade. The wide range of textiles sent to the colonies and the increasing influence of ever-changing fashion led merchants to convey information about taste rather than prices. The subjective nature of their orders and reports (they were based on individual perception) served to intensify competition because merchants always expected their assortment of clothes to be of better quality and more fashionable than those of their competitors. No doubt more research is needed to explore these three avenues more deeply.

Price Information under the 1778 'Free Trade', 1783–1820

The pinnacle of the Bourbon programme of economic reforms was the publication of the *Reglamento y aranceles reales para el comercio libre de España a Indias* (The Regulations and Royal Tariffs for the Free Trade from Spain to the Indies) on 12 October 1778. It meant, among other things, the abolition of Cádiz's monopoly. A similar measure had been taken in 1765, allowing nine peninsular ports to trade directly with the islands of the Spanish Caribbean, but now those same ports, plus four more, were given permission to trade with most of Spanish America (the measure would not apply to New Spain and Venezuela until 1789). In the colonies, twenty-seven ports were immediately open to 'free trade', five of which were on the Pacific coast. Soon after the *Reglamento* was published, a new war broke out between Spain and Britain that postponed the effective implementation of this more open (though never quite free) trade until 1783. When it was finally implemented, it generated more intense competition among merchants and also more risks associated with timing and decision-making.[42] The contrast with the pre-1778 conditions was stark. After 1783, making decisions in Cádiz was, as I have explained elsewhere, almost tantamount to gambling.[43]

Naturally the mid-1780s were years of great anxiety for merchants. Bankruptcies occurred at an accelerated rate due to the enormous glut of European merchandise in the colonies. Historians who have analysed the quantitative effects of the free trade regulations disagree in their conclusions, but three things seem clear: first, Cádiz still retained around 80% of the trade with America; second, on average, exports to America increased during the period 1782–96; and third, imports of American staples grew significantly in the same period. It was in 1787, just when it was clear to everyone that trading conditions had changed entirely, that for the first time a Cádiz merchant proposed the establishment of a monthly business gazette in which import and export data as well as commodity prices would be published. The proponent, Matías de la Vega, partially attributed the succession of bankruptcies to the inadequate information with which traders operated. In Vega's mind, if useful data could be compiled and made public, then capable merchants would thrive.[44] However, most Cádiz merchants do not seem to have shared Vega's view. The creation of the first business gazette that included information on colonial trade would take place in Madrid five years later, in 1792, and only then at the government's instigation. The *Correo Mercantil de España y sus Indias* would be criticized by merchants for the unreliability of the information it provided, and probably as a result it attracted a strikingly small number of subscribers.[45] Furthermore, it only provided prices of American staples.

What can we make of this apparent lack of interest in commercial information? It does not reflect merchants' real practice. As Jeremy Baskes has noted, in the 1780s and 1790s lists of current prices crisscrossed the Atlantic, and merchants even sent one another preprinted lists of commodities with the existing prices penned in.[46] Even though the evidence is limited (there are only four sets of private records in the Seville archive for this period), it seems that merchants were now hungry for information on prices. Preprinted lists of commodities with prices penned in the margins were intercepted by the British navy in 1796 and 1797. One such list, sent from Havana to Cádiz in November 1796, can be seen in Figure 5.3. It lists sixty-two *géneros extranjeros* (foreign goods: mainly textiles and clothing), thirty *géneros nacionales* (national goods: textiles and clothing), thirteen *comestibles* (foodstuffs), eighteen *ferretería* (ironmongery) and nine *frutas de la isla* (staples from the island). Were lists of this kind the first sign of a development that could have taken place decades earlier had the *flotas* to New Spain not been resumed? Or were these lists the consequence of a more competitive trade brought about by the free trade regulations? In any case, what they demonstrate is that private means of information, and the networks needed to acquire that information, were more important and reliable than the much-heralded (particularly in the English-American historiography) public means of information.[47]

However, the very long-distance trade with Peru continued to pose a major problem for merchants in Spain. Early in October 1804 the merchant Miguel Ventura Osambela replied to a letter his friend Francisco Miguel Lombardo had sent him from Tolosa (in the Basque province of Guipúzcoa, northern Spain) in February that year. Lombardo had requested a list of current Lima prices, to which Osambela replied that 'the prices of goods in this city vary depending on their scarcity or abundance ... [but] it is of no use to know the current prices, because when the ships that are expected in the coming months finally arrive, it will all change'.[48]

More business newspapers were founded in the 1800s and 1810s, on both sides of the Atlantic.[49] In them, current prices began to appear in listings similar to the preprinted forms. But they only concentrated on prices of American staples, a sign of the growing importance that staples had acquired in the post-1783 Spanish Atlantic trade.[50] Important questions still remain unanswered. Why were textile prices left out of these newspapers? Was the publication of prices of staples useful for exporters in America, or was it only intended for potential buyers located in Spain and Europe? Further research is needed to answer these questions and to find out more about the degree to which merchants' practice was altered, perhaps even transformed, by the transatlantic flow of price information.

Conclusion

Did the increasing flow of price information across the Atlantic contribute to the expansion of Spanish colonial trade? Unfortunately there is no straight answer to this question, though one must acknowledge that both variables, growth of trade and flow of price information, were positively correlated in the eighteenth

PRECIOS CORRIENTES DE LOS GENEROS, frutos y comestibles en la Havana: à saber.

GENEROS EXTRANGEROS.

Platillas imperiales, finas. . . . . à
Dichas, corrientes. . . . . à
Dichas, crudas, ó morleses. . . . . à
Dichas, de colores. . . . . à
Bramantes crudos. . . . . à
Dichos, floretes finos. . . . . à
Dichos, regulares. . . . . à
Kuanes legitimos. . . . . à
Dichos, contrahechos finos. . . . . . . à
Dichos, entrefinos. . . . . à
Roldanes? aplatillados. . . . . à
Dichos, ó caserillos finos. . . . . . . à
Dichos, entrefinos. . . . . à
Bretañas ancha, legitimas, superfinas. . à
Dichas, idem, regulares. . . . . à
Dichas, angosta legitimas, superfinas. . à
Dichas, regulares. . . . . à
Dichas, anchas contrahechas. . . . . . . à
Dichas, idem, entreanchas. . . . . à
[illegible] . . . . à
Dichas, corrientes. . . . . à
Dichas, clarines finas. . . . . à
Dichas, labradas. . . . . à
Libretes legitimos. . . . . à
Dichos, contrahechos. . . . . à
Listados finos de à 48 varas. . . . . . . à
Dichos, de à 14 idem. . . . . à
Dichos, ingleses de siete ochavos de ancho. à
Dichos, mas ordinarios. . . . . à
Lona de Rusia. . . . . à
Olan batista, superfino. . . . . à
Dichos, regulares. . . . . à
Dichos, clarines superfinos. . . . . . . à
Dichos, regulares. . . . . à
Dichos, labrados superfinos. . . . . . . à
Dichos, regulares. . . . . à
Rengues lisos, superfinos. . . . . à
Dichos, idem, finos. . . . . à
Dichos, pañuelos. . . . . à
Creas anchas. . . . . à
Dichas angostas. . . . . à
Anascotes. . . . . à
Filailes. . . . . à
Tripes. . . . . à
Bayetas inglesas. . . . . à
Sombreros de Castor. . . . . à
Paños finos del Sedan. . . . . à
Paños de tercera, ingléses. . . . . à
Canela [illegible] . . . . à
Dicha [illegible] . . . . à
Quesos de Flandes. . . . . à
Aceros de Milan. . . . . à
Clavo de comer. . . . . à
Pimienta. . . . . à
Estaño inglés en barritas. . . . . à
Aceyte de linaza. . . . . à
Bayetones. . . . . à
Bombasies. . . . . à
Cotines anchos. . . . . à
Coletas. . . . . à
Filipitsines. . . . . à
Hoja de lata. . . . . à

IDEM, NACIONALES.

Sombreros negros de Barcelona núm. 3. . à
Dichos, idem, núm. 18. . . . . à
Dichos, de Sevilla, núm. 4. . . . . à
Rasos negros de Valencia. . . . . à
Tafetanes dobles de Malaga. . . . . à
Dichos, de Sevilla. . . . . à
Tafetanes dobletes de [illegible] . . . . à

Figure 5.3: 'Precios corrientes de los géneros, frutos y comestibles en la Havana' (Current prices of goods, commodities, and staples in Havana), recto and verso; sent by Luis Rodríguez (Havana) to Juan Santos Salsamendi (Cádiz), 3 November 1796. National Archives, London, High Court of Admiralty 32/788 (1).

century. However, their evolution also ran parallel to the Bourbon reforms that opened up trade to more ports and more merchants. From a double system of fleets and fairs that served to conduct the exchanges between Spain and Spanish America for over two centuries, transatlantic trade experienced increasing levels of competition from the mid-eighteenth century onwards, when a new system of single ships was gradually adopted and there was an increase in the number of ports involved. The reforms brought more risk and uncertainty to the exchanges, and the merchants' response was to increase the flow of information across the Atlantic, even when a succession of wars seriously harmed the Spanish transatlantic trade in the period 1793–1820.[51] But more information on prices did not stop colonial markets from repeatedly suffering a glut of European merchandise, or merchants from going bankrupt. In fact quite the opposite happened.

As well as trading across the Atlantic, merchants established on both sides of the ocean also operated within the continent where they resided. Naturally in the intra-European and intra-American trades distances were far more manageable, often allowing merchants to employ price information successfully when taking business decisions. But across the Atlantic, and particularly in the Spanish colonial trade, distance posed a difficult problem for individual traders, and price signals were often of very limited use for making ex-ante decisions, unless a trader was inclined towards taking risks and gambling. For the merchant it was perhaps more useful to think in terms of scarcity or abundance of goods; prices would often be no more than a very broad numerical approximation to those notions, an approximation that could easily lead to disappointment. Furthermore, even when a sale was agreed at a favourable price for the seller, it only meant partial success because, under conditions of growing competition, more and more sales were made on credit in the final decades of the period under consideration here. As is well known, the general use of credit had far-reaching consequences.

Since all merchants, poor and rich, gave and received credit, a considerable part of their assets was inevitably scattered throughout the Spanish Atlantic world and beyond. This feature captures the essential vulnerability of these traders. Even those who were fortunate enough to have amassed vast wealth by the end of their lives found themselves with substantial receivable debts (*dependencias*) of which a large proportion, sometimes over 50%, were deemed lost or doubtful.[52] It is impossible to disagree with Pierre Gervais's argument (see his chapter in this book) that accounting was primarily a way to track credit rather than a means to calculate profit and loss. Merchants must have thought of their businesses not as a long succession of concluded exchanges, which they could terminate whenever they wanted, but rather as a constant circulation of assets that took the form of credit and debit entries in their ledgers. Only bankruptcy or death could truly bring an end to that circulation. Ironically, the unconcluded and vulnerable nature of long-distance trade could be exacerbated by the limited utility of price information for ex-ante decision-making.

6 PRODUCT QUALITY AND MERCHANT TRANSACTIONS: PRODUCT LINES AND HIERARCHIES IN THE ACCOUNTS AND LETTERS OF THE GRADIS MERCHANT HOUSE

Dominique Margairaz, translated from the French by Darla Rudy-Gervais

While quality appears as a crucial concern in early modern systems of control and regulation, in market 'policing', and in the dynamics of pre-industrial growth, historians have only recently come to focus on what was a key element of exchange operations and market growth. The issue of food quality has attracted researchers, particularly with respect to the interplay between public health concerns on one hand, and on the other hand references to honesty in transactions and the management of legal conflicts and violations stemming from fraud or adulteration of goods offered for sale.[1] In the latter vein, after several decades of work on consumption, researchers have concluded that traded objects were increasingly numerous, and the product lines increasingly diversified – an observation which has given rise to a whole series of discussions around quality in terms of innovation, productive organization and market strategies.[2] At the crossroads of the avenues of inquiry opened by economics of convention[3] and the anthropological approach to objects,[4] historians interested in taxonomy issues also explored the formal investments the various actors agreed to when they generated a hierarchy of merchandise within which the interaction between similarity and singularity underpinning market segmentation and the dynamics of trade could be played out.[5]

There has not been much research, however, on the way quality performed within the process of coordination between actors, maybe because the abundant literature on merchant networks obscured the extent to which the topic could be a fruitful one. Indeed, community solidarities, whether ethnic-religious or merely merchant, were thought to provide a universally valid key to the understanding of observed behaviours, besides ensuring almost automatic coordination. However, one fact remains: in order for there to be an exchange, there has to be agreement on what is being exchanged. No matter what the circumstances are in which a deal is made, whether it be in a face to face encounter at a fair, in a store or in a shop, or in a long distance exchange through correspondence or the sending of samples, agreement on a given product is always made with implicit or explicit reference to a set of products one could substitute for it, or to which it is preferred. The process of qualification of products is thus essential, and the rise of an economy based on variety was a genuine challenge for the actors, who had to be able to associate a name, and sometimes a ranking or an indication as to the origin, to objects or materials characterized by their appearance, by their intrinsic properties, or by properties having to do with the way they were used. The multiplication of dictionaries of trade and other encyclopedias of merchandise was one way of answering this challenge,[6] yet if the truth be told, testimony of the use or even the possession of these works by merchants is rare.[7] Work carried out to meet the needs of tax collection, seeking to benefit from the growth of trade, also contributed to the process of constituting merchant goods by giving structure and coherence to the diversity of tariffs and rules.[8] By the discipline it imposed upon actors, obliged to conform to protocols of declaration or displaying of exterior signs of quality, the tax-related processes appear as powerful agents in the construction of a unified area of knowledge and language.

Quality, however, is not just a matter of language. Admittedly, the extensive growth characterizing this period may be defined by the multiplication of variations of quality initiated by innovative producers or merchants, or in response to the needs and wants of a larger clientele.[9] Yet this diversification was magnified by the absence of product standardization. The same item was not always presented in the same state; each unit was subject to variations insofar as the conditions of strict reproduction made possible by machines did not exist and precarious conditions of preservation and transport exposed products and commodities, whether they were raw material or manufactured goods, to many forms and degrees of alteration. While the gap between consumer or merchant expectations and the reality of the product presented for their appraisal included necessarily an element of subjectivity, as it still does today, in the pre-industrial context this gap was the result of objective factors merchants necessarily had to include in their anticipations in order to reduce the uncertainty generated by such an environment as well as the potential costs linked to it. The continuous growth of the number of items in circulation necessarily made the acquisition of knowledge of merchandise and of what determined its quality a hazardous and costly process.

In the face of such difficulties, there are two possible outcomes. First, merchants could attempt to specialize in those few products they knew well, and in parallel record the data gained from their experience carefully in order to better specify their orders to their correspondents, whether factors or commission agents, and to eliminate those products, the trade of which brought about the most disappointment, whatever their origin might have been. In particular, were they attentive to the margin of profit generated by the qualitative position of a product? Wine, grain, fabric, and so on, with a single designated origin, included a fairly wide range of qualities, so that the possibility of such a calculation is plausible, and traces of it can be found in merchant accounting or in the accompanying appendices. The example of the exportation of French wine to Holland pleads in favour of this hypothesis: during the eighteenth century, one observes on the part of specialized tradesmen a move upscale in vintage red wine, the quality of which was stable and increased in value by ageing, the profit to be made from it being thus more predictable. At the same time the ordinary qualities were left to the 'wine makers' ('fabricants de vins'), who produced indeterminate liquids out of fruit juice and various alcohols.[10] A second possibility was always to trade with the same partners, those whose reputation was assured, and in whom merchants could reaffirm their confidence based on past experience. In the long run, perfect mutual comprehension of reciprocal expectations could translate into tacit agreement about what was wished for in the products traded, the only remaining uncertainties being hazards having to do with a third person or uncontrollable events, most notably during transportation. In this case, the issue of how the process began in the first place remains, that is, the way in which the partners came into contact and adjusted their expectations, their language or their representations for the first time. All the more so since in practice, the instability of personal networks seemed to be rather high, especially in the case of trading on commission.[11] But whichever hypothesis is correct, it remains true that the transaction appeared to be a cognitive process and not simply an automatic response to a price stimulus.

Thus, merchants seem to have been faced with a choice between product specialization versus partnership specialization. In the last analysis, this is the alternative from which we should start to question the notion of quality. The first elements of an answer provided here have been formulated from the analysis of merchant accounts and correspondence recorded in the context of the research programme MARPROF. The most intensive treatment was carried out on a little over eighteen months' worth of accounting and correspondence from the Gradis firm.[12] Over the period studied, the company was under the leadership of Abraham Gradis, a large trader from Bordeaux engaged in both transatlantic and European operations. The research was completed by results from the study of the accounts and correspondence of the house of Charand, based in Nantes, and engaged in even more diverse operations, and also clearly focused on the slave-trade, contrary to Gradis.[13] These two houses are not unknown. In both cases, these are merchants who belonged to the elite of their respective cities;[14] yet no study up until now has attempted to explore systematically and in parallel their accounts and their correspondence.

Gradis was an international trader, active in the French colonies. Much of his activity consisted in sending supplies to the French Caribbean and Canada, and importing colonial goods in return. In this capacity, he was engaged in operations for his own account or on a joint account with a partner, but also on a commission basis, especially for planters whose products – coffee, sugar and indigo – he received in consignment and endeavoured to sell on the French and European markets. Gradis was also involved in supplying operations for the stores and the King's armies in Quebec, both on his own account and on a commission basis. Thus simultaneously, he was in the position of being an agent for purchases, in a relationship with suppliers from whom he purchased supplies to fit out shipments he then sent to America, a sales agent and consignee when he received and sold colonial products, and finally, a merchant, buying and selling on his own account on the continent or in the Islands. Moreover, as owner of a vineyard in Talence, near Bordeaux, he traded in his own wines both domestically and in export. To this trading activity proper may be added fitting out ships or even naval construction, for while Gradis organized the fitting-out of ships on which his own merchandise or that of his associates were sent, with the cargo sometimes rounded out with goods taken on as freight, he was the owner, sometimes alone or sometimes in participation with others, of those ships which he bought, and for some of them had built.[15] As for the brothers Chaurand,[16] their activity, while even more diverse, will only be considered here from the point of view of the trading of goods, even though the question of quality was certainly not totally foreign to the slave trade.[17]

Whatever the degree of diversification of the activities of these large trading houses, merchandise was indeed at the centre of their business. Estimated by the number of entries in the accounts having to do with it, we are far from seeing only merchandise, however, since it appears in less than one third of all entries, and accounts for around 30% of the total recorded values. Yet it is important to keep in mind that each transaction on a product gave rise at once to many other entries due to flows of credit either mobilized or granted, movements of assets transferred from one account to another, or negotiations of bills of exchange. Straightaway, the range of merchandise mentioned in the accounting invalidates any hypothesis of a product specialization by Abraham Gradis: over ninety products, each one presenting a range of different types of quality, were the object of transactions over the eighteen months studied here.

Table 6.1: Distribution of goods traded and listed in Gradis's accounts, October 1754–December 1755.

Animals	Hens	Pork								
Fish	Cod	Sardines								
Furniture	Furniture	Table								
Paper	Paper	Playing cards								
Flour	Meal	Biscuit	Flour							
Metals	Silverware	Lead	Copper							
Alcohols	Liquor	Spirits	Wine	Vinegar						
Hardware, arms	Iron tools	Hardware	Chains	Rifles	Cutlery					
Clothes	Shoes	Hats	Silk stockings	Hosiery	Footware					
Packaging	Barrels	Hoop strips	Casks	Hogsheads	Boxes	Packaging				
Materials	Plate glass	Paint	Wood	Nails	Ropes	Planks				
Colonial products	Tobacco	Coffee	Indigo	Sugar	Cocoa	Quina				
Foodstuff	Vegetables	Grease	Plums	Butter	Cheese	Lentils				
Meat	Meat	Pâtés	Ham	Beef	Salted beed	Lard	Tongues	Cured pork		
Raw materials	Cotton	Wool	Feathers	Chalk	Grease	Tallow	Yarn	Wicker	Ivory	
Textiles	*Camelot*	Mouchoirs	Cloth	*Calemandes*	*Coitif*	Fabrics	*Florentine*	Tablecloths	Napkins	
Groceries	Candles	Ink	Soap	Powder	Tallow candles	Oil	Jam	Brine	Cinnabar	Salt Pistachios

The most frequent entries, however, have to do with a small number of products representing an important share of the total value generated by operations on merchandise which can be estimated overall at being on the order of 1.8 million *livres tournois* for the year 1755:

Table 6.2: Value of selected goods traded by Gradis, October 1755–May 1756.

Goods	Estimate of the posted values*
Flours	540/550,000
Colonial products	280/300,000
Wines and spirits	200/220,000
Meats	230/240,000
Total	1,250,000 to 1,310,000

* It is impossible to calculate for each product the exact value of amounts recorded in the postings, since in some postings it is impossible to determine what exact share of the total value posted had to be attributed to each product among the series of products mentioned, as in the following example, p. 467 of the Journal: 'Flour barrels in the sh.p L'aimable Roze capt Saley; & 300 quarts Salted Lard *amounting together* according to Bill of lad.g 95 br.s ⅞ at £ 105 100666.17.6' ('Barrils farine dans le n.re L'aimable Roze Cap Saley; & 300 quarts de Lard Sallé *faisant ensemble* Suiv. Connoissem.t 95 th.x ⅞ a £ 105 10066.17.6'); italics added.

Thus a few leading products, representing over two thirds of the value exchanged, seemed to monopolize this merchant's attention. This impression is reinforced by the fact that some products, counting for a large part of Gradis's activity, gave rise to the opening of a specific account in his books, as was the case with flour, wine, spirits and sugar. The other products purchased or sold were recorded under the account label 'general merchandise', or 'merchandise for the firm', or again under other similarly general labels such as 'ship X' or 'cargo n° N', for accounts opened at the time of the fitting-out of a ship. Even worse, some entries, fortunately not many of them, refer to products in allusive terms, as in the following example: 'merchandise for the company Dr. to Robert, Antoine £ 3982.12.6. for *various* that he sent'.[18] All in all, and considering the highly uneven consideration granted various goods in the accounting treatment, ought one to conclude that there was already a high degree of specialization in the house of Gradis?

First, let us set aside the question of the specific accounts created and that of the identification of merchandise. In his analysis of the structure of merchant accounting,[19] Pierre Gervais was able to show that these accounts were not created in order to track the profitability of certain products, but as a way of marking out a specific kind of lasting partnership formed around a certain product: the account 'flour', for instance, showed debits and credits having to do with supplies on behalf of the king, destined for stores and troops in Quebec, while mentions of barrels of flour also existed in various other real or personal accounts.[20] As for sugar and indigo, they gave rise to the opening of not one, but two accounts, which distinguished not between different segments of a given market (raw sugar versus refined sugar, for example, or indigo according to its origin), but according to the position of Gradis in the exchange, whether actor on his own behalf ('sugar for our account', 'indigo for our account'), or as a commission agent ('indigo for the account of sundries', 'sugar for the account of sundries'). Obviously, the association of two products in this latter account not only shows that these merchandise accounts could not provide a proper basis for an analysis of returns, but also suggests a relative indifference to the object of the transaction as far as accounting went. The creation of two different accounts for 'Wine purchased' and 'Talence wine' introduces another, more doubtful element, but this differentiation should be primarily analysed as a choice to single out the wines produced on the merchant's property, not necessarily in order to supply information for an operating statement of results of the wine-producing concern, but because the said property constituted a separate unit of capital investment. In fact, in the structural logic of this accounting, being able to track capital was more important than the qualitative identification of the product.

Whatever the nature or the weight of these products, their identification in the accounting artefact indeed generally did not follow any systematic descriptive pattern, and was downright vague at times. The following entry: 'Merchandise for The Company Dr. to Horutener & Cie £ 12561 f. their delivery of 14 Bales, 1 b[arrel] and 2 Crates As pr. the bill.g and Bill of lad.g of 29 January'[21] is an extreme example, of which, however, one meets many versions. Sometimes the deliveries were identified only by the marks on the bales or bundles: 'pr 7 Bales LRM N° 1 to 7' ('pr 7 Balles LRM N° 1 a 7'); sometimes they were listed under the label 'various merchandise' with a reference to the sender or to the place of origin: 'for various supplies from Baas' ('pour diverses provisions de chez Baas') or 'for various from Holland' ('pour diverses de Hollande'). At the same time, the 'Wine' accounts included miscellaneous notations, from the very vague mention: 'for 6 b[arrels] at various prices',[22] to formulae associating, without any regularity, references to places of origin, to prices, to colour or even to packaging.[23] Generally speaking, beyond specifications of the products by origin, whether geographical or commercial,[24] and by use (canvas 'for sails', glass 'for windows'), signs of actual quality appear tenuous at best.

Thus, it is clear that neither in its structure, nor in the way it recorded entries, was the accounting tool applied to the management of quality or as an aid in selecting the most profitable segments of the market. Despite the visibility of some products, the relative vagueness as to quality and the large array of merchandise marketed does not allow one to conclude that there was any rational process of specialization. On the contrary, the necessity of putting together outgoing cargoes, of responding to the demands of commercial partners, of stewards of plantations or of the *intendants*, who sent memoranda they expected to be perfectly executed, forced merchants to be able to respond to any and every request within a limited amount of time in order to fulfil the requirements of transatlantic crossings. Indeed, under these conditions the second option – partnership specialization – should be privileged, that of a delegation of competence to suppliers responsible for negotiating with producers for provisions. The configuration of the Gradis relationship network seems to plead in favour of this view, since it reveals the existence of a multiplicity of subsets organized around specific kinds of trade, having little to do with one another, except for the intermediation of Gradis himself.[25] However, the fact remains that expectations concerning quality had to be made explicit, and that any durability of commercial relations had to do with the ability of all of the actors to correctly meet the expectations of the final addressee. Yet one must also distinguish the positions from which the merchants were led to intervene: as sales commission agents and consignees for colonial products, Gradis had no more control than Chaurand on the quality of what was sent to him. Yet his own competence to judge these products underpinned his ability to obtain a good price from partners he could not, however, hope to deceive, because these partners were also competent, but also because of the detrimental effect such deception would have had on his reputation. In his position as buyer on his own account or for those who commissioned him, he could rely on a network of tested suppliers. Yet the ability of these suppliers to faithfully respond to his orders depended not only on their own abilities and on their own network of suppliers, but also on the merchant's ability to clarify his own expectations and those on the account of whom he was acting. That is what can be grasped from Gradis's active correspondence.[26]

In contrast to the dryness of the accounting documents, the correspondence reveals genuine attention paid to the various conventional ranges of quality, whether having to do with a shared knowledge, inscribed in lists or classifications, or stemming from a reciprocal adjustment of expectations among the suppliers, intermediaries and recipients of the products. For this reason, the correspondence makes it possible to grasp the structural and circumstantial determining factors of quality as well as the ways in which this issue was managed in relationships with commercial partners. The question of what kind of solution the merchant's relationship network could give to this issue of quality comes down first of all to the question of how expertise was shared. To what point could the merchant trust another person? Because he was the one accountable for the quality of products for the final recipient, he also constantly had to be in the position of discussing product prices, and thus able to situate them within a range of quality. *Ex ante* or *ex post*, he had to be able to demonstrate his competence in order to maintain his domination over his network of partners and to remain in an advantageous negotiating position, a prerequisite for the satisfaction of his clients and principals. From this point of view, the case of Gradis in the context of the Seven Years' War provides us with a wealth of information, since his investment in supplies for the king meant gaining more contacts. Within a limited amount of time, he was forced to meet extremely diverse orders, to which were added supplies for the crews and goods and for the ship-officers who traded on their own accounts. Thus, one can draw a parallel between two different configurations, one in which Gradis showed himself to be fully capable of judging the quality of products moving through his warehouses, a first set roughly corresponding to what was his day-to-day transatlantic trade; the other in which Gradis was obliged to rely on others in order to be able to face a potentially infinite variety of orders coming from the Islands or from Nouvelle-France, or addressed to him from the offices of the *Secrétariat d'État à la Marine* (Secretary for the Navy).

The first set is easy to distinguish and, unsurprisingly, what can be found here are the flagship products that showed up in the accounting: flour, wine, colonial commodities among other items. Gradis regularly sent barrels of flour and had at his disposal a network of suppliers from the Bordeaux hinterland providing him with the means to react quickly to orders he was given, or to additional clauses in them. The requested quantities had then to be sent for as quickly as possible to load ships leaving for America or the Islands. Obviously, Gradis mastered the scale of conventional qualities used on the markets, as in the tariffs for bread; for example, when he recommended that his suppliers in Moissac only deliver flour 'of the most perfect quality', that is, superfine wheat flour called 'fine fleur', of course free of any sanitary shortcoming.[27] Above all, he knew the local marketing customs and was sure enough of himself to consider the substitution of one quality for another in case there was a difficulty, as he did in October 1755: 'for 30 barrels of flour from Moissac, this will not be possible, it is necessary to ask for it on the spot. However, if I found some that was good from some other mill and on another ready occasion to send them to you, we shall do it'.[28]

Wine also belonged to a category of commodities differentiated within a scale of norm-based quality, more particularly established for the collection of internal customs duties, or of 'taxation', that is, the setting of maximum prices for ordinary qualities. According to this scale, which provided the framework for a hierarchy of prices,[29] wines were distinguished by their origin, their vintage, their colour, the year of harvesting – which provided the basis for the differentiation between 'old wine' and 'new wine', and finally by a classification from first to nth quality, this last varying even within the same vintage or the same year, not only from one *terroir* (producing micro-region) to another according to the type of grapes or to the whims of the microclimate, but also because of the multiplicity of processes of wine-making and conservation. This scale of quality is the one to which Gradis referred in his communications with correspondents. These communications demonstrate his competence and his familiarity with all of the wines from the south-west of France, and even beyond, since on occasion he imported Iberian wines (from Alicante, Sherry or Madeira) or Italian wines (wines from Monferat or Capri). In the latter case, he used the services of certified brokers who provided legal certification of the appellation under which the kegs of wine were to travel, as was the case here for Spanish wines: 'we have notified you that there is here no good wine from Alicante. I have some that I must have *qualified* and that we have thus received, we will see to having you sent some bottle which is very old and very good'.[30] However, Gradis mostly relied on himself to select what he sent, and was careful to have his correspondents address to him samples which allowed him to determine the gustatory qualities of the wines as well as the properties that made them more or less proper for storage or transport. It is in this spirit that the request he sent to one of his suppliers in Saint-Macaire[31] must be understood:

> We have the opportunity for around thirty kegs of wine from you, of the most perfect and the best, that we ask you to choose as long as the price does not go over 34 to 35 at the most ... also send us a bottle and a few other *shows* ... here we tasted those of Madame de Loupes with which we were not at all satisfied. Since we have had them, they have lost their color and have become as thin as water and at the same time they are very green.[32]

Thus the standard-based dimension of the appreciation of wines which Gradis produced or bought was combined with a subjective dimension, which still integrated as well the expectations of his correspondents. In this respect, the way Gradis worked does conform to the commercialization schemes which have been described for Madeira wines or for the sale of French wines in Holland.[33] Gradis's interlocutors were connoisseurs, with whom he maintained ongoing relationships, and who consumed all or part of the volumes they bought – with the exceptions of ordinary wines or wines sold on commission, for instance on the account of M[lle] de Beuvron d'Harcourt, who entrusted to Gradis the export to the Islands of her vineyard production, from an area near his own property in Talance. Gradis's expertise, combining institutional markers of quality and data drawn from his own judgement and from shared experiences, gave our Bordeaux trader, there again, a certain amount of freedom with regards to the orders he received. He would modulate his shipments according to the tastes and the needs of his correspondents. Thus he warned one of them: 'we will not send you the two barrels of Cahors wine included in your memorandum, since these are none too good this year, but we will replace them with the same quantity of excellent wine from Montferrand, which assuredly you will find to your satisfaction'.[34] To another, who had rejected up front any possibility of a downgrade in his order, he explained that

> the whole difficulty will come from the first quality Cahors wines and other wines from the *palus*, since we want neither those from Monferat nor those from Capri ... for the *palus* wines, most of those from the latest harvest are of bad quality ... The need in which you tell us you find yourself to have stock eventually prompted us to buy part of your *great* red wines, which seemed to us good for last year and which we trust will keep.[35]

Unlike with flour and wine, Gradis was not in charge when it came to the quality of the colonial produce sent to him on consignment from the Islands, and which he sold on commission. He was master only of the commodities he bought on his own account. Since he could not exercise his own judgement in these cases, he delegated it to local commission agents, but even more to some ship captains, deemed more able and above all more faithful than these local representatives. Such was the case of a Sieur Lareguy, whose services he vouched for to correspondents who wished to move goods into America:

> do entrust Mister Lareguy with their sale [of Morlaix linen] and collection and employment in good coffees. He will do so, and more advantageously and faithfully than commission agents would, indeed cheaper, since he will settle for 5 pr% for selling and buying whereas commission agents will charge you 10 pr% and they will ship you bad coffees anyway, and then at a higher price than the good ones.[36]

But to whomever it was he delegated, Gradis's own expertise would come into play on the return trip, once the sugars, coffees or indigoes reached his warehouses. Then only would he have to correctly assess their quality, so as to place them within a price scale which was both the result of past experience and a function of the current state of the market, in other words offer and demand. Quality could eventually become an excuse used with principals if the sale was delayed, or not sufficiently profitable. In September 1755, Gradis explained away unsatisfactory results as follows: 'The coffees you Sent us on the ship Le Patriarche (Captain Combal) remain unsold, their quality is very bad in part, we will endeavour to unburden ourselves of them as soon as possible', adding two weeks later that 'certainly whoever sold you the coffees you shipped us on the ship Le Patriarche served you very badly, they being of very bad quality. Still we just sold them today at 18^{s} a [pound] which is a good price considering their imperfection. Had they been good we would have been able to get 20^{s} or 20^{s} 6d. for them'.[37]

The examination of this first set of goods thus leads us to qualify somewhat the conclusions we derived from the accounting material. From the point of view of the knowledge of the goods traded, to which pride of place was given in so many textbooks and encyclopaedias such as those written by Savary or Savary des Bruslons, Gradis's practice was indeed specialized to a certain extent, if specialization is defined as the ability to master the elements determining a level of quality and to assess autonomously and expertly a small number of products, the commercialization of which was key to the profitability of the firm.[38] This profitability, however, was within reach only if outgoing cargoes could be put together, instead of having outgoing ships leave on ballast (as was the case in the Asian trade), with profits correspondingly reduced.

Yet things became much more complex when a merchant had to put together these outgoing shipments, which gave rise to surprisingly complex orders. The flow of goods was centred on cloth, mostly dress clothes, to which should be added sail cloths and oilcloths. Even if we consider only their main area of origin, Brittany and more particularly Morlaix, these cloths were already quite varied.[39] But the needs of the colonists and of the king's soldiers increased the list of requested merchandise to the point where there could be no hope of achieving any in-depth knowledge of this universe of items. One had to rely on others, and logic would demand that our merchant would turn to specialized and highly reputable operators, and rely on trusted, time-tested relationships.[40]

A first surprise comes from the analysis of the orders placed. While the geographical extension of the network of correspondents, which covered a large part of the French territory, as well as the well-established reputation of some merchants or merchant-manufacturers,[41] do support the hypothesis that the suppliers sought out were specialized, at least by broad product class, the orders themselves prove that Gradis also quite often used general suppliers, such as Horutener & Cie of Rouen, or Guillaume Nayrac & Cie from Amsterdam. These general merchants provided him with general assortments including ironmongery, haberdashery, cloths, linens, hosiery, building materials, dry goods, paper products and more.[42] Moreover, while some formulations, such as 'find attached Mssrs the memorandum of goods we request *this year* from you',[43] imply extended relationship and repeated, routine orders, the extent to which new partners were embraced is quite striking. Thus Gradis, on the recommendation of his Parisian bankers, Chabert et Banquet, contacted the firm Ferregeau & fils from Tours and ordered cloth from them.[44] But all suppliers, whether old partners or newcomers, were necessarily responsible for the selection of goods making up the assortments shipped, and Gradis had no choice but to rely on them for the quality of what he received, all the more so since the orders were often shipped directly to the ports from which his ships would sail, not only Bordeaux, but also Rochefort or Brest.

Beyond the repeated and incantatory formulations by which Gradis demanded that his suppliers make sure to provide 'fine and good quality' ('belle et bonne qualité'), the success and longevity of the business depended first and foremost on the certainty that there was a mutual understanding, manifested at the most basic level through the systematic albeit summarized repetition in the outgoing letters of the contents found in the letters received. Still, the summary descriptions of products which was meant to make expectations explicit left a wide margin of uncertainty, whether it focused on the outward characteristics of the product ('Dourgne curly and purple or blue'), on its format (paper sizes, widths of textile pieces), on the materials used (assorted buttons 'of fake gold and silver'), on the weight (iron anchors 'of 350 ... 450 ... 900 pounds'), or on some scale of prices. The whole extent of merchant vulnerability and risk-taking is perceptible in these abstract characterizations, which entirely eschewed physical testing, and even more clearly in the awkward answers Gradis sent to suppliers who presumably found themselves stumped by his terse orders, and at any rate requested further details from him. So it was with this Montauban merchant who asked for a clarification on an order of '77 pieces of flanelettes of which half in whites, a quarter red and a quarter blue', and was told in answer that 'concerning the articles of the flanelettes, we were not provided with explanations with regard to quality in the orders we were given, thus we are unable to tell you anything on this head, and beg you to *do your best*'.[45] When no precedent could be referred to,[46] Gradis found himself entirely dependent on the competence of his correspondents and on whether they were able to get from other merchants or merchant-manufacturers products which would fulfil his expectations. Of course he would try a variety of arguments aimed at stimulating the zeal of his interlocutors. First, there was the barely veiled threat to change suppliers in case there were a lapse: 'Be so kind madam, as to take care there be no delay in the shipment as there has been in the past, and the paper be of fine and good quality, otherwise we will be forced to find our supplies elsewhere', Gradis wrote to a papermaker from Angoulême, in spite of the fact that that particular house was well-established and highly reputable.[47] But his main tool was the cash payment, upon reception of the bill, most often paid directly by Chabert & Banquet[48] and credited to the latter in the accounts, and even in some cases paid in advance in part, as Gradis reported to a superintendent (*commissaire*) of the Navy: 'We had to pay cash for almost everything, and even before the delivery of the largest part of the goods, since we granted large advances *so as to be better served* and to get the goods at better prices'.[49]

The quality of goods was not only a question of competence or know-how, however. Quite a few parameters eluded both the art and the control of the merchant. First and foremost, there was the relative scarcity of a product: one could not get everything at all times. Moreover the production was so dispersed, as in textiles and metals for example, that no network, however extended one could make it, could provide a guaranteed supply of products continuously of the same quality. Ordering twenty thousand bricks, Gradis took care to explain: 'we expect that whoever will provide you with the bricks will take care that *they be well fired* and of the best quality' ('nous comptons que celui qui vous fournira cette brique aura attention *qu'elle soit bien cuite* et de la meilleure qualité'). Many passages in the correspondence refer to how hard it was to put together homogeneous assortments. Here the 'scarcity of fake gold yarn' ('rareté des fils d'or faux') delayed the shipment of bales of cloth, there *carises* could not be found at the Niort fair, elsewhere the 'scarcity of small barrelling' ('rareté du petit barillage') was a stumbling block to the completion of an order.[50] Loosened relationships had then to be tightened up: 'It is long since we had the honour of writing to you for lack of opportunity, we have one to do so today', writes Gradis hurriedly in the frantic activity of the winter 1755.[51] Sometimes, one had to give up, when no correspondent was found to answer to some request: to one of his Bayonne correspondents Gradis writes,

> As for the twenty dozen napkins which we had requested from you with their tablecloths, which are so expensive, the order must be cancelled and do not buy them. We don't know anybody in Ghent, we will ask around to see if we can be directed toward somebody so that something could be done in this respect.[52]

With shortened deadlines, as was the case in 1755–6 when Gradis received wave after wave of new orders added to his contracts with the state to supply the French troops in Canada, the balancing act became even harder: Gradis finally admitted in December 1755,

> We have the memorandum of supplies which you gave us which is different from the first which you had sent heretofore. We will work as hard as we can so as to answer to it as best we can, although we do believe it will be very difficult when it comes to this supplemental amount, *since there is so little time*.[53]

The diversification of suppliers was an answer to this structural constraint: strikingly, Gradis frequently shared the same order, drawn up in exactly the same way, between several suppliers. 'We give you preference for *the largest part* of our memorandum', Gradis wrote to one of them, 'for the affection and respect we have for you would not allow for any less on our part'.[54] And on the same day, he wrote to two other traders from Montauban, ordering from them the rest of the cloth he needed to complete his shipment.[55]

The aim of this strategy was not only to make sure that for a given product at a given quality level Gradis would get the quantity he needed for his business. This was also a way to spread other structural risks. First there was the packaging, a constant worry for our merchant, who kept warning his suppliers that a product had to be 'well packaged' ('bien emballé').[56] Sometimes, he would even tailor his shipments to what was available: 'We had to take a whole barrel of sugar ... this sugar will keep better in a barrel than if it had been put into bags, which is the reason why we decided to ship you a larger quantity than what was mentioned in your memorandum'.[57] Be it cloth, saddles, glass panes, silverware or wines, the preservation of which could be compromised by a defective barrelling or bottling process, the final quality of a product was dependent as much on the care with which it was kept from breaking, becoming damp or from any other deterioration, as on its intrinsic properties and use value. 'Do make sure that everything is well packed and packaged, so that nothing will go bad or break during the trip',[58] Gradis recommended to one of his correspondents; and to another, 'be careful to have these [glass] panes better packed than last time, which ended with more than half of them broken'.[59] These admonitions were also linked to another source of hazards: the transportation and storage of the goods, the integrity of which could easily be compromised in this high-risk period of the trading process. Shipped by waterway or by land, the goods did not necessarily end up in Gradis's own warehouses from which barks would take them onboard seagoing ships. Quite often they were sent directly under cover of the bonded customs transit system ('acquit-à-caution'), to the warehouses of the ports from which they would be shipped, and ended up sometimes in open spaces, where surveillance took place with a view to customs duties rather than the preservation of the stored goods. Along the way as much as in the final storing place, goods could be altered or degraded by accident, by rain or by careless handling. There again, diversifying the supply sources or fractioning shipment were ways to spread the risks, a fact of which Gradis himself was well aware: 'we reckon that it was better to send you this separate shipment either to split your risks or to make sure that if your wines happen to be delayed at least you will receive your other supplies'.[60] And then there was the time factor, which Gradis managed with considerable deftness, striving to minimize the costs and the risks of a prolonged stay in the warehouses. In particular, he passed on to his suppliers the storage costs, making sure that their shipments coincided as closely as possible with the loading of ships. This early example of 'just-in-time' management only required some organization, and some diplomacy. Thus, on 18 October 1755 Gradis sent a series of urgent orders to Lille, Tours, Rouen and Montauban, yet on 28 October already he dampened the zeal of his eager suppliers and asked them not to ship his prior orders without further notice to them. To his Lille correspondent who showed signs of impatience and worry, Gradis then explained:

> we have only requested that you hold back on shipping them until further orders from us, not to dump them on you but only so that we would write to you exactly whether you must ship them to us directly here, or by land to some other port which we will indicate to you very soon.[61]

The widow Tirand ended up having to wait, with all the other suppliers, until the following January, when all the conditions were in place for the ships to load the various parts of their cargoes with no time wasted in warehouses. The balance to be struck between the two risks, of the goods being delayed because of the hazards of transportation, or degraded or even stolen in storage, was a delicate one, and the arbitrage process complex, but both were integral parts of the construction of quality.

Conclusion

In standard economic theory, quality is regulated by the offer and demand on a market. Unwanted goods are not bought and 'good quality' is whatever will fit consumer demand. Lower prices may eventually lead to the sale of leftover goods, this being the way in which weak demand is recognized. In a word, a price carries all the information necessary to assess a quality – provided of course that market sellers offer a perfectly interchangeable product, and that information circulate perfectly. These conditions were far from being met in the economic environment of the 'Age of Commerce', and if truth be told, are never met in reality. As an intermediary acting both on his own account and on account of others, Gradis operated within a context marked by a multiplicity of conventions over qualities, themselves grounded in a multiplicity of systems of reference.[62] Trading in some goods such as sugar did respond to market coordination, with the interplay of offer and demand providing information as to the preferences of the agents, and the level of quality which they would seek. Other goods, such as cloth, were referred to by their marker of origin, as with the 'cloth from Morlaix', for instance; to these markers were associated norm-based characteristics made explicit in manufactory regulations, or, for wines, in merchant usage, confirmed through price scales built by town magistrates, or by their place in fiscal hierarchies. But a whole universe of goods did not belong properly to either of these two regimes of quality assessment, since the generic qualification of these goods did not coincide with any regularly occurring characteristic in them, whether in terms of appearance, of raw materials used, or of labour employed. Given this situation, it is logical to expect that Gradis relied on his own personal way of managing quality, which he inscribed into the repetitive occurrences of similar transactions, the effect of which was to reduce uncertainty over time. In concrete terms, we observe that most of his relations with his suppliers were built over time, and enabled him to refer to past experience. However, this regime of coordination did away only partly with uncertainties over quality, since a merchant's correspondents were themselves dependent on their own suppliers, and the limitation on one's ability to produce and collect goods meant that piecing together assortments was a particularly difficult process, especially if delays happened to be shortened. More than the longevity of relationships which were never immune to failure, the spreading of risks between a multiplicity of suppliers seems to have been the most adequate answer. This is why Gradis was not only careful to maintain a network of sleeping partners, making sure to send their way part of an order from time to time, but was also always on the look-out for new entrants, and was constantly trying to enlarge the group of his sellers. Moreover, the case of Gradis illustrates another aspect which is explored in the economic literature on quality, that of the very limitations of the term 'product'.

Gradis was not only buying and selling goods, he was also buying and selling services:[63] packaging, the organization of routing processes, the whole logistics making possible the concentration within a limited timeframe of highly varied merchandise. But these services were not external to his products, on the contrary they were fully incorporated into a 'model of the state of things',[64] expected as the result of the coordination between Gradis and the people he dealt with – in a word, into the quality of the products.

Thus the network was the basis of a solution to the issue of quality because of the risk spreading which it made possible, rather than because some magic wrought by a relation of trust always liable to be put into question because of the weak degree to which products were objectified. Beyond the particular case of Gradis, this observation should lead us to revise our assessments on the role of institutional tools such as the corporations, the certifying or trademarking offices ('bureau de marques', 'bureaux de certification')[65] which contributed to the construction of classes of equivalence within which a price-based competition could appear; to the construction, in other words, of product markets.

7 THE PINET FAMILY OF GAP AND THEIR BUSINESS RELATIONS, 1785–1816: OFFICIAL ACTIVITIES AND THE ISSUE OF COMMERCIAL RISK

Boris Deschanel , translated from the French by Darla Rudy-Gervais

Introduction

From a classical and neo-classical point of view, the concept of risk is closely linked to that of profit, in the sense that taking a risk legitimizes economic profit as it is perceived by the entrepreneur. As David Hume wrote, 'men must have profits proportionable to their expence and hazard'.[1] The rational agent is thus supposed to engage in evaluating risks ahead of time, in order to invest if and only if the rates of profit vary in the same direction as the intensity of risks. Such a procedure can be envisioned only when it is possible to determine ahead of time the probability of an event – hence the necessity of introducing the distinction between risk and uncertainty proposed by Frank Knight.[2] On the one hand, we would be dealing with predictable events, the probability of which could be expressed in quantified form after having been calculated. On the other hand, uncertainty would signify the opposite: that is, the impossibility of assigning a mathematical probability to any given event.

In the standard literature, the notion of risk reflects first of all a probabilistic grasp of the future, and secondly, a purely economic conception of profit and therefore of the notion of risk itself, in that this notion cannot be dissociated from that of profit. Furthermore, the notion takes on a differential function: the tendency to expose oneself to risk rationally, in classical and neo-classical theory, makes it possible to distinguish entrepreneurs from other investors. At the end of the day, the definition of risk is thus necessarily connected to the interpretation of the role and of the psychology of the entrepreneurs. This model, which we will call here the classical model, has deeply influenced business history, even when the latter attempted to define objects predating European industrialization, such as merchant societies of the eighteenth century. Implicitly, pre-industrial enterprise was thus reduced to individual initiative, based on the spontaneous attraction of the 'brains' for 'adventure', in the words of Joseph Schumpeter.[3]

This approach generates serious methodological problems, particularly because it can lead to a hagiographical rereading of entrepreneurial careers – in this case, that of European merchants. Moreover, it places at the centre of business practices the notion of risk, conceived of as being at the same time descriptive and prescriptive, in a social setting in which such a notion did not necessarily play the part it does today. While the current definition of risk appeared in the eighteenth century, in parallel with the development of the theory of probabilities,[4] the scope of the word was not strictly identical to the meaning it came to take on eventually, beginning at the end of the nineteenth century. Economic profit stemming from risk-taking did not necessarily have an aura of prestige compared to rents-based profit. On the contrary, in the economy of the Old Regime, it was this latter kind of profit which was more valued socially as a rule,[5] and would attract investments first and foremost.

The classical interpretation of risk thus suffers from two main limitations which basically recycle a mythologized vision of the relationship between the entrepreneur and time. On the one hand, it does not allow for the apprehension of risk as a historical concept, and in the end identifies an attraction to risk as a psychological trait, both distinctive and unchanging. On the other hand, this interpretation confines risk to the field of economics, disregarding all the social transformations which took place between the age of commerce and the era of industrialization, and which deeply transformed the very notion of profit.

Thus emerges an almost timeless vision of the entrepreneurial instinct, of which biographical and family narratives would serve in a way as empirical illustrations. It is precisely this relationship between risk-taking, profit and entrepreneurs that we intend to explore here, based on a case study. The Pinet family,[6] settled in Gap, in Haut-Dauphiné, from the middle of the eighteenth century on, seems at first glance to be the very archetype of a dynasty of merchant entrepreneurs of provincial importance, of the most ordinary kind in Old Regime France. Within three successive generations, the Pinets rose to prominence through banking and trade speculation to become one of the richest families in the area. Yet the family firm based this rise less on constant and calculated risk-taking than on strategies intended on the contrary to reduce exposure to risk, in particular during the uncertain period extending from the end of the Old Regime to the beginning of the Restoration.

Trade and participation in public affairs were closely linked in the Pinet family trajectory. This dual activity took place over three successive generations. As early as the first half of the century, André Pinet was simultaneously a merchant and a low-ranking *officier de finances*.[7] His son, Pierre-Daniel, developed the family firm from the 1750s, while concurrently purchasing offices and titles. Finally, from the 1780s onwards, Pierre-Daniel's children, and in particular the eldest, Jean-Joseph-André, took over, and throughout the Revolution and the Empire turned to commercial, administrative and commercial offices. Thus, it is important to study the articulation between these apparently very diverse functions, in the service of supposedly clearly differentiated interests. It is worth examining in particular the commercial advantages linked to official activities taken up in a period of domestic and international political tensions. In this respect, we have first and foremost attempted to understand how holding several offices concurrently made it possible to reduce merchant exposure to risk. We will show that this strategy was based on the prior existence of regional and national business relationships which were mutually reinforcing. These were mechanisms, the solidity of which we can finally measure, as they stood the test of revolutionary dynamics, in the diverse shapes they took over time and space.

The Relationship between Commercial and Public Activities

Initial Conditions of Public Involvement

Interest in the public sphere was a characteristic of the end of the early modern era, as one can see in the reflections begun during the Enlightenment on the public spirit, the public interest or even public service. Nevertheless, these concepts took on meanings specific to their own period, in which public order was essentially viewed in opposition to private matters.[8] The antagonism which opposes today what is public and what is private did not exist as such. Public activities were defined less by the context in which they were practised than in their contribution to general interest: thus, they were not the privilege of agents of the State, but could be carried out by private individuals. The issue was what could confer a public dimension to any type of activity. In this respect, the State and the intermediate institutions dependent upon it played the indispensable part of mediator, defining (and legitimizing through definition) what exactly was or was not a matter of general interest.

In this sense, the Pinet family became involved in a series of activities which could be assimilated to manifestations of public service. The first form of involvement, and also the most visible, had to do with the offices the family had accumulated throughout the eighteenth century. André Pinet first obtained the office of *receveur des tailles* (tax collector) in 1719, then was licensed as *changeur* (money changer) in 1726 in Veynes. Using income from his paternal inheritance, Pierre-Daniel purchased the office of *receveur particulier* (special tax assessor) in the *élection*[9] of Gap in 1763,[10] and of royal secretary in the Besançon Parliament in 1784,[11] along with seigniorial titles in Manteyer (1783). Finally, the eldest of his sons, Jean-Joseph-André, took over in turn the responsibilities of *receveur particulier* until the abolition of the position in 1792.[12]

Far from limiting their activity to the offices listed above, the Pinets also took up the resupplying of French armies in some parts of Briançonnais and in Embrunais. The family had garnered great success in this area, the highest point being in the first half of the 1790s. While no member of the family line ever officially joined a military administration, still, unlike ordinary commercial exchange, transactions carried out with the authorities were supposed to be subordinate to the general interest, and were thus defined as a form of *de facto* public activity. On one hand, the war economy was to be in the service of the State – which consequently intervened heavily in the transactions, whether before or after the Revolution.[13] On the other hand, family speculation was presented as being a profitable operation for the regional community as a whole, and not just as a purely private business matter.[14]

All the activities described above implied being able to mobilize considerable resources. The purchase of offices called for large investments: in order to become *receveur des tailles*, for example, Pierre-Daniel Pinet, in August 1763, had spent 55,000 *livres tournois*.[15] Similarly, supplying the military meant having abundant enough financial and relational assets in Haut-Dauphiné and Haute-Provence to organize the storage and distribution of the supplies: preparing the convoys, renting the warehouses, packaging the goods ... Consequently, the concentration and transmission of offices was underpinned by previous accumulation of wealth and integration into the business circles of the area.

Thus involvement in the public domain did not exist prior to the merchant expansion of the family. On the contrary, it was this very expansion which allowed the Pinets to create those conditions indispensable for their engagement in the service of the monarchical State: their acquisition of new offices was generally preceded by phases of development of their private business. Thus it was André's successes which brought in enough money for him to purchase his first fiscal offices. In the same way, Pierre-Daniel was able to become *receveur* in Gap thanks to an inheritance from his father. Finally, the acquisition of the office of secretary to the king and of the seigniorial titles came about precisely at the same time as the family firm was gaining importance. Indeed, at the beginning of the 1780s, the yearly volume of business treated with Lyon reached nearly two million *livres tournois*[16] – a figure all the more remarkable for a merchant from Haut-Dauphiné[17] when one considers that it included only a part of the family operations.[18]

Commercial Advantages and Public Activities

All in all, profit – by its loose definition – earned from trade was massively used to acquire a series of offices, the benefits of which were both administrative and honorific. The behaviour observed was not exceptional among the various economic agents of the time, whether they came from the ranks of large French traders[19] or from the middling or small merchant bourgeoisie of Dauphiné.[20] The question here is how we should understand the meaning of these investments (whether financial or relational) made in the public sphere. The issue has been the focus of numerous discussions among historians, who remain divided between two main, and contradictory, interpretations.

On one hand, it is possible to view this phenomenon as a symptom of the weaknesses proper to French trade in the Old Regime, the aspirations of which mimicked the aristocratic model and its attributes (landed property, titles, independent income). More implicitly, this interpretation fits with an overall analysis aiming at explaining the difficulties French entrepreneurs had adapting to the mechanisms of modern capitalism, particularly compared to what was happening in England. But more recent studies have tended to question this thesis, adopting an approach less oriented towards the critique of the supposed 'backwardness' of the actors than towards the analysis of their motivations. Most notably, they stress the fact 'that finding as one of the goals of wealth accumulation the consumption of status goods by oneself or one's family is a perfectly normal phenomenon'.[21] The acquisition of public offices must be considered in its specific social and economic context rather than being evaluated in the light of twenty-first century criteria.

This more recent working hypothesis is attractive, to the extent that it avoids tacking teleological considerations onto the analysis of a historical phenomenon. Even so, it contains the implicit presupposition that trade and public activities were separated, since in this view the public functions mainly constituted an object of consumption to which commercial profit gave access. Still, even though an overall trend of retreat into investment and rents or the service of the State did exist and can be clearly observed in the collective trajectory of the Pinets, the process remained slow. Only under the Restoration did Pierre-Daniel's son, Marie-Edouard, end up giving up trade entirely, a fact noted in the 1829 census, where he appears as a '*bourgeois, membre du conseil municipal*' (bourgeois and councilman), and not subject to trader's fees (the *patente*).[22] For more than half a century, the family thus combined public offices, public service and private merchant transactions, without really wielding trade as a mere tool, the use of which was limited to acquiring enough money to rise to political and administrative functions. The avid collection of these functions has led us to reassess the articulation between general and private interest. The aim is not simply to study the passage from one sector to another, from tarde-based to rents-based income, but to analyse the interaction between two modes of action, differentiated in the final analysis by their relationship to State institutions.

Let us start by examining the commercial advantages generated by public functions. In the case of the Pinet family, we may distinguish four main categories, which work for the Old Regime, but also for the Revolutionary and post-Revolutionary period.

First of all, public offices guaranteed relatively stable financial revenues which complemented the generally more uncertain income to be derived from trade. The office of *receveur*, for instance, provided the family with a fixed yearly payment.

Secondly, service to the State eased access to economic information in a context in which it was unequally shared. Two factors thus came into play. On the one hand, certain administrative tasks presupposed obtaining the information necessary to carry them out: fiscal responsibilities, for example, provided useful indications on the local distribution of wealth. On the other hand, by forging links with political and administrative personnel, the Pinets were able to obtain information liable to benefit their own transactions. In this fashion, in the year VIII of the republican era (1799), Pierre-Daniel Pinet and Jean-Jacques Chauvet attempted to obtain from one Boutin, head of the *Bureau des lois*, first-hand details on the evolution of French–British relations. Such a step could be considered only by actors able to make use of reliable relays in the State apparatus. The goal of the two merchants was unambiguous: it was, they wrote, to anticipate 'peace with the English' in order to carry out a 'speculation on the Colonies', offering in passing to the administrator a profit-sharing agreement, the details of which remained to be defined.[23]

Thirdly, such official actors benefited also from privileged access to certain markets and commercial and financial opportunities, which followed in part from the information advantage previously described. The perfect military supplier had to be '*au fait du service*' (aware of the way the service worked), and in this capacity he had to combine three indispensable qualities: a good knowledge of military circles, close familiarity with the demands of resupplying and solid financial means.[24] Actually, behind these individual abilities stood the family situation, which to a great degree conditioned the ability of the actors to win army contracts. The quasi-monopolistic situation enjoyed by the Pinet family in the middle of the 1780s can only be accounted for by their maintaining close ties with the military administration (in Embrun, for example) and by the experience they had accumulated since the War of the Austrian Succession.[25] The same was true for other merchants of Haut-Dauphiné: over the same period, Alexandre Barillon had also used family and marriage ties with several officers to buttress his influence in army procurement.[26]

Lastly, merchants could hope to spread and consolidate the systems of relationships on which their individual merchant operations were founded. Public activities implied making contact with political and administrative representatives, which could then be called upon for commercial ends. Moreover, the prestige attached to the offices they had taken on reflected on their reputation as merchants and enabled them to take on the role of intermediaries between other commercial actors and the authorities.

Distributing Risk: Complementary Activities

The advantages we have just referred to all had a common thread: they contributed to reducing the commercial risks to which the family firm was confronted, sometimes through a diversification of the sources of profit, and at other times by relying on asymmetrical relationships between agents. To sum up the situation, in the 1780s, the income of Pierre-Daniel and Jean-Joseph-André Pinet was drawn mainly from their various offices, from transactions carried out under contract with the military administration, and lastly from ordinary merchant speculation, especially in the silk, wool and almond trades.

Gaps in the archival record prevent any quantitative comparison between the amounts of profit they drew from the various areas of activity listed above.[27] But using their correspondence, one can nonetheless propose a typology of these activities according to the regularity of gains they generated. Thus on the one hand, merchant speculation represented potentially high but very variable sources of profit; on the other, tax offices produced regular (or partly regular) revenues,[28] which still could fluctuate, but only very exceptionally.[29] The brutal reduction in value of the tax farm granted the *receveurs* in 1789 was thus seen as exceptional, and justified only in the context of the financial difficulties of the monarchy.[30]

Thus, it is possible to argue that the combination of various public and private functions was part of an overall strategy aiming at distributing risk in order to lessen the exposure of the family to the hazards of trade.[31] Admittedly, by its very nature, business carried out on behalf of the State did not entirely exclude uncertainty; military contracts, for example, had the reputation of being highly unstable, particularly during periods of war.[32] But owning offices allowed agents to be able to rely on a regular income, and thus to compensate for potential unexpected losses.

At the same time, commercial activities and relationships made up for difficulties occasionally encountered in the course of administrative management. In December 1788 for instance, Jean-Joseph-André Pinet was experiencing great difficulties carrying out his function as *receveur*. To a Parisian correspondent, he wrote the following:

> You will have received [from M. Sain Costard and the Pinet brothers of Lyon] a new remittance which will reduce my debt to 300 400 l[ivres]t[tournois], which I cannot hand over to you at this moment, having not yet been able to obtain enough funds to face the commitments I have been obliged to make in Lyon ... In order to be able to pay you during the whole time of upset in our province, our collection, in spite of all of my meticulousness, is again behind by more than 60,000 lt. Since I had not

counted on this inconvenience at the beginning of the year, I had not been able to take any precautions.[33]

In order to solve his difficulties, Pinet had to call to the rescue the Perier family of Grenoble, to which he was linked through his merchant and financial operations since at least the 1760s.[34]

The accumulation of public offices thus cannot be reduced to a backup strategy, meant to compensate for speculative risks. On the contrary, one must insist on the constant complementarity between public activities and trade, whether it be from the point of view of the financial profits that were amassed or from that of the networking resources one could mobilize.

Family Relationships in the 1780s

A Geography of Merchant Relationships

The various sets of family relationships developed by the Pinets were situated at the intersection of their private occupations, whether commercial or financial, and their public attributions. What remains to be determined is how these different functions were articulated one with another. In order to study these relationships at the outset of the Revolution, I have used three sources: copies of letters sent by the firm,[35] a journal (1788–93)[36] and a complete inventory of Pinet's claims on his debitors in 1788.[37]

For the most part, these documents reveal the regional character of the family activities. This is especially true of the trading transactions recorded in the journal, almost none of which took place outside of the limits of Haut-Dauphiné or Haute-Provence in 1788–9. Similarly, the great majority of the recorded active debts were local in character. Debts from outside of Dauphiné in 1788 represented less than 2.6% of the total amount listed (see Table 7.3 below).

Statistical analysis of the letters confirmed these observations, but brought to light some finer points: even though more than half of the letters sent between 1785 and 1786 were destined for Dauphiné, it can be pointed out that during the same period outside centres of attraction also appeared (Lyon, Paris or to a lesser degree, Aix), and that numerous ties existed with Provence (Tables 7.1 and 7.2).

Table 7.1: Destination of Pinet's correspondence, 1785–6.

Destination of the letters	Proportion of overall correspondence (N = 665 letters)
Dauphiné	53.7%
Provence	12.5%
Lyon	17.9%
Paris	9.6%

Source: Archives Départementales de l'Isère, 14 J 5-9.

Table 7.2: The main cities in Pinet's epistolary network, 1785–6.

Rank	Places	Proportion of letters sent (N = 665)
1	Grenoble	20.8%
2	Lyon	17.4%
3	Embrun	15.2%
4	Paris	9.5%
5	Sisteron	4.4%

Source: Archives Départementales de l'Isère, 14 J 5-9.

Two distinct networks (in terms of scale) appear in these preliminary observations. The first was spread between the Alps of the Dauphiné and of Provence, around Gap and the neighbouring local territories (Bochaîne, Champsaur, Dévoluy). The second stretched further, to areas immediately outside the region, to Bas-Dauphiné – mainly to Grenoble – as well as to the rest of France (Lyon, Paris, Aix), and to other areas contacted occasionally (see Map 7.1). These systems of relationships did not take on identical functions. The nature of the activities dealt with (whether public or not) in all likelihood varied considerably according to the scale of action under consideration. Thus, it is necessary at this point to take another look not only at these differences, but also at the possible overlap between the two networks.

Regional Network, Trade and Notability

At the regional level, business relations were characterized by an overlap of trade relationships and family or friendship bonds. The network that becomes apparent thus covered a large part of Haute-Provence and Haut-Dauphiné. These bonds remained remarkably stable, including during the Revolution. After the division of the country into *départements*, Pinet's correspondents remained concentrated in Hautes-Alpes and Basses-Alpes, following a spatial distribution which recalled the period of the Old Regime. Within this geographical area, the sources provide evidence of a diversification of roles. The family activity divided itself mostly into three parts: commercializing local products (wool, almonds), fulfilling the public functions presented above (taxes, military resupply), and finally, financial activities.

This latest element deserves particular attention in that it is what distinguishes Pinet from all the other commercial actors in the area. Actually, the family played a central part in regional banking, including informally, through advances granted throughout Haut-Dauphiné. The inventory of debts from 1788 gives an idea of the geographical extension of the family's financial network (see Table 7.3). The document proves that Pinet's influence stretched mainly over Gapençais and neighbouring areas.

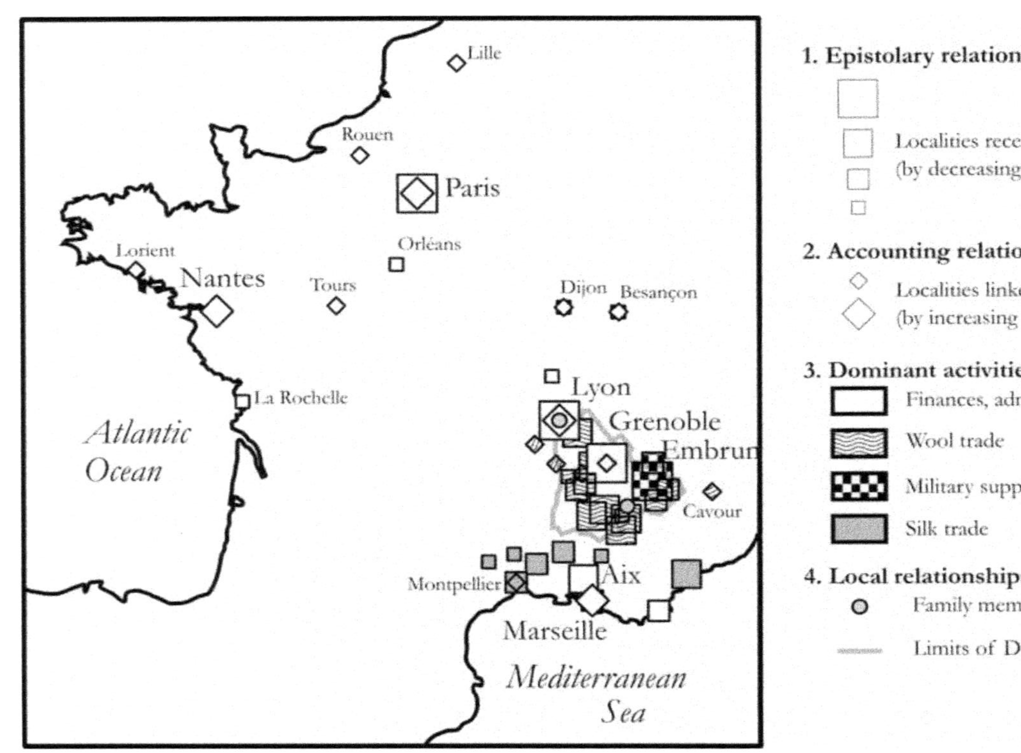

Map 7.1: The Pinet networks.

These debts were very unequal in volume as in quality, since the reimbursement periods turned out to be extremely variable.[38] Family documents on this topic show that there were very different in nature according to the case chosen. While there were sums of money advanced in order to provide financial means to entrepreneurs from the area (whether they were commercial or not), there are also traces of a number of debts from individuals and impoverished family groups endeavouring to obtain financial assistance from the Pinets.[39] These loans were for small amounts and their reimbursement was generally spread out over a long period. The family was thus guaranteed a heterogeneous *clientèle* (in every sense of the word). Overall, these emergent relations of indebtedness confirm the presence of relations of domination within the regions of Haut-Dauphiné and Haute-Provence.[40]

Table 7.3: Debts due to Jean-Joseph-André Pinet in 1788.

Local territories	Due debts	Average amounts recovered daily	Percentage in the total of due debts
Bochaîne	4 145 lt.	0 lt. 2 s. 7 d.	3.7%
Champsaur	20 505 lt.	5 lt. 12 s. 9 d.	18.2%
Dévoluy	969 lt.	0 lt. 2 s. 0 d.	0.9%
Diois	15 506 lt.	1 lt. 13 s. 4 d.	13.8%
Gapençais	66 237 lt.	1 lt. 3 s. 7 d.	58.9%
Lyonnais	2 546 lt.	0 lt. 13 s. 4 d.	2.3%
Provence	310 lt.	0 lt. 1 s. 9 d.	0.3%
Valentinois	405 lt.	0 lt. 0 s. 4 d.	0.4%
undetermined	1 714 lt.	0 lt. 12 s. 0 d.	1.5%
total	112 341 lt.	1 lt. 12 s. 7 d.	100%

Source: Archives Départementales de l'Isère, 14 J 23.

The Pinets' position, within the social and geographic space which was theirs, was thus closely linked to their situation within the personal economic relationships they had with local agents. By taking on the status of main merchant and financier in the region and by alternating forms of action having to do both with the pursuit of private trade interest and the service of the public interest, the family group demonstrated that it was part of the regional notability. However, local mechanisms would not have been enough on their own to establish this social predominance, it also called for outside legitimation.

Distant Horizons, a Source of Legitimacy

It is precisely through this necessity for institutional recognition – in the wide sense of the term – that relationships between regional and national networks were brought about. In the race to hold on to the leading role regionally, the Pinets's commercial and financial activities served as the basis for the maintenance of their relationships of trust with their individual and collective partners. However, merchant operations were not in and of themselves sufficient to achieve the desired result.

Chronologically, the Pinets had gone into commerce before becoming interested in financial or public activities. Nevertheless, the family does not seem to have progressed much in the business of being merchants until the second generation, that is, until the time when Pierre-Daniel acquired the office of *receveur*, and a few years later, began taking up speculation on a larger scale. From that point on, a significant milestone had no doubt been reached, and one begins to witness the development of extra-regional relationships. Admittedly, commercial relations with the Perier were attested as early as the middle of the eighteenth century.[41] However, it was only at the instigation of Pierre-Daniel that these relationships were transformed into lasting and regular financial links, and that the Pinets would thus become the local intermediaries of the Grenoble traders, representing their interests locally. The most likely hypothesis is that the family's recently acquired public functions had increased their notoriety nationwide, and especially in the commercial centres of Grenoble, Lyon or Paris.

Indeed, the extension of their system of relationships during the Old Regime took place in three main directions: towards Grenoble, where the Periers as well as several officials of the fiscal or military administrations were based; towards Lyon, where the Pinets opened up a commercial firm; and towards Paris, finally, for reasons which originally seem to be related to purchasing the office of *receveur des tailles*, and secondly to banking and financial operations. This network gained even greater importance during the Revolution. For example, while over half of the mail was addressed within Dauphiné in 1785–6, this proportion fell to only 28% in 1803–5.[42] Around thirty circular letters (1792–1815) moreover, bear witness to the existence of links with many firms outside of Dauphiné, established mainly in Paris, but also in Cologne, Limoges or Poitiers, for example.

Regional and extra-regional networks had mutual ties. The fact that they held many offices within Gapençais turned the Pinets into choice intermediaries for outside merchants. At the same time, recognition by central government authorities and by business milieux from outside of Haut-Dauphiné was an asset and an advantage, because it reinforced the social status of the family and granted it a very particular role in local transactions. It was by playing on both scales at the same time, and thus by dominating a large part of exchanges between the area and the outside, that the Pinets were able to make their enterprise last.

Commercial Risk and Revolution

Risk and Uncertainty in 1788–9

The sudden outburst of the Revolution raises the issue of the joint evolution of social and economic relations and of political organization. Ordinarily, the distribution of risks between public and commercial activities was built on the premise that the current existing political and administrative regimes were meant to last. The Pinets' business relations were well adapted to the institutional environment of the Old Regime, in both its formal or informal dimensions, to its usual mechanisms as well as to its dysfunctions. In contrast, our merchants did not anticipate the possibility of a relatively rapid fall of the monarchy and of a substantial revamping of the State apparatus. Thus, the question arises of the adaptation of commercial networks and merchant practices to a new and uncertain situation. Before considering the family's medium-term response, it is important to examine its attitude at the outset of the movement.

In Haut-Dauphiné, it was the peasant rebellions in the spring and summer of 1789 that attracted Pinet's attention,[43] whereas he had almost entirely ignored the events of 1788. 'The troubles which have been occurring during the last two or three days totally upset our plans', he wrote. 'We are all distressed. What is most dangerous is the evil intentions of the peasants toward their lords'.[44] Fears were expressed for commercial reasons (on property rights,[45] or the security in the material conditions of trade), but also much more widely, touching the Pinets' social status and the defence of their prerogatives. Hostility towards the uprising was frequent in merchant circles in Dauphiné, even if it was most often coupled with very liberal positions, notably in Bas-Dauphiné.[46] But this kind of liberalism, much less present in Haut-Dauphiné anyway, was not at all characteristic of the Pinet family. At the very time of the Vizille assembly, Jean-Joseph-André wished above all 'that God would rouse spirits to their true duties and submissions toward the king'.[47] Indeed his own brother, François, was added to the *émigrés* lists,[48] and the authorities tried – vainly – to confiscate his belongings.[49]

An Example of Adaptation: The Military Contracts of the 1790s

During the Revolution, the former offices would be done away with. The office of *receveur*, which had brought about the family's heyday, was suppressed in 1792. Pinet's intervention in the fiscal administration from then on was almost non-existent. In contrast, activities related to military resupplying expanded. Pinet won several contracts in the 1790s, with one Lesbros, and then with the Gayde brothers from Basses-Alpes. The archives on this topic have been rather well conserved, and the dispute opposing the Gaydes and the Pinets in the 1800s and 1810s help us understand better how the business of our Gap merchant was carried out. An 1813 document notably comments on Jean-Joseph-André's activities:

> Mr. [Jean-Joseph-] André the eldest having become, after his father, *receveur des tailles,* continued to engage in the same speculation. Having received in the year 1792 an immense quantity of *assignats* [depreciated State paper currency] as reimbursement for the financing of his fairly considerable charges and claims, he had to find a way to use them, and he couldn't find a more advantageous use, and which would expose him less to the persecution directed at those who appear rich, than in times of abundance, to purchase foodstuff which he then gave over to public administrations or firms, when State necessity would demand it, and when he would be able to make such investments with some security as to the reimbursement of his funds.[50]

Pinet thus attempted to restore some balance to his activities, with a constant will to reduce risks which took into account revolutionary transformations. His decision is all the more interesting in that it entails massive investments in the area of military food procurement, which, as we have already seen, had a reputation for uncertainty under the Old Regime. Nonetheless, economic risks in this case were compensated for by a reduction in the public exposure of the firm and the merchant.

Indeed, any risk-taking of a commercial nature included a political component, but to various degrees. Revolutionary dynamics had contributed to exacerbating this latter aspect because of social tensions (and their institutional consequences), expressed in particular during the first half of the 1790s.

Within this context, military resupplying carried with it four decisive advantages. First of all, it was a function, the mechanisms of which were well known to the Pinets since they had participated in procurement throughout the entire eighteenth century, during both peace-time and war-time. As a second advantage, the responsibilities in this case left some leeway, since the operations were carried out in the context of contractual agreements between private actors and public authorities. Thirdly, the merchant's own resources were bolstered by the administration both at the financial level (with the paying out of amounts earmarked for making purchases) and at the logistical level (a share of the means of storage and transportation was provided directly by State agents). Finally, the fourth advantage was that the war effort had in the end been recognized as indispensable to the very survival of the Revolutionary State. From this point of view, the organization of resupplying the armies did not come under the kind of political attacks which could sometimes affect other administrative functions.[51]

Pinet was already in full possession of all the material means necessary to gain access to these military contracts. Continuity in the military administration before and after the Revolution guaranteed that he had numerous contacts in official circles. Jean-Joseph-André moreover had considerable funds which he would reinvest in this speculation. He found in this type of activity a golden opportunity to get rid of a large quantity of *assignats,* taking advantage of the fact that he was supposed to be serving not his own interests, but the army of the Alps and the government.

Merchants on the Coat-Tails of Political Power

There was a very real public involvement of the merchants studied here during the Revolution. This involvement represented an adaptation to trade conditions and to the social and political relations of the day. It was not systematic, and corresponded mostly to a kind of commercial strategy which had to take into account three major parameters: the accessibility of public service, the influence of this kind of service on commercial risks and the level of exposure to political attacks of the public offices thus accepted. Investment into military supplies was the best compromise between the various constraints listed above.

What was the impact of this implication? Is it possible to maintain, in particular, that being close to political power allowed the family to get through the Revolution without experiencing economic instability? Actually, merchant activity seems to have been very much disturbed, especially towards the middle of the 1790s. Until 1793, the situation had remained rather favourable: the revenues of the house of Pinet increased (Figure 7.1) and the volume of mail sent out by the company did not change much. On the contrary, from 1794 on, there was a complete collapse in the number of letters sent (Figure 7.2), lasting until the 1800s. The phenomenon coincided with changes in the international context, and with troubles for the family, including the proceedings against Jean-Joseph-André's brother, and a lawsuit against the Gayde brothers.

Nonetheless, the impact of these events on the family must be put into perspective, for at least two reasons. On the one hand, these difficulties did not spare the other merchants of the region or the surrounding areas. On the other hand, the Pinets's collective resources were far from having been destroyed: at the end of this somewhat chaotic sequence, the family maintained its prerogatives. However, the heart of the family's activities was reoriented towards public affairs. This transition, no doubt furthered by the Revolutionary experience, is nevertheless situated within the context and with the dynamics initiated during the Old Regime. In the end, what was important was to complete the work of social ascent already undertaken, by abandoning trade for what were becoming increasingly prestigious positions.

Thus Jean-Joseph-André Pinet really took up politics under the Empire, becoming in turn mayor of Gap and president of the *conseil général*[52] until the Restoration. This type of orientation was not rare in Dauphiné merchant circles, as has been shown by a survey carried out in the Hautes-Alpes, Drôme and Isère *départements*.[53] Within what was formerly Dauphiné, a majority of merchants (52.4%) had been active in the administration or in politics between 1789 and 1809–12. In Hautes-Alpes, the proportion was lower, but a strong minority of the local merchant bourgeoisie (41.9%) was or had been linked to public affairs. The analyses carried out in neighbouring *départements* confirm these observations, even when one considers territories which were more active from an economic point of view: in Rhône, for example, it has been estimated that nearly 46% of commercial actors had taken on public functions during the same period.

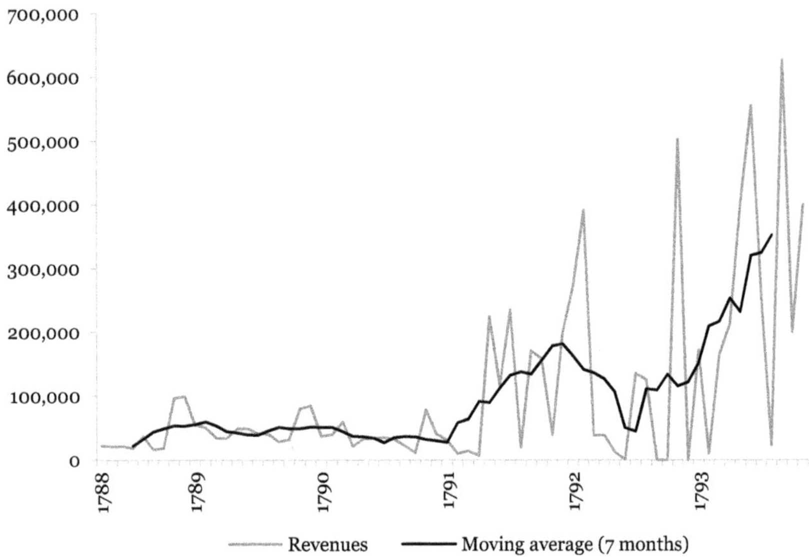

Figure 7.1: Revenues of the Pinet house listed in its Journal, 1788–93 (in £ tournois).

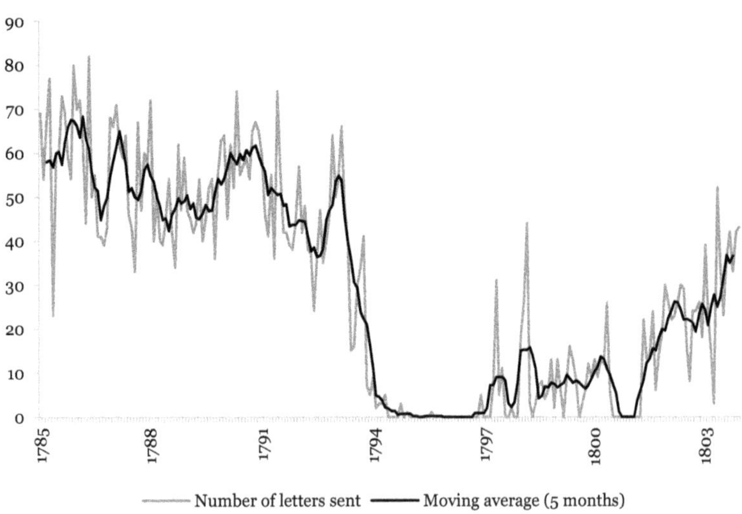

Figure 7.2: Quantitative evolution of the Pinets' correspondence, 1785–1803.

This is not to say that Pinet's trajectory is representative of that of those other merchants and tradesmen involved in the administration or in public life; for most of them were only active at the local level (27.9% of individual cases identified in the Hautes-Alpes). Only a minority were involved in public activities at the national level (fewer than 1% in the whole of the Dauphiné) or even at the *département* level (13.9% in Hautes-Alpes). Jean-Joseph-André Pinet, through his relations with the military administration and the part he played as *conseiller général*, was part of this small number of individuals belonging mainly to the upper levels of merchants who alone disposed of adequate means to reach their position and to accomplish the duties inherent to it by relying not only on administrative means, but also on their own private resources, whether these were financial, relational or more generally, social.

Conclusion

The considerable commercial profit made by the Pinet family during a large part of the eighteenth century was less the result of permanent risk-taking than of the ability of the actors to reduce their exposure to a great variety of risks and uncertainties. In the very discourse of the merchants studied here the concept of risk-taking was never glorified in and of itself. The gains obtained instead supposedly rewarded personal and collective qualities characterizing the actors, those qualities which made the Pinets 'good merchants' within a pre-established moral framework inseparable from the economic field.

More generally, the economy is not autonomous: the notions of risk, profit, or entrepreneurship may be used to describe the Pinets' activities under the sole condition that they be considered as elements associating at the same time merchant and moral or symbolic considerations, that is, if one agrees to break with the classical interpretations to which we referred in the introduction.

Indeed, the Pinet family never considered that its commercial or banking activities were an end in themselves. What moved these merchants was not a taste for adventure or for entrepreneurial adventure – these ideas in fact turn out to be totally absent from the discourse studied here. Involvement in business was the result of a very different kind of incentive, having more to do with family influence, routines followed as a group, or imitative behaviour in an area in which the practice of trade was a good path towards social promotion. The interpretation which turns the founding of a firm into a solitary and rational act must thus be strongly questioned. In the case studied here, the actors began at a very young age to be trained in merchant techniques. Immersion in the world of trade fit into a collective decision, organized by the rest of the family circle and in the service of social and economic ambitions which were both personal and collective.

We begin to see just what kind of profit entrepreneurs such as the Pinets coveted. Economic gain, expressed as a numerical value, in the end was but one of many elements of a more general kind of profit. When they were purchasing offices, participating in military resupplying or going into banking and financial operations, the Pinets were not content to hope for merely monetary gains. They also expected greater social prestige and a set of symbolic gains which would contribute to the family's repositioning within established social hierarchies. This did not in any way mean that economic activity would be more or less inhibited by moral considerations, or that it would essentially be constrained by the archaic rules and social norms characteristic of pre-industrial societies. On the contrary: it was indeed non-economic incentives that motivated the actors studied here to create new firms and to stay in merchant activities.

From this point on, involvement in public affairs in the Ancien Régime participated in two different yet converging kinds of logic. On the one hand, it was important to distribute risk and to accumulate complementary forms of remuneration, achieving a balance between potentially large but hazardous speculative gains, and gains linked to holding office, which were distinctly less lucrative but much more regular. On the other hand, these initiatives take on significance within strategies of social enhancement: financial offices, the office of secretary to the king (which carried with it a title of nobility), and seigniorial titles bestowed increased symbolic prestige upon the Pinets. At any rate, these two dynamics contributed to reinforcing the social and economic power of the family group while at the same time reducing the risk of a drop in social status, with economic risks being merely one particular manifestation of this wider risk.

The strategies engaged in by the Pinets appear to have been crowned with success during the 1780s, when the family finally succeeded in entering the nobility. Nonetheless, the Revolution upset this situation by modifying material conditions of exchange, but above all – and that is notably what distinguishes it from past military conflicts – because it gave concrete shape to an evolution of social and symbolic relationships which gave to the notion of commercial risk a whole new significance, with the political dimension gaining an ever larger weight in it. Under such conditions, the opposition between risk and uncertainty lost some of its relevance. The Pinets were indeed confronted with a totally unpredictable event (uncertain, in the classical meaning of the term), which modified radically the conditions within which one could anticipate events deemed predictable (that is, risks).

The hazards inherent to the Revolution could only be faced by relying on resources already acquired during the Old Regime: financial capital, relationships and merchant proficiency would be mobilized in order to reinforce group positions. On the basis of their former social and economic positions, the Pinets were thus able to make themselves indispensable not only in the commercial sphere, but also in the public space. Their involvement in political life and in the administration – especially in military supplies – gave them such importance that it allowed them to efficiently reduce the various risks to which they were otherwise exposed. This family adaptation would not have been possible if a number of practices developed before the Revolution had not been maintained. The Pinets' trajectory tends to show in particular that the interaction between economic and symbolic profit lasts even through times of Revolutionary breakdown. It was by relying upon the various forms of socially accepted profit-making that the family group was able to perpetuate its rise, despite the collapse of the institutions and structures of the Old Regime.

8 'THE WAY TO MAKE A HUGE FORTUNE, EASILY AND WITHOUT RISK': ECONOMIC STRATEGY AND TACTICS AMONG TOBACCO-SOUTH PLANTERS IN THE EARLY NATIONAL UNITED STATES

Steven Sarson

Introduction

As historians of colonial British America have shown, the essentially rural, agricultural economy of the Chesapeake region, comprising upper North Carolina, Virginia, Maryland and lower Delaware, depended on Atlantic commerce. While some have argued that the regional staple crop of tobacco exhausted the land, and indebtedness to British merchants further eroded entrepreneurial energies by the late colonial era, others, more recently, have portrayed a generally prosperous economy, at least for larger planters. So, while tobacco cultivation was replaced by wheat farming in parts of the eastern and northern Chesapeake in the late eighteenth century, and even more extensively and rapidly during and after the American revolutionary war, the tobacco south was actually growing larger, expanding in the late eighteenth and early nineteenth centuries into swathes of Kentucky and Tennessee. Indeed, tobacco was temptingly profitable enough that, once American Independence annulled the Navigation Acts and freed planters from dependence on the merchant houses of Glasgow and London, freeing them to seek out the most profitable markets, some became merchants full-time and more became part-time merchants. Also, planters filled the gap left by resident Scottish factors in the Chesapeake, buying up tobacco and other produce from poorer farmers and selling that on too.[1]

On the face of it, then, profit-oriented tobacco planters seem to have conformed to modern notions of classical rational-choice economic behaviour. And yet profit making and accounting was, as Pierre Gervais, Yannick Lemarchand and Dominique Margairaz explain in the Introduction of this volume, often more complicated than that. First of all, because tobacco was a cash crop that required overseas markets, planters needed to diversify to avoid dependency in case price fluctuations, embargoes and wars interrupted business for long periods of time. Unlike sugar, tobacco did not reap the scale of profits that allowed West Indian planters surpluses enabling them to ride out years without trade. What Trevor Burnard and others have said of colonial Maryland planters was true of their post-revolutionary descendants: they were profit-oriented but necessarily risk averse. In any case, tobacco could be a soil-exhausting crop and thus required long-term field rotation. Though tobacco was a staple, then, there could never be a tobacco monoculture as there was a sugar one in the West Indies. Also, after Independence, the newly autonomous American economy meant planters could invest more than ever in extra-agricultural and non-agricultural enterprises such as tobacco and land speculation, road building, railways, manufacturing, banking and government bonds.[2]

Planters' approaches to profit-making and accounting were further complicated by the role of the household (as both a place and a cultural entity) in social and economic networking. Networking relied to a great extent on particular forms of southern hospitality, and planters considered expenditure on dinner parties and other social events in their calculations of profit margins. Yet, while they (or more often planters' wives) could accurately assess the costs of a dinner party, translating that into a calculation of profit margin from any subsequent business transactions was another matter. Hence the sporadic use of account books in the tobacco south. The absence or at least partial conflation of what we have come to think of, thanks to Jürgen Habermas, as separate spheres, thus complicated the calculation of the costs of doing business. In turn, the fact that the home was a public as well as private space, a place of business as well as a family retreat, allowed women a prominent role in planter profit-making and accounting. And it was more than an instrumentalist role in which women might perform pre-defined profitable tasks. Because the household end of profit-margin calculation was complex, because it was difficult if not impossible to account numerically the relationship between the expenses of hospitality and the profits of business, women necessarily obtained significant agency in defining what profit was and how it could best be made, allowing them crucial agency at the heart of the planter economy.[3]

It is worth noting that the nature of profit-making in tobacco south had powerful implications for race and class as well as gender. Tobacco cultivation in particular was labour intensive and was most profitable and efficient when the work was done by slaves. It was also capital intensive, as were various forms of diversification, both in terms of financial and social and cultural investment. Only wealthier planters had sufficient means to diversify when international tobacco markets closed during the years of embargo and war (1807–15), and only they could invest in barns of sufficient quality or hire warehouses to store hogsheads while waiting for markets to open again. In the meantime, smaller farmers with poor or no storage facilities and in need of ready cash to pay taxes and other day-to-day expenses had little choice but to sell to rich planters at low prices. And prices in overseas markets were higher, but only those able to pay transportation and insurance as well as storage costs could fully benefit from them. Also, exporting required mercantile connections in European cities that were available only to the wealthiest Americans. Furthermore, only the wealthiest could afford dinner parties with other members of the economic and political elite among whom access to knowledge about and opportunity to engage in profitable enterprises was far more extensive than it was among others. And indeed rich tobacco planters maintained a near-monopoly on access, knowledge and trust by inviting only the most 'genteel' to the dinner tables at which they built their business networks. As Pierre Bourdieu has shown, 'social capital' of this kind served to exclude the many as well as to include only a few.[4]

Among the few were the Calverts of Prince George's County, Maryland. At the death of his father in 1788, George Calvert, a descendant of the colonial proprietors of Maryland, took control of his 2,000-acre Mount Albion plantation worked by over sixty slaves. He obtained full ownership when his mother died ten years later. By 1803, he owned over 3,000 acres and that year married Rosalie Stier and moved to the 730-acre Riversdale plantation, with a mansion built by his new father-in-law, Henri Stier, a Wallonian refugee from Napoleon's invasion of the Low Countries. When Rosalie died in 1821, the Calverts were the richest family in Prince George's County, with over 5,000 acres of land and 124 slaves, and a total taxable wealth of $47,245.16. When George Calvert began to distribute property among his children in 1835, he owned 13,925 acres of land and 173 slaves, and total wealth of $222,198.25. Rosalie Calvert's 230 letters to her family, written after their return to Europe following Napoleon's 1803 amnesty to refugees, reveal a great deal about how the Calverts and others like them made and accounted profits. Other evidence from across the tobacco South shows that the Calverts were untypical in that they were extraordinarily successful in their endeavours, but were nonetheless exemplars of tobacco planters' economic mentality and behaviour.[5]

Fighting for Profits

Some tobacco planters kept account books, others did not. George Calvert did not, at least before he married, but Rosalie kept detailed and daily accounts and encouraged her evidently reluctant husband to help her, with limited success. As she wrote her to father in 1804:

> Finally, I have found a way to make my husband keep an [account] book – I began it myself! At the beginning he laughed at me for my awkwardness in doing it. Then he became impatient because I asked him every day how much he had spent. But at last he is going to do it himself, because he says I do it so badly that he will never be able to get away. Now every evening after supper we enter how much has been received or expended during the day.[6]

A little over a year later, however, Rosalie expressed regret for not having maintained the account book, but then pointed out that the new one she had begun would 'convince you that we manage our affairs not only with all possible economy but also with system, and that our method accords exactly with the plans you have often advised us to follow'. A few years later, to her father's query as to whether Riversdale was producing the 4% returns that he predicted, she replied, 'I have kept an exact account of everything I have received since my marriage, both in gifts and allowance ... I will send ... a note of what Riversdale produced the past year, which I think you will see exceeds $1,600'.[7]

Unfortunately, none of Riversdale's account books survive from George and Rosalie Calvert's time. Her letters, however, as well as tax and probate records, include extensive detail on the family's economic pursuits, sometimes including what they made profits from, how much they made and how they accounted for them. One thing that is soon clear is that the Calverts were first and foremost tobacco planters. On their various properties fully enumerated in the Federal Direct Tax of 1798, there were fifteen barns, and the two for sheltering animals and two more for storing grain demonstrate a degree of agricultural diversification. The eleven devoted to the drying and curing of tobacco, however, show how dominant this staple cash crop nevertheless was. One reason for this dominance was the difficulty in redeploying enslaved labour. Responding in 1804 to her father's question about why her husband did not make the developments in horticulture and forestry he had recommended, Rosalie explained that George insisted that 'a tobacco planter doesn't have time to attend to the details of a farm because his workers are always and without respite busy [with that crop] ... The work necessary to grow tobacco employs the negroes every day of the year'. As Joseph Mobberly, the Jesuit manager of St Inigoes Plantation in nearby St Mary's County, observed, planters had to grow tobacco because 'their slaves must have employment – hence they must cultivate extensive fields which are much too large for their stock to manure – but their people must not only be employed, they must also be supported – hence the necessity of the corn & tobacco systems'. Thus, 'as long as we hold slaves', he continued, 'we must make those crops'.[8]

More than that, however, tobacco was simply very profitable most of the time. At the end of the first season after the Stiers' return to Europe, for example, Rosalie wrote,

> Our affairs here are going pretty well now. My husband sold his last tobacco crop a few days ago for $10 for the best quality and $8 for the second quality. He had 51 hogsheads which will bring him more than $4,500, since most of it is of the best quality ... We will now have enough to live splendidly here, to improve our properties ... and to buy some bank shares from time to time.[9]

The Calverts did not even cease tobacco production when international trade came to a standstill after 1807 and until 1815. To be sure, the Calverts found trade disruption and war worrying for various reasons, and Rosalie vehemently opposed the embargo, non-intercourse and the War of 1812 as a Federalist and an Anglophile. But her objections were also based on fear of possible economic and social disruption. As she wrote in 1807, with embargo impending, '[i]f things continue, a huge number of people, especially merchants, are going to be ruined, and we probably won't be able to send our tobacco to London anymore'. The following year she complained that the 'effects of the embargo here are quite ruinous. If it continues much longer, all the merchants will fail. The farmers and planters can't sell their commodities – nobody pays and everything is expensive'. On a personal note, she also complained that '[o]ur tobacco crop looks very promising this year, but that is small consolation when it is predicted that there won't be any market'. In March 1812, as war with Britain looked ever more likely, Rosalie Calvert showed signs of being disheartened. 'We still have all of our tobacco [on hand]', she glumly told her father, 'and yours too. I see little hope of ever selling it at a tolerable price'. The Calverts thus decreased tobacco cultivation, but only to a limited extent, for, as Mrs Calvert explained in 1812 in regard to Buck Lodge, 'we haven't grown tobacco for a long time and are working towards putting it entirely into meadowland for pasturing the cattle. However, this requires time and doesn't produce revenue right away'. In February 1814, looking back over five years of trade disruption and almost two years of war, Rosalie Calvert wrote regretfully to her brother, Charles Jean Stier, '[y]ou ask me if my husband continues to make improvements in farming and I in my gardens, etc. It is with much regret that we have abandoned all work of that description for the last two years, which will not surprise you when you consider that we have the tobacco harvest of several years in store, and that since this abominable war with England everything is double and triple the price, so that we must exercise the most scrupulous economy'.[10]

Those economies included Rosalie renewing her efforts in clothing slaves from the family plantations' own resources and, as we shall see a little later, further diversifying their agricultural enterprises. Yet, while this allowed survival, only tobacco allowed profits. After detailing various endeavours in 1810, Rosalie noted that 'all this together only defrays the expenses of farming, tools, overseers' salaries, etc. Our tobacco was net income'. Similarly, when English traveller Charles Varlo visited Edmund Plowden's Bushwood plantation in St Mary's County, Maryland, shortly after the War of Independence, he noted that Plowden

> farms his own estate, being about fifteen hundred acres, as good land as most in the county; he keeps thirty negroes, men, women, and children, and though he always lives in the country on his own estate, at as little expense as possible, yet he told me he had enough to do make all ends meet; that the negroes eat up his produce, though he

> generally makes about thirty hogsheads of tobacco yearly, besides raising great quantities of India corn and other crops, but these were all destroyed in his own family; he had never anything to sell but tobacco.

Bayly Marks calculated that to feed all of St Mary's livestock in 1840 would have required 94% of the county's corn crop and that 17,320 hogs would have eaten 75% of the potato crop.[11]

The Calverts therefore continued growing tobacco, hoping to be able to be able to sell it later. In 1807, as soon as trade disruptions began, Henri Stier counselled abandonment of the crop, but his daughter disagreed. 'I believe you are mistaken', she wrote, 'in advising us to stop growing it. This is a commodity which cannot be dispensed with; its consumption will not diminish and its culture is fact. We could not undertake any other crop with the same profits'. And thus it was that she wrote, seven years later , '[w]e have continued to grow [tobacco] each year in the hope of being able to sell it. It is the same with the 100 hogsheads bought for you [which are] in storage and [which] I hope will soon bring us a good price. At present [tobacco] is being sold at $5 and $7, and I have no doubt that it will go higher'.[12]

Because planters had brick barns or were able to afford warehouse fees, they were able to store their tobacco as they waited for markets to reopen. They were even able to speculate in the tobacco of smaller farmers who did not own and could not afford to rent storage space, and who needed cash for daily expenses. As Rosalie wrote in 1808, concerning the last season before the embargo began,

> At present the way to make a huge fortune, easily and without risk, is through buying tobacco. It can be bought for $4 and $3 – even for $2.50 a hundred for ready cash. Our last, which we sent to Murdoch, brought an average of $12 a hundred net, after all expenses, etc. were paid. There hasn't been a year [recently] when you could fail to make a good speculation by buying tobacco from the small farmers at the beginning of the season.

Mrs Calvert was ruthless in pursuit of these kinds of profits. In 1809, she wrote, in a phrase she used more than once, of buying '100 hogsheads at $5 and $3 – and this sometimes one or two [hogsheads] at a time from people who had the sheriff at their heels'.[13]

This kind of merchant activity had been possible for planters since the American Revolution had nullified the Navigation Acts, leaving them free to market tobacco where they could get the highest prices. Initially, Chesapeake planters reopened trade with those they knew, London and Glasgow merchants. Gradually, though, merchants in Richmond, Annapolis and Baltimore began buying Virginia and Maryland tobacco and finding new markets through their long-held associations in grain trading in the West Indies and Europe, especially France during their monopoly but also Germany and the Netherlands. When the Annapolis trading company Wallace, Johnson and Muir went bankrupt in 1790, Baltimore merchants became the principal local buyers and sellers of Maryland tobacco. Planters indeed became bullish about how they might use their new options. In 1793, 'the Planters and Farmers Friend' told the readers of the *Maryland Gazette* that they should abandon consignment to Europe altogether and sell locally.[14]

In late August 1810, Rosalie enumerated the Calverts' stockpile, grown by themselves and bought from others, as 'more than 100 [hogsheads] of tobacco a year now ... three hundred in storage, with 100 more in the barns waiting to be packed'. That was the year she took to speculating in tobacco on her father's behalf, although the risks of doing so became clear four years later after the 24 August Battle of Bladensburg, the cannon fire from which rattled the windows of Riversdale, and after the 'Bladensburg Races' when defeated American soldiers scattered and left the area undefended. 'Of the 100 hogsheads that I bought for you in 1810', Rosalie told her father in 1815, 'seven were in one of the warehouses which the British partially looted; they took five and left two'. Even this was no catastrophe, though. As she optimistically informed her father, 'I hope the price we can get for the remainder will compensate you for this loss. I am most anxious to sell yours as well as some of our accumulated crops, but at this point there is no stable price for anything. Everything is in a state of constant fluctuation'.[15]

The Calverts did not have to wait much longer, however, before reaping their reward. They were able to export their crops at the war's end, and, with the advantage of having their own factor in Europe, they could have their tobacco stored abroad awaiting the best possible price. Rosalie wrote to her father in November 1815,

> The ship carrying this letter has 104 [hogsheads] of your tobacco on board ... They ought to bring a very good price, being for the most part of a superior quality and even [having] some [barrels] of yellow tobacco among them ...
>
> There is another ship which will sail in a month with more than 70 barrels of ours on board, [and] still another leaving this week from the Patuxent to England with 410 barrels. That will make nearly 500 – the yield of our harvest for seven years.[16]

Things were really looking up by March 1816. 'I have learned that the *General Lingan*, carrying your 104 barrels [of tobacco]', Mrs Calvert told her father, 'reached Holland at a time when the price was very high. I do hope this made you a good profit'. She also mentioned that the Calverts' own 410 hogsheads had arrived aboard the *Oscar* in Rotterdam. At this point, however, 3,000 miles of Atlantic Ocean became a problem. 'My husband had written to Mr. Murdoch', she wrote of the family's factor,

> quite explicitly not to be in a rush to sell since there is very little tobacco on hand here and the price would certainly continue to rise. However, [Murdoch] sold it right away for 10 ½ stuyvers, and a fortnight later the price went up to 11 ½, which with the 20 percent higher exchange resulted in a $10,000 loss on this cargo.[17]

They did not actually make a loss. What Mrs Calvert meant here was in fact $10,000 less profit than they might otherwise have made. This misfortune evidently played on Mrs Calvert's mind over subsequent weeks, especially when she learned that the tobacco had been resold again at an even higher price. On 8 April, she wrote to her brother that

> Our shipment of 410 barrels on the *Oscar* turned out badly ... because of Murdoch's stupidity. Despite the fact that my husband had written him in November that he wouldn't draw anything on him before spring and that since there wasn't any tobacco left here, it would greatly increase in value, [Murdoch] persisted in thinking the opposite and sold the cargo before the ship had even arrived in Rotterdam. Two days later this same cargo sold for a profit of $10,000 to a second party, and since then to a third for $20,000 – all, moreover, without even seeing the tobacco! If Murdoch had followed our instructions, which were explicit, we would have had $20,000 more, since two-thirds of the cargo belonged to us – which he caused us to lose by his timidity and obstinacy.[18]

Rosalie Calvert's anger is understandable. Nevertheless, the Calverts still made a gross profit of around $85,000 for the 410 hogsheads they sold in Europe that year. They also did well out of the others, which they did not ultimately export but sold on the home market where they could trade at their own discretion. As Rosalie wrote to her father in March 1816, '[w]e have sold 39 hogsheads here at $13 and $15 [a hundredweight], including five of yours which were stored in the warehouse; the sixth is still here and will be sold with the rest of ours if we can get $20 for it before May. If not, we will ship it all to Amsterdam'. It is not known whether they sold the remainder at such a good price, although Mrs Calvert seemed confident enough of being able to do so. As she told her brother in April, '[w]e just turned down $16 [a hundredweight] for our last year's crop (which is not even completely packed), and I am sure we will easily obtain $20'. Certainly, the Calverts did better out of their speculations than those who were so much in need during the years of privation that they had to sell to planters at knockdown prices.[19]

Diversification

While the above shows that tobacco agriculture remained the most profitable pursuit among upper south planters, it was equally clearly not without problems and risks. As Rosalie Calvert worried about tobacco markets and other matters during the War of 1812 and the embargo and non-intercourse acts before it, her father lost some of his tobacco to British soldiers raiding the Bladensburg warehouses. Her own brother-in-law lost more than stored tobacco. As Rosalie wrote to her father in October 1816, 'Many people, Edward Calvert included, lost some of their negroes, and some lost all of theirs, plus their tobacco, grain, etc. without being able to recover anything'.[20]

And the years between 1807 and 1815 were not uniquely problematic for tobacco profits. The price per hundredweight of Common or Potomac tobacco was quite high at $5.39 after the end of the War of Independence in 1784. Post-war uncertainties and depression saw it slip to $4.37 the following year, however, and $3.94 in 1786. After a rise to $4.09 in 1787 it then slipped steadily to a low of $2.59 in 1791, whereupon it rose slowly and then more rapidly to a high of $7.48 in 1799, before slumping amid electoral uncertainties to $4.63 in 1800. Prices then remained fairly steady, with an upward trend to $5.50 in 1807, slipping to $5.12 the following year as relations with Britain deteriorated, and then sank to $3.80 in 1809 due to President Jefferson's embargo, and as the War of 1812 began they bottomed at $2.10. As the end of the war approached, prices began to rise rapidly, from $2.66 in 1813 to $4.65 in 1814 and $8.04 in 1815. When trade fully reopened in 1816, prices reached $11.25, much to the aforementioned benefit of the likes of the Calverts. They reached a peak of $13.33 in 1818 but then began to fall again, to $10.35 in 1819 and then more precipitously in the aftermath of the Panic of 1819, reaching as low as $2.66 in 1823. The price did not reach $4 again until 1832 and after that made a high of $5.25 in 1839 and a low of $1.94 in 1847. Higher-quality Kites foot or Yellow tobacco was not so susceptible to dramatic downswings. It was as high as $13 a hundredweight in 1840, but was still $6.50 in 1809. It went to $29.75 in 1825, despite depression, but then mostly remained below $20 through the 1830s. And, of course, as prices tended to fall in wartime, so insurance and other transportation costs rose, narrowing profit margins from both sides. As much as tobacco was fundamental to the profitability of upper southern plantation agriculture, then, diversification was essential to protect planters as far as possible from the price fluctuations inevitable in Atlantic trade, as well as to avoid soil exhaustion.[21]

Besides the fact that in 1798 the Calverts used four of their fifteen barns for purposes other than tobacco storage, there is little quantifiable evidence of the extent of agricultural and other forms of entrepreneurial diversification. Yet it is clear that there was extensive diversification and that it was carefully considered in light of the primary imperative to cultivate tobacco. Having commented to her father, in June 1803, that her husband had just relocated slaves from Riversdale, 'where it hasn't rained enough', to Mount Albion, she went on to mention that the 'corn looks beautiful and today [the hands] are busy cutting the rye. After that, they will cut the hay'. Less than two months later she told her father that the field tobacco 'has succeeded very well' and that the tobacco 'growing in the orchard also looks good, as does the corn ... the oats and hay have not been as successful – in part, I think, because the pigs were in the fields so much during the spring. My husband had a large number of them slaughtered and [that has helped]'. After floods in 1804 destroyed much of that year's crop and caused a credit contraction in 1805, the Calverts confined tobacco planting to their Mount Albion and Buck Lodge properties. Of Riversdale, Mrs Calvert wrote, 'in future we won't grow tobacco – only meadows, oats, clover, and enough maize for the consumption of negroes, horses, etc'. Indeed, the following year she noted, '[w]e don't grow any [tobacco] at Riversdale, but we made a nice crop of hay and 1200 bushels of oats last summer'. Rosalie described the continuing diversification of Riversdale and the carefully considered reasons for it to her father in June 1807:

> Next year nearly all the plantation will be in meadowland, which is preferable to all other kinds of culture here for several reasons: our land's location and its susceptibility to flooding, the higher profits of hay as a crop, and certainly nothing gives so much embellishment [to the land]. We also found that by closing off part of the woods three years ago in a way that keeps the animals out, young trees spring up in abundance and replace the old, decaying ones fourfold. I hope the fir trees develop well and I'm delighted with the other tree seedlings, especially the larch which I have wanted for a long time.[22]

The Calverts also contemplated diversifying one, but not both, of their other plantations. 'My husband intends in the future', Rosalie wrote in a continuation of the above,

> to give up growing tobacco at [Buck Lodge]. The terrain is unsuitable and the costs high in proportion to the profits. We have decided to continue [growing] it on the Patuxent [Mount Albion], and this year we have fine prospects, barring mishap, of making a very good crop at that plantation.

By the early 1820s, the Calverts were cultivating tobacco at Riversdale once again, despite what Rosalie said earlier. In June 1820, describing to her father a 'plain to the north of the house' that her husband had 'sown in oats' some seventeen years before, Rosalie explained that her husband had 'replaced it as a meadow and for over ten years had good crops of hay, but as the grass there had begun to deteriorate, he has just had it cultivated in order to make a crop of tobacco there. He covered the entire area with manure and in October he will again seed it with grass'.[23]

The Calverts also profitably husbanded animals. Accepting her father's offer of some Spanish sheep in 1805, Rosalie wrote that '[a]t present we have the finest bull, the best donkey, and the finest male hog in the county, so if you could send us a male and some female sheep, our collection would be complete'. These 'very valuable' sheep were probably Merinos, known for having the softest wool, which were also popular in St Mary's County and which were worth $20 per head, as opposed to $3 for common sheep. The Calverts even engaged in extra speculations in livestock, as they did in tobacco. As Mrs Calvert recounted in 1809, '[t]hese last two years, we have made a nice profit by buying some lean young steers in the spring at $11 to $14 each and selling them in the fall for $22 and $30 apiece. Similarly, we bought sheep for $3 and sold them for $5, sometimes $7'.[24]

Diversity in crop and animal husbandry is also apparent in George Calvert's probate inventory of early 1838. There was no tobacco recorded and, the inventory having been taken in February, the 1837 crop had probably been sold. In various barns and lofts, however, there were 116 barrels and 143 bushels of corn, worth $433.80, and oats, rye, hay, straw and animal fodder, together worth $633.75. There were also ninety-one sheep, worth $378, seventy-four head of cattle, worth $1,304, sixty-two pigs, worth $150.50 and twenty-five horses, worth $1,595. An additional 3,138 pounds of bacon was worth $235.35. These non-staples were worth $4,730.40 in total, nowhere near as valuable as tobacco, but valuable enough to add significantly to the Calvert family fortune and to insulate the family from Atlantic political and economic storms.[25]

The Calverts were not alone. In 1790, William Thomas Jr of Delabrooke Manor in St Mary's County produced 10,702 pounds of tobacco, 113 bushels of wheat, 190 barrels of corn, and had sixty-seven sheep, fifty-four hogs and fifty cows. Samuel Abell of Beaverdam Manor produced eight stacks of hay in 1801, and William Somerville produced 10,000 pounds of it at Medley Neck and eleven bushels of clover at Mulberry Fields, mostly as animal fodder. In 1807, wealthy planters in St Mary's County founded a Board of Agriculture that was allied to the State Agricultural Society, and they later formed a St Mary's County Agricultural Society as a local chapter of the Maryland Agricultural Society when that was constituted in 1819. In their articles of association, the St Mary's men agreed to keep agricultural accounts, experiment with new crops, disseminate their findings and subscribe to the *American Farmer*. They also had annual meetings with prizes awarded for the best crops and ploughing contests for horses and oxen. Its records and therefore presumably its activities ended in 1821, but some of this who had been involved probably continued their attempts at agricultural improvement individually. Athanatius Fenwick of St, Mary's County remained active in the state society until he died in 1824.[26]

The Calverts also engaged in extra-agricultural economic activity. In 1805, after explaining that the family 'had just shipped 102 hogsheads of tobacco, the harvest of two years', she wrote that 'I must not forget to tell you that I am also a dairymaid and make $7 a week from my butter at a quarter of a dollar a pound, over and above our own consumption'. She added in her next letter, 'I am now making 25 pounds a week, and at the height of the season was making 40 pounds. It is quite renowned for its quality'. Within a short while success inflated her pride and ambition: 'I made so much profit last year from my butter (which has a fine reputation) that I am going to have a nice little dairy built under the stairs of the north portico, vaulted like your wine cellar at the Mick'.

Bayly Marks found that most St Mary's County planters had 'milch cows' and made and sold butter too. The 1840 census for that county listed $10,225-worth of dairy products, and as cheese was usually purchased from outside the county, and as milk was too perishable to have around very long, most of this produce was probably butter.[27]

Whether the Calverts eventually built the dairy or not is unknown, but Rosalie was active in other areas too. 'Another of my diversions', she wrote in 1805, in a passage that reveals yet another crop cultivated on Calvert soil, 'is to make cloth for the negroes, which lasts twice as long as what we can buy and, everything considered, is much cheaper. For summer I also make cloth from cotton (which grows well here) for my servants ... Much of the manipulation is done by some little girls who in the future will become good maids [for her daughters Caroline and Marie Louise]'. Small-scale cotton textile production was still occurring at Riversdale four years later, when Rosalie told her father, 'I, too, am a manufacturer – all the women in my house are dressed in pretty cloth made right here. All told, it costs me about three shillings a yard for one-yard width'.[28]

Riversdale also contained a sawmill, and indeed the Calverts invested much effort and money in different kinds of milling. In February 1812, George leased a mill and race near Bladensburg to Thomas Ewell for $500 per year plus $5 daily for exclusive use of mill-race water during the dry season. He also leased a Bladensburg plot in 1820 to Thomas Ferrall for $6 annually, although the lease required Ferrall to build a granary or store on the site, adding a substantial improvement to the family's property portfolio. The Calverts were never as successful in the milling business as they hoped to be, however. They intended, for example, to build what they believed would be a highly profitable commercial grist mill at Riversdale. Spotting a gap in the market in 1803, or at least a chance to give an economic rival a run for her money, Rosalie Calvert wrote that they aimed to build one as 'Mrs. Diggs' [Digges's] mill has three times more business than it can do'. Soon thereafter the Calverts came close to building one. 'A very capable Baltimore mill builder was here some time ago', Mrs Calvert told her father, 'to look over the land, see what type of mill would be best, and now he is busy drawing up plans'. At the same time, again demonstrating considerable savvy, she enumerated the expenses and potential profits of this putative enterprise:

> It will cost between $3,000 and $4,000, and will yield 20 percent, possibly 25, by leasing it out. Subtracting 3 percent for the cost of repairs would leave 17 percent [return], quite apart from the plaster of paris, which we would supply to be processed – it is more and more in use and its toll would return a great deal. Another big benefit would be not having to produce any Indian corn at all – just contracting with the miller to deliver so much meal for the negroes. A second benefit is that half the cost of the mill has already been expended in the dam and race, which have to be maintained without yielding the return they should.[29]

The Calverts did not ultimately build this grist mill, although their intentions endured. 'Every day', Rosalie fretted in 1812, 'I regret that we have still not been able to build a mill'. As she reiterated, '[t]here is none in the neighborhood except for Digges' which earns $1,000 a year, and the mill and everything are not worth $5,000. Besides, it is in such bad condition that it often breaks down completely. I am sure that a mill which cost $10,000 would earn a 15 percent return, not to mention the benefit of manure produced by the animals one would fatten here'. As late as 1820 Rosalie was saying of her husband that 'this year he is going to build a large mill', although for unknown reasons it never materialized. In earlier years it was again diplomatic uncertainties that prevented capital investment on this large a scale. In 1810, for example, the Calverts rented an acre of land near Spa Spring 'to build a tannery', which they intended to rent out, but the initiative was, as Rosalie put it, 'thwarted by the Emperor of the French'.[30]

The Calverts also invested in non-agricultural enterprises. George was, for example, as Rosalie told her father in 1810, 'director of the Bank of Washington, which takes a day every week, [and] director of a manufacturing company in Georgetown'. Unfortunately, the Calvert letters contain no further details of manufacturing activities, but they do have ample information about investments in and profits from public roads, government bonds and bank stocks. Initially opposed to a proposed Baltimore–Washington Turnpike running through their land, the Calverts eventually accommodated themselves to it by making money from it. 'Yesterday people came by here to survey and fix the right-of-way', as Rosalie wrote in 1807, with rather imperious irritation, 'and they dared to mark it all through this property, passing very close to the stables. We will oppose this and it is only by force that they will obtain my consent. If they would make it on the other side of the Eastern Branch, it would be a great benefit for us, giving us an excellent road to Washington and Baltimore which would greatly diminish the distance'. Yet the Baltimore–Washington Turnpike eventually went through the Riversdale side of the Eastern Branch, and did so with the Calverts' say so. George was elected President of the Turnpike Company on 12 March 1813, a position that allowed him to maximize profit while minimizing inconvenience. Toll charges were 6 ¼ cents per ten miles for a single horse and rider, 12 ½ cents for a one-horse chaise with two wheels, 25 cents for a two-horse coach with four wheels, and 37 ½ cents for a four-horse coach with four wheels. The Calverts and Rosalie's father, Henri Joseph Stier, owned a 15% share of the road. Rosalie Calvert expected eventually to make 10 ½% annual profits from the $10,000 that she and her husband invested in it, and for the $5,000 she invested in it for her father, a tidy sum when loans and bank investments usually yielded 5 or 6%. So, the price of the Calverts' consent was profit of a bit over $1,000 per year for her own family and $750 for her father. Mrs Calvert also invested an unspecified quantity of her father's money in the Frederick Road. And in 1834, George sold a nineteen-acre strip of land at Riversdale to the Baltimore and Ohio Railroad Company for $11,000.[31]

The Calverts also profited from government bonds and bank stocks. There is no account of the exact amount that Rosalie invested for her father, but, as Margaret Law Callcott calculates, Henri Stier appeared to be receiving and reinvesting about $25,000 every six months, which, at an average rate of 6% interest, indicates an enormous principal of about $800,000. Rosalie also acted as stockbroker for her brother, Charles Jean Stier, and brother-in-law, Charles van Havre, husband of her sister, Isabelle. She took pride in her own skills and offered a great deal of advice to her father, especially when times arrived for reinvestment of principals when investments reached maturity. In 1805, Rosalie illustrated how much care she took when considering such investments. 'As for buying land', she explained to her father, 'I admit that it is a more secure investment and my system would be to have a certain proportion, but we already have so much and no stocks. I think it is better to use our savings to buy [stocks] now, [but] for you, with already a lot in the banks, perhaps it would be advantageous to buy some land'. A few months later she expressed her gratitude for $1,500 Henri Stier had sent for her children. In explaining what she intended to do with it, she demonstrated again her willingness to diversify capital investment, but not to take great risks. 'I am going to invest it in stock of [the Bank of] the United States', she wrote, 'I don't like the private banks – even though they pay more interest, I don't think they are as safe'. This perception was heightened by the difficulties created by embargo and the insecurities created by possible war in Europe. 'There is no danger to the public bonds', Rosalie wrote in 1807, 'but there is fear that the banks will suffer greatly. I think you would have done well to have sold your Alexandria and Baltimore [bank] shares long ago'. During the War of 1812, however, she worried that government bonds might 'become worthless' and thus reinvested in 'the public highways' as described above.[32]

The Calverts maximized profits and minimized risks in stock broking by ruthless use of insider information. In 1811, when reinvesting her own and her father's capital after Congress declined to recharter the Bank of the United States, in which the Calverts and Stiers had stocks, the Calverts invested in private banks, one in particular. As Rosalie explained to Henri Stier:

> Several things made me buy in the Bank of Washington. This bank is better managed and has a number of advantages over the others, such as [receiving] the government's deposits. Being one of the directors, my husband can know precisely what degree of confidence it merits, [and] even if the other banks fail, I think this one could sustain itself. Another advantage is that in case of a general upheaval in this country, with [this bank] being so nearby and with the certificates in my name, I could convert them more easily if it became necessary. So you now have $30,000 there and all payments made, that is to say, at $10 a share.[33]

The profits secured by George Calvert's insider knowledge proved to be huge. In 1817, Rosalie increased her father's stake in the Bank of Washington, explaining,

> You will be surprised to hear that I have sold $24,600 worth of 6 Pcts. to pay for your [Bank of] Washington shares, but here is the explanation. I had always kept these shares uncompleted because I foresaw that this stock would increase in value. Being a director of this bank, my husband knew that there was a surplus of $80,000, which was to be divided among the shareholders this summer. [This] caused me to complete payment on [the shares] last November 1st when they were only $10 – after which they went to $20 a share. You will receive [dividends of] five percent on May 1st, June 1st, August 1st, and November 1st, and there will still be a $20,000 surplus in the bank (but this is just between us).

That this activity may have been seen as unethical by others is suggested by Mrs Calvert's recommendation of secrecy. At the very least, secrecy would have ensured exclusive control of economically advantageous information. Otherwise, neither Rosalie Calvert nor her husband seems to have had any ethical aversion to or misgivings about using insider information. In fact, she seems to have been rather proud of her accomplishments in using it. 'Since the $24,600 had only been producing six percent and this way you would make twenty percent', she proclaimed triumphantly, 'I trust that you will approve of my speculation'.[34]

It was privileged knowledge also that prompted the timing of Rosalie Calvert's converting her father's Bank of Washington stock back into government bonds in 1819. 'Since this stock is presently selling at from nine to ten percent above par', she told her father, 'it seemed advantageous to sell it'. She did not mention who the losers were in these transactions, but it is clear that she was perfectly willing to sell stock that she knew was going to fall in value. She also knew to be careful, given her special position. 'I would have sold more', she explained, 'but it had to be done secretly and in small amounts because, with my husband a director of this bank, the value would have fallen considerably if we had offered all your stock for sale'. Also, Rosalie was as willing to profit from the desperation of others in stock broking as she was in tobacco speculating. 'You will note', she wrote to her father in 1810, 'that I now have 2,000 shares of Washington Bank stock for you. I don't think there will be any more available at par for the present. All the shares I bought were from people who had the sheriff at their heels'.[35]

Conclusion

As is already clear, Rosalie Calvert played a key role in producing the Calverts' fortunes. The use of a family account book was her initiative, she ran aspects of the plantation business, she personally played a hand in investing in stocks and bonds, and she gave opinions about every aspect of economic life, including calculating the best ways to balance profits and risks. Women like her were able to play such key roles because the households to which gender convention nominally but far from entirely confined them were not entirely private spaces. Such households were also places where much of the business described in this essay was carried out, where economically useful information was exchanged and where networks were weaved.

Of course, as with other economic matters, how much to invest in socialization was sometimes subject to contestation. Henri Stier occasionally rebuked his daughter for what he saw as her extravagance. In some instances she defended herself on aesthetic grounds, but more often on economic ones. 'You must take into account when making a comparison between our expenditures and yours', she wrote her father in 1805, 'that we are obliged to receive more people, which is very costly. We have to have more household goods, more bedding, etc. – things you already had ... Each of our dinner parties costs over $20 on average'. And it was to her father's question in 1808 whether she could 'become acquainted with [Albert] Galatin [Gallatin] and if it would be advantageous to be on close terms with some members of the Treasury', that she responded that '[n]othing is easier. Our situation, rank, and connections here make it quite convenient, and as soon as it could be of the least use to you, I will do it with pleasure'. Indeed, George and Rosalie sought advice in social settings from US Treasury Secretary Gallatin about government bond issues at least three times, once through the mediation of their friend Gabriel Duvall, Comptroller-General of the Maryland Treasury. On another occasion Rosalie wrote to her father of having spoken on these matters to other 'high government officials'. Over the years the Calverts hosted many dinner parties, and Albert Gallatin and Gabriel Duvall were far from their only guests who thereby became friends in high places. In 1819, for example, Rosalie reported to her sister on a Riversdale dinner party of 9 January 'for twenty people', including French and Prussian ministers and their wives. The Bagots, the British ambassador and his wife, would have attended too, but were mourning the death of Queen Charlotte, and visited on other occasions anyway. They were present, for example, at a five-day Riversdale exhibition of a family collection of sixty-three paintings by, among others, Brueghel, Rembrandt, Rubens and Titian, shown in the spring of 1816 before packing them to send to Henri Stier with the assistance of Charles Bird King, Rembrandt Peale, Thomas Sully and John Trumbull. The Calverts also visited the Monroe White House on several occasions, including a state one, as their daughter Caroline had been at private school in Philadelphia with Maria Hester, daughter of James and Eliza.[36]

Thus it was that in 1806 Rosalie Calvert sent her father 'a list of the silver items I most want', comprising '2 pairs of candlesticks; 2 pairs of candlesticks having 3 branches if possible, or else 2; 6 salt cellars; 1 vinegar caddy; 4 butter and sauce boats; 4 wine "coolers" like the ones placed at the four corners of the table with a bottle of wine inside; 1 bread basket; 2 small cabarets, 9 inches long, 7 inches wide, or approximately; 1 large cabaret, 34 inches long, 36 inches wide, or approximately; 2 soup toureens [*sic*] '. The inventory of Calvert possessions taken after George's death in 1838 included household items worth in total $4,372.56 ½. Among them were seventy-eight wine glasses, twenty-three cut-glass tumblers, fourteen cut-glass dishes, a china dinner set of 157 pieces, a chandelier and 372 ounces of silver. They also had an 'Open Carriage & harness', a 'Chariot with harness for 4 horses' and four other carriage horses. As is evident from Mrs Calvert's words, these items were not mere luxuries. They were necessary for business, or at least for creating a social environment suitable for economic networking, and their costs were therefore considered in calculating profits from any transactions that followed.[37]

As well as implications for gender, planter profit-making had profound implications for the structure of southern society. Social-economic inequality had been growing in the Chesapeake since the 1660s in older-settled areas, as the growing slave population disproportionately drove up planters' profits, which in turn drove up land prices, all of which diminished opportunities for social-economic mobility for the less well-off. Hence the emergence of a recognizable Chesapeake gentry by the 1690s and decline in land-ownership rates from 70% of household heads in the tidewater in 1660 to 50% by 1760. After the Revolution provided even greater economic opportunity for wealthy planters, social-economic differentiation grew faster than ever.[38]

Planters such as the Calverts were members of a tiny elite. They were among just fifteen families in Prince George's County who owned 2,000 acres of land or more (an acreage capable of employing the labour of fifty slaves or more) in 1800. They thus formed 0.9% of all 1,712 households, and yet they owned fractionally less than 15% of taxable wealth. In 1820, after the hardships of years of embargo and war, twelve large planters still formed 0.7% of 1,795 householders, but held just over 18% of taxable wealth. Furthermore, landowners with a minimum of 280 acres, those who could employ seven labourers or more (say, five slaves and two family labourers) in tobacco growing, constituted just over 11% of household heads in 1800, but possessed two-thirds of taxable wealth. By 1820, they possessed over three-quarters of taxable wealth. Meanwhile the rate of non-landownership rose from 50% on the eve of the Revolution to just less than 70% by 1800 and just under 75% by 1820. A principal reason for this acceleration in social-economic differentiation is the ability of the better off to market their own tobacco, the ability of the best off to market other people's tobacco as well as their own, and of course the inability of the less well-off to do likewise.[39]

Also, in 1800, 782 household heads, 46%, did not even own the $40-worth of taxable wealth to qualify to pay the county levy. In 1820, the number was 1,006, or 56% of household heads. In 1816, on the back of embargoes and war, and in the wake of drought that destroyed much of the Chesapeake wheat crop, the Maryland Assembly passed an Act for the Temporary Relief of the Poor, authorizing wealthy patrons to distribute money to those 'they may discover to be such objects of distress as to require immediate relief'. In the spring and summer of 1817 the Prince George's County Levy Court thereby disbursed $3,140 to 217 people for whom the tobacco economy was not nearly as profitable as it was for George and Rosalie Calvert.[40]

CONCLUSION: REORIENTING EARLY MODERN ECONOMIC HISTORY: MERCHANT ECONOMY, MERCHANT CAPITALISM AND THE AGE OF COMMERCE

Robert S. DuPlessis

At least since the Greeks, European languages have employed the notion of profit to denote advantage, gain, benefit and utility in domains ranging from spiritual condition to progress in learning.[1] 'For what shall it profit a man, if he shall gain the whole world, and lose his own soul?' demands the apostle Mark.[2] Less dramatically, a grateful insomniac profits from the absence of the sun and a listless student profits from the efforts of a devoted teacher.[3] Beyond its multiple uses in popular discourse, 'profit' has been invoked to define the outcome of numerous economic activities, as Gervais, Lemarchand and Margairaz point out in the Introduction: wages, interest on loans, land rent, manufacturing revenue, income from trade.

Over time, some meanings of and some synonyms for 'profit' in both general and specialist usage have fallen by the wayside. We are no longer likely to quote Jeremy Bentham's deliciously wicked epigram, 'The profit of an offence is a lot of pleasure', and we rarely speak of 'profits' to signify tips given to household servants.[4] If anything, however, profit has moved to the centre of learned and quotidian economic analysis, for rational profit-seeking is usually taken to be vital both to the operation of market economies and to the fortunes of entrepreneurs within those systems. Thus the careful scrutiny of profit margins, heartfelt eulogies of profit maximizers, frantic searches for profit centres, worried notices of profit warnings and even, if occasionally, thundering denunciations of profiteering.

Yet as the essays in this volume demonstrate, merchants in the Age of Commerce, often considered pioneers of the modern economy, did not focus on profit. To be sure, they were in business to make a profit, and unless they did so they failed. They did not, however, attempt to determine profits or losses by comparing final to opening balances, nor did they calculate rates of profit for guidance on how to maximize returns. Likewise, they neglected systematically to gather and employ price data to guide commercial decisions, they dispensed with consistent guidelines for granting credit and collecting debt and they disdained to draw a firm distinction between trade and office, private affairs and public duties. Whether local retailers, regional players or major international traders, in short, early modern merchants did not employ the tools, techniques and tactics that scholars have considered definitional to economic modernity, not to mention indispensable to commercial success. How can this situation – so strange to us – be explained?

Merchant indifference to all this did not arise from the nature of their business. Though hardly strangers to gifting and bartering (and not only at the geographic margins of their ventures), they were firm and full participants in the world of market exchange. Nor can their disregard be attributed to lack of knowledge, much less to an inappropriate business ethic or insufficient entrepreneurial acuity. Archive shelves groan under kilometres of bulky tomes that testify to the far-flung commercial networks that early modern merchants established and carefully nurtured; the dizzying array of foodstuffs, raw materials, semi-finished goods and manufactures that they bought and sold; the complex financial operations in which they engaged across political, cultural and linguistic frontiers; and the fortunes and misfortunes that attended their enterprises. This all went on, however, within a distinctive economic ecology. Merchants of the Age of Commerce did not fail to scrutinize their affairs nor did they act blindly. But structural characteristics of early modern markets obliged them to develop modes of analysis and business strategies appropriate to their environment.

The richly detailed, fine-grained essays in this book have delineated that historically specific economic context and the merchant principles and procedures – successful and less so – that emerged in response to this economic context. As noted below, many relevant issues regarding the contours and dynamics of the merchant economy remain obscure. But the significance of this collection goes beyond an anatomy of the Age of Commerce. For one thing, it provides a healthy portion of the material needed to answer the large question posed in the editors' Introduction: whether the 'practices, activities and representations, system of production, [and] legitimizing structure, characterizing the older, merchant capitalism ... were specific to this "old" capitalism', or were essentially those of 'the "new" [capitalism] postdating the Industrial Revolution'.[5] The volume might also profitably reinvigorate the once vibrant debate about a yet more sweeping subject, the evolution of the European (and eventually global) economy since the close of the Middle Ages – or, to restore its earlier name, the transition to capitalism.

I.

Structurally unstable and segmented markets, non-standardized products, slow and incomplete communications, substantial time lags between ordering goods and selling them, reliance on networks of interdependent yet substantially autonomous agents, ubiquity of credit transactions combined with varying payment rhythms and expectations among merchants and customers: these attributes defined the early modern world of commerce. Merchants had to anticipate that wartime blockades might close ports, cargoes arrive out of season or after competitors', fabric be badly woven, tastes change, shipping containers leak, uncollectible debts mount up. Under these conditions, profit was unlikely to be earned by systematic application of lessons learned from carefully calculated rates of return in the past as deduced from the study of account books, no matter how well kept. Every venture, every product or every market – and often all of these – was sure to deviate radically from those previously encountered. Nor was much to be gained by close attention to publicly available prices, for they were typically long out of date by the time merchants received them and in any event largely disconnected from actual sales prices. Those who, like the dismayed European creditors of hong merchants, counted on replicating past results found that they were no guarantee of future performance.[6] Rather than generic rules, policies and information, merchants required flexibility that could take advantage of variable economic circumstances; specific knowledge about particular products, markets and prices; and mechanisms to manage credit flows.

The case studies in this volume explore the mutually supportive strategies that merchants employed as they attempted to master both this structural market environment and the particular markets that comprised it. With diversification, they sought to reduce risk and uncertainty, as well as problems of information asymmetry and market access. Merchants did not branch out into non-commercial activities indiscriminately, nor to escape from commerce: no sprawling conglomerates or 'treason of the bourgeoisie' were involved. Rather, diversification entailed undertakings that would support and extend trade: public office and government contracting, money-lending, even (as with the Calverts that Sarson studies) construction and investing in stocks and bonds. Besides providing alternative sources of income to compensate for the vagaries of commerce, ventures like these could yield insider intelligence about and privileged entry to markets. No single activity would be consistently profitable. But as Gervais, Deschanel and Villain all detail, in combination they could both smooth out the inevitable ups and downs of markets and allow a merchant to maintain a positive business reputation and its corollary and foundation, a constant supply of credit.

Other strategies advanced the same goals. Specialization in a delimited group of goods that they knew well gave the Gradis detailed knowledge about product quality and market conditions, as Margairaz spells out, but their successful trading relied as well on long-term relationships that they developed with reliable associates. The latter were equally valuable for the type of on-the-spot negotiations essential for obtaining the best possible results in any given situation, as Lamikiz reveals. And because credit was essential (even when illegal, as Grant underlines) yet always problematic (even when legal, as Villain explains), trustworthy agents who could manage the personalities and payments involved in maintaining viable credit flows were indispensable.

Indeed, in the analyses offered by most of the essays in this volume, agents play a crucial role: earning a profit was a collective enterprise engaging factors as much as principals. Faced with inadequate information about key components of commerce – goods, markets, participants – merchants carefully nurtured networks of trustworthy representatives. Lamikiz deems agent quality more important to remunerative Spanish American trade than current price information, which at best indicated no more than general market conditions, and Margairaz notes how crucial responsible partners were for effective risk management in French long-distance commerce. A good agent could exploit information and connections to capture advantage – not permanently, but by obtaining the right price for specific goods in a specific market – and he or (if rarely) she could ensure that funds were available to sustain network participants' assets and thus their reputation and their credit, in all senses of the word. Of course, if agents were key to earning profits, they could also run up losses, whether by exploiting privileged information for their own advantage, by granting credit recklessly, by negotiating lazily or simply by not being sufficiently attuned to local conditions. Uncollectible loans made by Canton agents were at the root of the debacle that Grant analyses, and their factor's 'stupidity' (as Rosalie Calvert acerbically put it in a letter that Sarson cites) lost Rosalie and her husband a handsome profit on Rotterdam tobacco sales.

Agents implied – or should have – conscientious and continuous monitoring. The manner in which early modern merchants sought to do so goes a long way towards clarifying the surprising fact, noted above, that in their correspondence and account registers merchants paid so little regard to profits and prices. As Lemarchand, Pineau-Defois and McWatters, and Gervais demonstrate in their essays, determining the rates and levels of these data was simply not the point of all that voluminous documentation. Rather than quantitative intelligence enabling calculations about profit rates and current prices, accounts and letters provided qualitative information about current assets, credit flows, reference prices, agent performance – in other words, they served to organize and monitor networks and their activities. To a large degree, eighteenth-century merchant networks functioned by collapsing the principal–agent distinction. Everyone had to supply information, buy and sell goods, grant credit and collect debt, establish and maintain trust. As profits were earned through networks, it was incumbent on all participants to ensure network health and longevity; hence much of merchant practice was devoted to those ends.

II.

Illuminating at once the distinctive context within which early modern merchants traded and the characteristic ways they went about doing so, the essays included in this book take major strides towards understanding the merchant economy in a more historicized manner than heretofore. But if the papers published here make it clear that the Age of Commerce obeyed logics and obligated practices specific to it, much remains to be learned about its structure, dynamics and history.

To begin with, we need to map its boundaries in time and space, within Europe first of all. Two sites are obvious candidates for consideration. During the Renaissance, as is well known, numerous innovations in trading practices – many of them subsequently appropriated by neighbours and rivals – were central components of the remarkable commercial expansion that occurred in northern and central Italy. Again, the seventeenth-century Netherlands was not simply the leading European economy, its predominance built on a powerful trading sector. 'Golden Age' Holland was also the benchmark against which other European states measured their own economic development, the adversary with which they competed and conflicted and the source from which they borrowed a great deal. Yet both of these initial commercial powerhouses saw their hegemony wane: they were destined neither to be the avatars of modern capitalism nor the progenitors of industrialization. Does this 'failure' indicate that their experience differed in kind from that of the eighteenth century?[7] Or did they represent an early version (dare one say 'stage'?) of the Age of Commerce?

Deciding between those alternatives, or coming up with another explanation altogether, involves examining the points of convergence and divergence between, for example, the great Italian and Dutch merchant houses and the enterprises of Gradis, Hollingworth and their contemporaries. Like their eighteenth-century colleagues, the Medici, the Tripp and their peers engaged in trade over long distances, buying and selling an array of non-standardized commodities in a variety of quite diverse markets, dealing with slow communications and market volatility (not to mention repeated exogenous shocks), managing complex credit relations, building up networks of factors and partners with whom they corresponded incessantly – and they also developed or improved many of the purported tools of rational enterprise, including double-entry bookkeeping. So were they the 'first-born' of the Age of Commerce?[8]

Though usually situated within European economic history, the Dutch and Italian cases should also encourage a geographical broadening of the historiographical horizon. Both Renaissance and Golden Age merchants operated in an imperial context, comprised mainly of less formal trading posts and factories but including settlement colonies as well. Thereby they encountered opportunities and constraints with which their eighteenth-century counterparts were all too familiar. Scholars of the Age of Commerce emphasize that merchant networks focused on goods and markets rather than specific empires or regions (whether Atlantic or other).[9] But cultural comfort, ease of forming networks and mercantilist strictures certainly facilitated commercial activities within imperial structures, while encouraging merchants to remain largely inside them. Several of the essays in this book uncover complications that merchants faced both as a result of imperial limitations and when trying to earn a profit outside the protections that empires offered. Still, not only does the articulation of empire with merchant economy remain to be theorized but more empirical studies are required before we will adequately understand the effects of empire on the economic environment in which traders operated.

Chartered companies were related to but not identical with empires. As Gervais notes in passing, with their legions of employees, not to mention their privileges and political interventions, the companies had a fundamentally different structure than the networks through which most merchants operated. At the same time, issues of quality monitoring and market volatility were as salient for them as for any other participant in early modern trade.[10] It is not clear, however, whether chartered companies functioned according to *sui generis* principles and practices or simply represented variants of the procedures outlined by the authors in this volume. Integrating their histories into the Age of Commerce thus holds the promise of further elucidating the operations and the contours of the merchant economy.

European colonial trade constantly interfaced with other systems. The commercial arrangements described in this book were found within societies in which the 'basic trust, shared cognitive frameworks and rules' that markets require 'if they are to function' were rooted in broadly shared and recognized understandings, discourses and practices of a rather homogeneous larger culture.[11] Yet Grant's case study of the Chinese debt crisis indicates that even in places with resident European merchants and long traditions of trade with the West, trust could be in short supply, relevant knowledge sadly lacking among all parties and enforcement mechanisms weak. So even though credit was as requisite to commercial life in Canton as it was in Bordeaux or Philadelphia, monitoring and collection methods failed, with disastrous results.

Much merchant business, moreover, was conducted in situations where even the flimsy but shared socio-cultural foundations found in Canton were wanting. Take the important North American fur trade. 'A striking feature' of that commerce, Carlos and Lewis observe, 'is the extent to which buyers and sellers had different cultural, ethnic, and linguistic backgrounds. For commerce to be successful, they had to overcome these differences'.[12] Solutions were devised. But it remains an open – yet significant – question whether these solutions represented an extension of the merchant economy or marked its outer limits.

The merchant economy is usually, if implicitly, treated as a European phenomenon, even if broadened to include European empires and interactions with non-Europeans across colonial borders. But did it extend further, perhaps encompassing those parts of Asia that scholars like Pomeranz have argued were as economically and materially advanced as north-western Europe through the eighteenth century?[13] Admittedly, Pomeranz has also claimed that together with accessible coal supplies, New World trade promoted European industrialization by making primary products easily available, and these were advantages that Asia did not enjoy. Surely, however, comparisons such as Pomeranz's between market economies and capitalism in Europe and Asia deserve to be elaborated from an explicitly merchant economy perspective. Similarly, studies of trading systems (including those shaped by European chartered companies) in the early modern Indian Ocean and Southeast Asia suggest the urgency of research that will more firmly demarcate the reach of the phenomena examined in this volume during a period of early globalization.[14]

Scholars also need to determine how much the practices delineated in this book permeated the commercial sector, even within Europe and its colonies. Did shopkeepers, for instance, exploit similar tactics of diversification and network participation as large wholesalers, and did the two groups of merchants imagine and manage prices, profit and credit in the same ways? Villain's essay suggests similarities. Like the international traders analysed by Gervais, for instance, Lorraine retailers were enmeshed in credit relations and therefore used accounting to track credit rather than to determine profits. Yet unlike wholesalers, shopkeepers had to negotiate between a rigorous short-term credit cycle imposed by wholesalers and a more relaxed payment rhythm demanded by consumers. Retailers therefore found it difficult to accumulate capital, resulting in a stratified merchant community which might be expected to pursue different profit and market strategies, depending on what was appropriate to their needs and circumstances. Yet as Villain also notes, some shopkeepers engaged in both wholesale and retail trade, so that boundaries between merchant groups were fluid, suggesting that attitudes and practices were likely to migrate between the one and the other.

Finally, just as the boundaries of the merchant economy need to be identified, so the interconnections between trade and other sectors of the early modern economy need clarification. The most common terminology – merchant economy, Age of Commerce – implies that traders defined and directed the entire economy, and certainly urbanization, industrial change and colonial development made merchants ever more vital intermediaries between producers and consumers. They enjoyed and exploited privileged access to the economic lifeblood that was circulating capital. Yet this was not merely a time when agrarian classes continued to be demographically preponderant, politically paramount and socially hegemonic. It was also a time of agricultural transformation, with new crops, new techniques and tools, new tenures and a new degree of market orientation. Equally important, a plantation order founded on chattel slavery became dominant within European empires. In the process, this system produced not only boundless misery for enslaved men and women but great wealth for their owners, and it made a significant if still controversial contribution both to European economic development and, thanks to new products and new tastes, to what is now termed the 'consumer revolution'.[15]

The early modern centuries also witnessed industrial restructuring. This involved some technological innovations, increasingly so as the eighteenth century progressed, announcing the advent of the mechanized factories characteristic of the Industrial Revolution. But primary and most far-reaching were interlocked organizational, locational, demographic and entrepreneurial changes. Together comprising what is usually referred to as 'proto-industrialization', they greatly expanded manufacturing (especially but not only in rural areas), engaged increasing proportions of the population in production for the market and re-shaped both work habits and consumption patterns.[16]

Scholars typically assign merchants a central role in the organization and operation of proto-industries thanks to their privileged access to capital as well as to raw material and product markets. As several of the studies in this volume suggest, merchants were likewise pivotal to the growing commercialization of agriculture, global exchanges of plantation commodities and consequent shifts in consumption. Merchant activities not merely extended across all these domains: more significant, merchant networks linked them together. In their own ways, the conceits of 'merchant–manufacturer' and 'merchant capitalism' seek to incorporate these pursuits. Yet these concepts have not been sufficiently investigated. Even in England the merchant contribution to industrialization has been little studied.[17] And though merchant involvement in agriculture – which often took the form of colonial plantation ownership – is well attested, its implications for economic development have not been spelled out.

So there is much work to accomplish before a satisfactorily historicized interpretation of the Age of Commerce comes to fruition. But the essays in this book suggest a promising path to follow. On the whole, merchants succeeded remarkably at expanding trade at home and abroad; what is more, merchant activities reached into all sectors of the economy. It therefore seems opportune to examine systematically the ramifications beyond the commercial sphere of the strategies and practices anatomized herein. Accomplishing this task will allow historians to understand the contours and specificity of the early modern economy. It also makes it possible to take up the question whether the merchant economy exemplified an old capitalism or the new. Were its structures, procedures and *mentalité* inextricably intertwined with a pre-industrial economic formation, or did they provide a bridge to the novel order that the Industrial Revolution announced?

III.

Answering that question entails defining capitalism and then accounting for capitalist industrialization, first in England, then in Continental Europe and North America, and increasingly around the world. Interest in these issues goes back at least to the eighteenth century, when the political economists sought both to encourage economic change and to understand the changes going on around them. But it became more urgent in the nineteenth century, as Marx and his followers, as well as Weber, Sombart and other members of the German Historical School, analysed the emergent factory system as the epitome of a new economic structure.[18] Explaining the origins of capitalism was, indeed, fundamental to the rise of economic history as a discipline.

Important contributions to the history of capitalism and industrialization continued to be published across the early twentieth century. But the subjects were renewed in the years following World War II. Though Marxist, neo-Marxist and marxisant scholars focused particularly on the emergence of the capitalist economic order, like their non-Marxist peers they were concerned as well to explain the precocious industrialization of England and the retardation of its great eighteenth-century rival France, and by extension the factors accounting for varied patterns of industrialization in Europe and beyond.

This is not the place to review the fecund scholarship and debates that ensued.[19] Suffice it to say that the major historiographic focus relevant to this volume has been the purported role of commerce and merchants in assembling the monetary and other resources needed for industrialization, whether through outright expropriation, the slow incremental gains of proto-industry, super-profits earned in the slave trade and imperial trade or the transfer of surplus earned by unequal exchange in the (essentially colonial) 'periphery' to the 'core' of European metropoles.[20] Alternatively, merchants have been assigned the role of necessary intermediaries for the raw materials and demand required to initiate and sustain factory industrialization.[21] All these interpretations are controversial; more salient, all consider merchants and trade secondary actors in the great industrialization drama.[22] As a result, little attention has been devoted to the types of actual merchant practices considered in this book, and virtually none to the merchant economy *per se*. Even those historians who employ the term 'merchant capitalism' tend to use it generically to denote a situation within which capitalist elements can be discerned rather than to signify a determinate economic formation.

This has begun to change. 'Atlantic world' and globalization scholars have been at the forefront, and if many concentrate on commodities and consumption, merchant activities are also receiving close attention in detailed empirical studies, as this book attests. For all that, there is as yet no testable model to focus research and organize findings. Here, again, the essays in this volume can serve a vital function. By specifying the structural conditions of the merchant economy, they have provided the means for determining whether that economy constituted a distinct phase of economic history or simply a variant of other arrangements, be they capitalist or not. More generally, by delineating the dynamics of the merchant economy they enable explanation of its dénouement. Unstable, segmented, stratified markets, non-standardized products sold far away and after long delays, poor communications, incomplete information, problematic credit, extended networks, constant agent monitoring: if all this characterized the functioning merchant economy, why, when and where did the balancing act break down? And what happened when it did? How, in particular, did the crisis of the merchant economy affect the rise of capitalist industry? Were the merchants swept aside? Did some form of diversification, some aspect of the flexibility that they had learned to deploy in trade and related activities rescue them? Did some metamorphose from merchant to merchant-manufacturer to manufacturer? These are not easy questions to answer, and in fact no answer is possible given the present state of knowledge. But this volume offers a good sense of where to begin to consolidate understanding of the merchant economy, to uncover the reasons for its disappearance and to account for the emergence of its successor – where to begin, that is, to explain the transition from the 'old' to the 'new', from the merchant to the industrial economy.

NOTES

Gervais, Lemarchand and Margairaz, 'Introduction: The Many Scales of Merchant Profit: Accounting for Norms, Practices and Results in the Age of Commerce'

1. For an extremely rare in-depth look at profit, see W. T. Baxter, *The House of Hancock: Business in Boston, 1724–1775* (New York: Russell & Russell, 1965). Data from France can be found in G. Daudin, *Commerce et prospérité: La France au XVIIIe siècle* (Paris: PUPS, 2005), pp. 274–360. For other countries, some evidence can be found in T. Doerflinger, *A Vigorous Spirit of Enterprise: Merchants and Economic Development in Revolutionary Philadelphia* (Chapel Hill, NC: University of North Carolina Press, 1986); D. Hancock, *Citizens of the World: London Merchants and the Integration of the British Atlantic Community, 1735–1785* (Cambridge: Cambridge University Press, 1995) and D. Hancock, *Oceans of Wine: Madeira and the Emergence of American Trade and Taste* (New Haven, CT: Yale University Press, 2009); C. Matson, *Merchants and Empire: Trading in Colonial New York* (Baltimore, MD: Johns Hopkins University Press, 1998); and F. Trivellato, *The Familiarity of Strangers: The Sephardic Diaspora, Livorno and Cross-Cultural Trade in the Early Modern Period* (New Haven, CT: Yale University Press, 2009).
2. Schumpeter, *Histoire de l'analyse économique*; translated by Jean-Claude Casanova; Gallimard; Frank H. Knight, *Risk, Uncertainty and Profit* (1921; Chicago, IL and London: University of Chicago Press, 1985), XXX.
3. D. Diderot and J. d'Alembert (eds), *Encyclopédie ou Dictionnaire raisonné des sciences, des arts et des métiers* (1751–65; University of Chicago: ARTFL Encyclopédie Project, 2013), R. Morrissey (ed.), at http://encyclopedie.uchicago.edu/, article 'Bénefice, Gain, Profit, Lucre, Émolument', vol. 2 ([1752]), p. 202; article 'Profit, Gain, Lucre, Émolument, Bénéfice', vol. 13 (1765), p. 428; and related entries within these articles [accessed 31 May 2013].
4. Such a view of the profit margin as socially controlled underpinned the price sheets of the *Maximum général*, the Revolutionary decree of February 1794 (ventôse II) aiming at setting prices for goods on the basis of a fixed 5 % margin for wholesalers and 10 % for retailers over and above the price of goods delivered to the warehouse or store, transportation costs included.
5. R. Cantillon, *An Essay on Economic Theory*, ed. M. Thornton (1755; Auburn: Ludwig von Mises Institute, 2010), c. 9, p. 49; A. Turgot, *Reflections on the Formation and Distribution of Wealth* (London: J. Ridgway, 1795), pp. 51, 62–6, **§ n°** XLIX, LX, LXI.

6. J. F. Henry, 'Adam Smith and the Theory of Value: Chapter Six Reconsidered', *History of Economics Review*, 31 (2000), pp. 1–13; T. Aspromourgos, *The Science of Wealth: Adam Smith and the Framing of Political Economy* (London: Routledge, 2009), p. 97–8. Even if one rejects Henry's contention that Smith is using a labour theory of value, it remains clear that natural profit is stringently limited in the latter's view.
7. S. Chassagne, *Oberkampf: un entrepreneur capitaliste au siècle des Lumières* (Paris: Aubier-Montaigne, 1980); S. Chassagne, *Le coton et ses patrons* (Paris, Éditions de l'EHESS, 1991). See also L. Bergeron, *Banquiers, négociants et manufacturiers parisiens du Directoire à l'Empire* (Paris: EHESS, 1999), pp. 223–30.
8. Cantillon, *An Essay on Economic Theory*, c. XIII, p. 75.
9. I. de Pinto, *Traité de la circulation et du crédit contenant une Analyse raisonnée des fonds d'Angleterre et de ce qu'on appelle commerce ou jeu d'actions* (Amsterdam: M.M. Rey, 1775).
10. C. Carrière, *Négociants marseillais au XVIIIe siècle* (Marseille: Institut Historique de Provence, 1973); C. Carrière, M. Coudurier, M. Gutsatz and R. Squarzoni, *Banque et capitalisme commercial. La lettre de change au XVIIIe siècle* (Marseille: Institut historique de Provence, 1976).
11. M. Weber, *The Protestant Ethic and the Spirit of Capitalism* (New York: Charles Scribner's Sons, 1950), p. 18.
12. See R. S. Bryer, 'The History of Accounting and the Transition to Capitalism in England. Part One: Theory', *Accounting, Organizations and Society*, 25:2 (2000), pp. 131–62; R. S. Bryer, 'The History of Accounting and the Transition to Capitalism in England. Part Two: Evidence', *Accounting, Organizations and Society*, 25:4/5 (2000), pp. 327–81; and J. S. Toms, 'Calculating Profit: A Historical Perspective on the Development of Capitalism', *Accounting, Organizations and Society*, 35:2 (2010), pp. 205–22.
13. Toms, 'Calculating Profit', pp. 213–14.
14. B. S. Yamey, 'The "Particular Gain or Loss upon Each Article we Deal In:" An Aspect of Mercantile Accounting, 1300–1800', *Accounting, Business & Financial History*, 10:1 (2000), pp. 1–12, on p. 6.
15. J. Bouvier, F. Furet and M. Gillet, *Le mouvement du profit en France au 19e siècle* (Paris: Mouton, 1965), pp. 16–20.
16. N. Bourne, *Principles of Company Law* (London: Cavendish Publishing Ltd, 1998), pp. 94–6.
17. Y. Lemarchand, 'A propos des dispositions comptables de l'Ordonnance de 1673', *Revue de Droit Comptable*, 3 (1994), pp. 17–37; also J. A. Sallé, *L'esprit des ordonnances de Louis XIV, Tome Second: Contenant l'ordonnance criminelle de 1670, l'ordonnance du commerce de 1673 et l'édit de 1695 sur la jurisdiction ecclésiastique* (Paris: Vve Rouy, 1758); or F. de Boutaric, *Explication de l'ordonnance de Louis XIV roi de France et de Navarre concernant le commerce* (Toulouse: G. Henault, 1743). For British standards, which are legal more than statutory, see R. J. Chambers and P. W. Wolnizer, 'A True and Fair View of Position and Results: The Historical Background', *Accounting, Business & Financial History*, 1:2 (1991), pp. 197–214; W. Wills, *The Theory and Practice of the Law of Evidence* (London: Stevens and Sons, 1894), p. 194; K. M. Teeven, 'Seventeenth Century Evidentiary Concerns and the Statute of Frauds', *Adelaide Law Review*, 9:2 (1983), pp. 252–66, on p. 254, n. 18, p. 256; J. S. Rogers, *The Early History of the Law of Bills and Notes: A Study of the Origins of Anglo-American Commercial Law* (Cambridge: Cambridge University Press, 1995), pp. 14–31.
18. P. Gervais, 'Mercantile Credit and Trading Rings in the Eighteenth Century', *Annales. Histoire, Sciences Sociales*, 67:4 (2012), pp. 1011–48. Quotes on the relationship between

profit analysis and tetbooks from J. R. Edwards, G. Dean and F. Clarke, 'Merchants' Accounts, Performance Assessment and Decision Making in Mercantilist Britain', *Accounting, Organizations and Society*, 34:5 (2009), pp. 551–70. See also P. Gervais *infra*.

19. 'Astute merchants must settle their accounts at the end of each year, and open new ones at the beginning of the next' ('Les habiles marchands doivent solder leurs comptes à la fin de chaque année et en ouvrir de nouveaux au commencement de la suivante'), J. Savary des Bruslons, *Dictionnaire universel de commerce, contenant tout ce qui concerne le commerce qui se fait dans les quatre parties du monde*, 3 vols (Genève: Cramer, 1742), vol 1, art 'Compte', p. 1002.
20. On the 'moral economy', see C. Muldrew, *The Economy of Obligation: The Culture of Credit and Social Relations in Early Modern England* (Basingstoke: Palgrave, 1998); M. C. Finn, *The Character of Credit: Personal Debt in English Culture, 1740–1914* (Cambridge: Cambridge University Press, 2003); L. Fontaine, *L'économie morale: pauvreté, crédit et confiance dans l'Europe préindustrielle* (Paris: Gallimard, 2008). On networks and their consequences, see Hancock, *Citizens of the World* and Hancock, *Oceans of Wine*; Trivellato, *The Familiarity of Strangers*.

1 Lemarchand, McWatters and Pineau-Defois, 'The Current Account as Cognitive Artefact: Stories and Accounts of *la Maison Chaurand*'

1. W. Funnell and J. Robertson, 'Capitalist Accounting in Sixteenth Century Holland', *Accounting, Auditing and Accountability Journal*, 24:5 (2011), pp. 560–86.
2. Ibid., p. 561.
3. R. A. Bryer, 'The History of Accounting and the Transition to Capitalism in England. Part Two: Evidence', *Accounting, Organizations and Society*, 25:4–5 (2000), pp. 327–81.
4. In this essay we use the following French terms: *le négociant* – merchant, but distinct in that the individual was engaged in wholesale trade but was prohibited from retail activity; *l'armateur* – a ship owner-entrepreneur who was involved in maritime trade and operated a diversified business. The scope ranged from vessel selection, acquisition of investment capital, hiring of experienced captains and management of the trade with significant amounts of personal capital at risk. A detailed analysis of the emergence and evolution of these terms is given by O. Pétré-Grenouilleau, *Les négoces maritimes français. XVIIe–XXe siècle* (Paris: Belin, 1997), pp. 35–101.
5. These archives are housed in the Archives du département de Loire-Atlantique (101 J): *le fonds Chaurand*. This collection has already been the subject of various studies, notably by D. Rinchon, *Les armements négriers au XVIIIe siècle d'après la correspondance et la comptabilité des armateurs et des capitaines nantais* (Bruxelles: Académie Royale des Sciences coloniales, 1956), pp. 77–136, and much more recently by L. Pineau-Defois, 'Les plus grands négociants nantais du dernier tiers du XVIIIe siècle. Capital hérité et esprit d'entreprise (fin XVIIe – début XIXe siècles)' (PhD dissertation, Université de Nantes, 2008), and A. Forestier, 'A "Considerable Credit" in the Late Eighteenth-Century French West Indian Trade: the Chaurands of Nantes', *French History*, 25:1 (2011), pp. 48–68.
6. W. Sombart, *Der moderne kapitalismus* (München and Leipzig: Duncker & Humblot, 1919).
7. M. Weber, *General Economic History* (London: George Allen and Unwin Ltd, 1923).
8. As well as those of other *négociants* studied in the context of the Marprof programme such as the Maison Gradis of Bordeaux.

9. 'Un instrument artificiel conçu pour conserver, rendre manifeste l'information ou opérer sur elle, de façon à servir une fonction représentationnelle'. D. A. Norman, 'Les artefacts cognitifs', in B. Conein, L. Thévenot and N. Dodier (eds), *Les objets dans l'action* (Paris: EHESS, 1993), p. 28.
10. G. Saupin, 'Les marchands nantais et l'ouverture de la route antillaise 1639–1650', in J.-P. Sanchez (ed.), *Dans le sillage de Colomb. L'Europe du ponant et la découverte de la route antillaise, 1450–1650. Actes du colloque de Rennes (5, 6 et 7 mai 1992)* (Rennes: PUR, 1995), pp. 173–83; C. Laucoin, 'La naissance du trafic antillais 1638–1660' (Maîtrise d'histoire, Université de Nantes, 1999).
11. The term *la droiture* designated the shipment of products to colonists in the Antilles and the acquisition and stocking of colonial staples, primarily sugar and coffee, in return; as opposed to the 'triangular trade' of the slave trade.
12. P. Butel, 'La croissance commerciale bordelaise dans la seconde moitié du XVIIIe siècle' (PhD dissertation, Université Paris I, 1973).
13. 'L'armement de navires n'est qu'une forme de commerce parmi d'autres, essentielle certes, mais ne le recouvrant qu'en partie', J. Meyer, *L'armement Nantais dans la deuxième moitié du XVIIIe siècle* (Paris: SEVPEN, 1969), p. 93.
14. S. Marzagalli, 'Stratégies marchandes et organisation du monde du négoce en Europe et aux Amériques (fin XVIIe début XIXe siècle)' (HDR, Université de Paris Panthéon-Sorbonne, 2004), vol. 1, p. 8.
15. We employ the French adjective *nantais*, 'of Nantes', to simplify.
16. A bottomry loan, in French a *prêt à la grosse aventure* or *cambie*, was designed to finance high-risk maritime expeditions, the interest rate premium was very high, but in the event that the vessel was lost, the lender received neither interest nor principal.
17. Notaire Boufflet, acte du 29 janvier 1748, Archives départementales de Loire-Atlantique, Nantes (hereafter AD LA), 4 E2/364.
18. Notaire Girard de la Canterie, acte du 12 décembre 1768, protest by Chaurand for the restitution of the sum of 20,000 livres owed by Antoine Bérard and Louis Rateau, at Portier de Lantimo, AD LA, 4 E2/935.
19. Meyer, *L'armement Nantais dans la deuxième moitié du XVIIIe siècle*, p. 192.
20. These offices and positions, in this case conferring noble status, were frequently purchased and sold subject to market forces. The Crown had well established administrative decrees and procedures to regulate these transfers and the royal treasury benefitted from a portion of the sales proceeds. Cf. B. Barbiche, *Les institutions de la monarchie française à l'époque moderne (XVIe–XVIIIe siècle)* (Paris: Presses Universitaires de France, 2001).
21. Actes de propriété de navires, AD LA, B 4500 to 4504.
22. *Le Minage* refers to a royal or seigniorial duty received on grains and other merchandise sold in the fairs and markets. Cf. M. Marion, *Dictionnaire des institutions de la France aux XVIIe et XVIIIe siècles* (Paris: Auguste Picard, 1923), p. 380.
23. Tribunal commercial, arbitrated judgement of the Chaurand beneficiaries, filed 29 May 1830, AD LA, 21 U 144.
24. Rinchon, *Les armements négriers au XVIIIe siècle*, p. 77.
25. According to what they themselves reported (Letters addressed to America, mail of 14 January 1785, to le Cap, Saint-Domingue, AD LA, 101 J 3).
26. Tribunal commercial, arbitrated judgement of the Chaurand beneficiaries, filed 29 May 1830, AD LA, 21 U 144.
27. 'Art. I. Les négocians et marchands tant en gros qu'en détail auront un livre qui contiendra tout leur négoce, leurs lettres de change, leurs debtes actives et passives et les deniers employez à la dépense de leur maison. Art. VII. Tous négocians et marchands, tant en

gros qu'en détail, mettront en liasse les lettres missives qu'ils recevront, et en registre la copie de celles qu'ils écriront'.

28. On the functioning of *les comptes d'armement et de désarmement*, cf. Y. Lemarchand, 'Les comptes d'armement revisités. Les particularités comptables des sociétés quirataires à Nantes au XVIIIe siècle', *Revue d'histoire moderne et contemporaine*, 42:3 (1995), pp. 435–53; C. S. McWatters, 'Investment Returns and *la traite négrière*: Evidence from Eighteenth Century France', *Accounting, Business and Financial History*, 18:2 (2008), pp. 161–85.
29. B. S. Yamey, 'Scientific Bookkeeping and the Rise of Capitalism', *Economic History Review*, 1:2–3 (1949), pp. 100–13; B. S. Yamey, 'Accounting and the Rise of Capitalism: Further Notes on a Theme by Sombart', *Journal of Accounting Research*, 2:2 (1964), pp. 117–36.
30. S. Pollard, 'Capital Accounting in the Industrial Revolution', *Yorkshire Bulletin of Economic and Social Research*, 15:2 (1963), pp. 75–91.
31. J. O. Winjum, 'Accounting and the Rise of Capitalism: An Accountant's View', *Journal of Accounting Research*, 9:2 (1971), pp. 333–50.
32. K. S. Most, 'Sombart's Propositions Revisited', *Accounting Review*, 47:4 (1972), pp. 722–34.
33. B. G. Carruthers and W. Espeland, 'Accounting for Rationality: Double-Entry Bookkeeping and the Rhetoric of Economic Rationality', *American Journal of Sociology*, 97:1 (1991), pp. 31–69.
34. M. Nikitin, 'Et si Sombart avait raison?', *Cahiers d'histoire de la comptabilité*, 2 (1992), pp. 29–35.
35. Y. Lemarchand, 'Werner Sombart, quelques hypothèses à l'épreuve des faits', *Cahiers d'histoire de la comptabilité*, 2 (1992), pp. 37–56.
36. R. A. Bryer, 'Double-Entry Bookkeeping and the Birth of Capitalism: Accounting for the Commercial Revolution in Medieval Northern Italy', *Critical Perspectives on Accounting*, 4:2 (1993), pp. 113–40; R. A. Bryer, 'The History of Accounting and the Transition to Capitalism in England. Part One: Theory', *Accounting, Organizations and Society*, 25:2 (2000), pp. 131–62. R. A. Bryer, 'The History of Accounting and the Transition to Capitalism in England. Part Two: Evidence', *Accounting, Organizations and Society*, 25:4–5 (2000), pp. 327–81.
37. B. S. Yamey, 'The Historical Significance of Double-entry Bookkeeping: Some Non-Sombartian Claims', *Accounting, Business and Financial History*, 15:1 (2005), pp. 77–88.
38. E. Chiapello, 'Accounting and the Birth of the Notion of Capitalism', *Critical Perspectives on Accounting*, 18:3 (2007), pp. 263–96.
39. J. R. Edwards, G. Dean and F. Clarke, 'Merchants' Accounts, Performance Assessment and Decision Making in Mercantilist Britain', *Accounting, Organizations and Society*, 34:5 (2009), pp. 551–70.
40. S. Basu, M. Kirk and G. Waymire, 'Memory, Transaction Records, and The Wealth of Nations', *Accounting, Organizations and Society*, 34:8 (2009), pp. 895–917.
41. J. S. Toms, 'Calculating Profit: A Historical Perspective on the Development of Capitalism', *Accounting, Organizations and Society*, 35:2 (2010), pp. 205–21.
42. Funnell and Robertson, 'Capitalist Accounting in Sixteenth Century Holland'.
43. Chiapello, 'Accounting and the Birth of the Notion of Capitalism'.
44. Toms, 'Calculating Profit'.
45. Funnell and Robertson, 'Capitalist Accounting in Sixteenth Century Holland'.
46. Weber, *General Economic History*.
47. Ibid., p. 275.

48. 'Die wesentliche Eigenart der doppelten Buchhaltung, die zweifellos darin besteht, den lückenlosen Kreislauf des Kapitals in einer Unternehmung zu verfolgen, ziffernmäßig zu erfassen und buchmäßig festzulegen ... Erst mit der Einstellung dieser Konten kann sich der von der doppelten Buchhaltung zu erfassende Kreislauf des Kapitals ohne Unterbrechung vollziehen: aus dem Kapitalkonto über die Bestandskonten durch das Gewinn- und Verlustkonto in das Kapitalkonto zurück', Sombart, *Der moderne kapitalismus*, p. 114; authors' translation.
49. Yamey, 'Scientific Bookkeeping and the Rise of Capitalism'.
50. Yamey, 'Accounting and the Rise of Capitalism'.
51. Yamey, 'Scientific Bookkeeping and the Rise of Capitalism', p. 110.
52. Yamey, 'Accounting and the Rise of Capitalism', p. 119.
53. Ibid., p. 122.
54. Bryer, 'The History of Accounting and the Transition to Capitalism in England. Part One: Theory'; Bryer, 'The History of Accounting and the Transition to Capitalism in England. Part Two: Evidence'.
55. Funnell and Robertson, 'Capitalist Accounting in Sixteenth Century Holland'.
56. The emergence of the profit concept has also been examined in other later contexts. In the nineteenth century, the Calvin Company did not see the need for annual profit determination despite its diversified operations and international network until such time as its institutional environment motivated changes in its internal strategies and structures. Cf. C. S. McWatters, 'The Evolution of the Profit Concept: One Organization's Experience', *Accounting Historians Journal*, 20:2 (1993), pp. 31–65.
57. This word referred to articles which officers and certain members of the crew had the right to bring on board, over and above the normal cargo of the vessel, without paying freight – *le port-permis* – and to sell on their own account, thus providing them with supplementary revenue. Individuals could finance all or part of the officers' purchases and receive a share of the profits; in short, a variation of the Italian *commenda* (commission contract).
58. Yamey, 'Accounting and the Rise of Capitalism', p. 134.
59. A rich example of this process of recording, synthesis, re-recording and reporting are the *comptes d'armement* and *de désarmement* referred to earlier.
60. M. de la Porte, *La science des négocians et teneurs de livres* (Paris, 1704).
61. C. F. Gaignat de l'Aulnais, *Guide du commerce* (Paris, 1773).
62. E. Degrange, *La tenue des livres rendue facile* (Paris, 1799–1800).
63. P. B. Boucher, *La science des négocians et teneurs de livres* (Paris, 1803).
64. Norman, 'Les artefacts cognitifs', p. 28.
65. W. T. Baxter, 'Early Accounting: the Tally and the Checkerboard', *Accounting Historians Journal*, 16:2 (1989), pp. 43–83; L. Kuchenbuch, 'Les baguettes de taille au Moyen Âge: un moyen de calcul sans écriture?', in N. Coquery, F. Menant and F. Weber (eds), *Ecrire, compter, mesurer. Vers une histoire des rationalités pratiques* (Paris: Éditions Rue d'Ulm, 2006), pp. 113–42.
66. 'Une petite pièce de bois, en laquelle par osches ou inciseures on marque le compte et nombre de quelque chose, et lors vient de ce mot latin *Talea*. Selon ce on dit, prendre du pain, du vin, et autres telles choses à la taille, *Taleae caesuris ac crenis amphorarum vini, panum, modiorum alteriusve rei numerum notare*. Et de cette signification vient taille, pour tribut imposé sur le peuple pour estre payé au Prince, d'autant peut estre que les impositeurs, ou asséeurs, ou distributeurs de tel subside, bailloyent anciennement à chascun taillable, sa quotité du tribut, merquée et oschée en tels petits bastons. Selon ce on dit, imposer ou asseoir la taille et taillable, celuy et celle qui sont subjets à payer la taille'.

A. de Ranconnet and J. Nicot, *Thrésor de la langue françoise, tant ancienne que moderne* (Paris, 1606).

67. S. Jubé, *Droit social et normalisation comptable* (Paris: Librairie générale de droit et jurisprudence, 2011).
68. *'De la preuve des obligations et de celle du paiement'* – *'Les tailles corrélatives à leurs échantillons font foi entre les personnes qui sont dans l'usage de constater ainsi les fournitures qu'elles font ou reçoivent en détail'*. On the legal aspects and jurisprudence, cf. M. Vidal, 'Discordances doctrinales sur la preuve par les tailles au XIXe siècle', in *Etudes à la mémoire de Christian Lapoyade-Deschamps* (Pessac: Presses universitaires de Bordeaux, 2003), pp. 345–60, and V. Perruchot-Triboulet, 'Commentaire sur l'article 1333 du Code civil', *Revue Lamy Droit Civil*, 7 (2004).
69. 'L'institution de la confiance – du *crédit* – suppose que chacun soit rappelé à la juste exécution de ses obligations'. Jubé, *Droit social et normalisation comptable*, p. 53.
70. 'Il y a compte courant entre deux négociants, dès qu'il y a crédit et débit entre eux pour affaires commerciales. Ce sont là des notions élémentaires en cette matière, et pour lesquelles il suffit d'interroger le premier teneur de livres'. Dalloz, *Jurisprudence du XIXe siècle*, 28 vols (Bruxelles, 1827), vol. 6, pp. 312–13.
71. In law, 'novation was defined as the changing of an obligation into a later one, as such the novation destroyed the previous obligation and created a new one' ('le changement d'une obligation en une autre postérieure, ainsi la novation détruit l'ancienne obligation, et elle en constitue une autre'. C.-J. de Ferrière, *Dictionnaire de droit et de pratique, contenant l'explication des termes de droit, d'ordonnances, de coutume et de pratique, avec les juridictions de France, Tome 2: nouvelle édition, revue corrigée et augmentée par M.* *** (Paris, 1769), p. 245.
72. Cf. Jubé, *Droit social et normalisation comptable*, pp. 47–111.
73. 'Pour revenir aux comptes courans il faut poser pour principe fondamental que l'on n'envoye un compte courant à un correspondant, qu'afin qu'il puisse le vérifier et voir si tous les articles répondent à ceux du compte qu'il tient sur ses livres. Or cette vérification ne se pouvant faire que très difficilement si tous les articles tant du débit que du crédit ne sont pas spécifiez en détail, il est nécessaire de les distinguer tous afin que celui auquel on envoye le compte, puisse trouver sans difficulté tous les articles qui répondent à ceux qu'il a couchez sur ses livres'. J.-P. Ricard, *L'art de bien tenir les livres de compte en parties doubles à l'Italienne* (Amsterdam, 1724), p. 23.
74. 'Nous venons d'arrêter Monsieur, suivant notre usage à la fin de l'année N/C Ct avec vous, vous le trouverez ci-joint et après examen il vous plaira nous créditer à nouveau de £ 68 833.11.9 y compris le solde des intérêts de nos avances que nous portons à 5% suivant le CCt aussi ci-joint'. Letter addressed by *les Chaurand* to Grieumard at Le Cap Français at Saint-Domingue, 3 January 1784, AD LA 101 J 1.
75. De la Porte, *La science des négocians et teneurs de livres*.
76. 'Nous avons reçus la lettre ... par laquelle vous faites diverses observations sur l'extrait de votre compte à vous remis, en voici un nouveau où nous avons ajoutés et rectifier tout ce qui nous a paru être juste, il résulte de ce nouveau compte, que vous êtes nos débiteurs de 5 316. 7. 9 [livres, sols, deniers], veuillez le faire examiner et le passer de notre conformité s'il n'y a plus d'erreurs'. Letter addressed by *les Chaurand* to Laval et Wilfesheim of Paris, 6 February 1785, AD LA 101 J 79.
77. Basu, Kirk and Waymire, 'Memory, Transaction Records, and The Wealth of Nations'.
78. Jubé, *Droit social et normalisation comptable*.
79. Bryer, 'The History of Accounting and the Transition to Capitalism in England. Part Two: Evidence'.

2 Gervais, 'Why Profit and Loss Didn't Matter: The Historicized Rationality of Early Modern Merchant Accounting'

1. H. Derks, 'Religion, Capitalism and the Rise of Double-Entry Bookkeeping', *Accounting, Business and Financial History*, 18:2 (2008), pp. 187–213, on p. 188.
2. J. R. Edwards, G. Dean and F. Clark, 'Merchants' Accounts, Performance Assessment and Decision Making in Mercantilist Britain', *Accounting, Organizations and Society*, 34 (2009), pp. 551–70.
3. For the stagnation of commercial accounting, see J. R. Edwards, *A History of Financial Accounting* (London: Routledge, 1989); also A. C. Littleton, *Accounting Evolution to 1900* (New York: American Institute Publishing Co. 1933); or S. P. Garner, *Evolution of Cost Accounting to 1925* (University, AL: University of Alabama Press, 1954); and more recently D. L. King, K. M. Premo and C. J. Case, 'Historical Influences on Modern Cost Accounting Practices', *Academy of Accounting and Financial Studies Journal*, 13:4 (2009), pp. 21–39. Compare with discussions on costs in R. K. Fleischman and L. D. Parker, *What is Past is Prologue: Cost Accounting in the British Industrial Revolution, 1760–1850* (New York: Garland Publishing Inc., 1997); also D. Oldroyd, 'Through a Glass Clearly: Management Practice at the Bowes Family Estates c. 1700–70 as Revealed by the Accounts', *Accounting, Business and Financial History*, 9:2 (1999), pp. 175–201. For other countries see E. Carmona and D. Gómez, 'Early Cost Management Practices, State Ownership and Market Competition: The Case of the Royal Textile Mill of Guadalajara', *Accounting, Business and Financial History*, 12:2 (2002), pp. 1717–44. For a neo-Marxist view also focused on cost accounting in agricultural and industrial firms, see R. A. Bryer, 'The History of Accounting and the Transition to Capitalism in England. Part One: Theory', *Accounting, Organizations and Society*, 25:2 (2000), pp. 131–62; R. A. Bryer, 'The History of Accounting and the Transition to Capitalism in England. Part Two: Evidence', *Accounting, Organizations and Society*, 25:4/5 (2000), pp. 327–81; also J. S. Toms, 'Calculating Profit: A Historical Perspective on the Development of Capitalism', *Accounting, Organizations and Society*, 35:2 (2010), pp. 205–21. For the specific advances purportedly accomplished by joint-stock companies, cf., for example, A. M. Carlos and N. Stephen, 'Theory and History: Seventeenth-Century Joint-Stock Chartered Trading Companies', *Journal of Economic History*, 56:4 (1996), pp. 916–24.
4. P. Jeannin, *Marchand du Nord: espaces et trafics à l'époque moderne* (Paris: Presses de l'ENS, 1996), p. 82. Another attempt at profit calculations in D. Hancock, *Citizens of the World: London Merchants and the Integration of the British Atlantic Community, 1735–1785* (Cambridge: Cambridge University Press, 1995), pp. 411–24; it focuses on produce imported from a plantation, thus on the sphere of production, and uses a complex set of approximations to complement the account books. See also D. Hancock, *Oceans of Wine: Madeira and the Emergence of American Trade and Taste* (New Haven, CT: Yale University Press, 2009), which gives only some capital and inventory overall values. Hancock also quotes a few other works on Great Britain, none as detailed as his own. For France, see G. Daudin, *Commerce et prospérité: La France au XVIIIe siècle* (Paris: PUPS, 2005), pp. 274–333. Daudin is highly critical even of basic capital accumulation ('profit rate') figures previously offered, especially in the slave trade, because most such figures were not annualized, and therefore did not provide the true internal rate of return ('Profitability of Slave and Long-Distance Trading in Context: The Case of Eighteenth-Century France', *Journal of Economic History*, 64:1(2004), pp. 144–71, on p. 147).
5. More detailed narratives, though without attempts at reconstructing accounts, can be found in W. T. Baxter, *The House of Hancock: Business in Boston, 1724–1775* (New York:

Russell & Russell, 1965) or K. W. Porter, *The Jacksons and the Lees: Two generations of Massachusetts Merchants, 1765–1844*, 2 vols (Cambridge, MA: Harvard University Press, 1937). Later works contain even fewer quantitative data; see T. Doerflinger, *A Vigorous Spirit of Enterprise: Merchants and Economic Development in Revolutionary Philadelphia* (Chapel Hill, NC: University of North Carolina, 1986) or C. Matson, *Merchants and Empire. Trading in Colonial New York* (Baltimore, MD: Johns Hopkins University Press, 1998); also the various authors in special issues of the *Business History Review*: 'Reputation and Uncertainty in America', 78:4 (2004), pp. 595–702; 'Networks in the Trade of Alcohol', 79:3 (2005), pp. 467–526; 'Trade in the Atlantic World', 79:4 (2005), pp. 697–844 and also 'The Atlantic Economy in an Era of Revolutions', *William and Mary Quarterly*, 62:3 (2005), pp. 357–526.

6. An analysis developed in B. Yamey, 'The "Particular Gain or Loss upon Each Article we Deal In": An Aspect of Mercantile Accounting, 1300–1800', *Accounting, Business & Finacial History*, 10 (2000), pp. 1–12; Hans Derks partly concurs in 'Religion, Capitalism and the Rise of Double-Entry Bookkeeping'. I developed the same points in P. Gervais, 'Neither Imperial, nor Atlantic: A Merchant's Eye View of International Trade in the 18th Century', *History of European Ideas*, 34 (2008), pp. 465–73 and P. Gervais, 'Mercantile Credit and Trading Rings in the Eighteenth Century', *Annales. Histoire, Sciences Sociales* [English version], 67:4 (2012), pp. 1011–48. See above all the insights in Jeannin, *Marchand du Nord*, and also P. Jeannin, *Marchands d'Europe. Pratiques et savoir à l'époque moderne* (Paris: Presses de l'ENS, 2002).
7. 7 Jac. 1 c. 12, copied from *The Statutes at Large, from Magna Charta, to the End of the Last Parliament, 1761. In Eight Volumes. By Owen Ruffhead, Esq.*, 8 vols (London, 1768–70), vol. 3, p. 84. The Act is quoted in W. Wills, *Theory and Practice of the Law of Evidence* (London: Stevens & Sons, 1894), p. 194. I could not find in secondary sources cases of account books being contested, and do not know whether this Act was significant at all (and also whether it actually concerned traders, or merely craftsmen).
8. J.-A. Sallé, *L'Esprit des ordonnances de Louis XIV*, 2 vols (Paris: Chez Samson, 1758), vol. 2, pp. 335–448, on pp. 355, 356. Sallé was a lawyer in the Paris Parliament.
9. Definition from Toms, 'Calculating Profit', p. 212. Bryer, 'A Marxist Accounting History of the British Industrial Revolution: A Review of Evidence and Suggestions for Research', *Accounting, Organizations and Society*, 30:1 (2005), pp. 25–65, makes on p. 29 a distinction between the 'semi-capitalist mentality' comparing merely the consumable surplus to the initial capital, and what to him is the real capitalist computation, assessing profit as the net return on employed capital. I have taken Toms's wider definition in order to guard against any underestimation of profit calculations among the actors I study.
10. Gervais, 'Mercantile Credit and Trading Rings in the Eighteenth Century'.
11. This may seem counter-intuitive, partly because our banks send us regularly an account drawn from *its* point of view, which is actually a mirror image of what our account should be. Our 'debits', and 'credits', at the bank are debits and credits from the point of view of the bank, since the bank holds us 'debitor', when it gives us value, and 'creditor', when we give it back. A proper account at the bank *from the customer's point of view* should list the bank as 'debitor', each time we entrust it with money (the bank has received value from us), and 'creditor', each time the same bank gives back that money, either directly to us or to a third party for our account (it has given back value, for which it is not accountable any more).
12. Y. Lemarchand, 'Style mercantile ou mode des finances. Le choix d'un modèle comptable dans la France d'Ancien Régime', *Annales. Histoire, Sciences Sociales*, 50:1 (1995), pp. 159–82; also Jeannin, *Marchands d'Europe*, pp. 331–5, 341–51.
13. From 1701 to 1800, 387 of the 621 textbooks listed by Jeannin (*Marchands d'Europe*, p. 351) had been printed in Great Britain, Ireland or British North America. For Great

Britain, the number of reprints was estimated for each title using the Eighteenth Century Collections Online database at http://www.gale.cengage.com/EighteenthCentury [accessed 15 september 2013]. The database is not perfect (it does not include four of the thrity-two authors listed by Edwards et al. as published in the eighteenth century) but any widely printed author should show up in it (of the four missing authors, three cannot be found either in the British Library or in the Bodleian Library catalogs, and one has only one edition listed at the Bodleian). By number of editions in the ECCO database, John Mair is most represented (nineteen editions), followed by William Gordon and William Webster (twelve editions each). Only four other authors in Edwards et al.'s sample are listed as reprinted more than three times, Thomas Dilworth (eight editions), Edward Hatton (seven editions), Robert Hamilton (six editions) and Daniel Dowling (four editions). In France during the eighteenth century, the most popular textbooks were those by Mathieu de La Porte, Jacques Savary and François Barrême. See Jeannin, *Marchands d'Europe*, p. 382, and Y. Lemarchand, 'Jacques Savary et Mathieu de La Porte: deux classiques du Grand siècle', in B. Colasse (ed.), *Les grands auteurs en comptabilité* (Colombelles: EMS, 2005), pp. 39–54. Jacques Savary's extremely popular textbook, *Le Parfait Negociant*, only mentioned accounting in connection with inventories, and ignored double-entry entirely.

14. See a shorter version of this analysis in Gervais, 'Mercantile Credit'.
15. J. Mair, *Book-keeping Methodiz'd: or, A Methodical Treatise of Merchant-Accompts According to the Italian Form* (1746; Edinburgh: W. Sands, A. Murray, and J. Cochran, 1749), p. 20; original italics. I must thank Yannick Lemarchand for referring me to these editions and teaching me how to use them.
16. Ibid., p. 17.
17. Ibid., pp. 76, 140–1; and p. 116 for expenses recorded in a merchandise account.
18. Ibid., p. 1.
19. Ibid., p. 6.
20. K. Polanyi, *The Great Transformation* (New York: Farrar & Rinehart, 1944). Also M. Granovetter, 'Economic Action and Social Structure: The Problem of *Embeddedness*', *American Journal of Sociology*, 91:3 (1985), pp. 481–510.
21. Ibid. p. 6.
22. Ibid. p. 26 for goods, pp. 29–30, 31–4 for debts.
23. Ibid. p. 17. Cf. also p. 36.
24. W. Gordon, *The Universal Accountant and Complete Merchant*, 2 vols (Edinburgh: A. Donaldson and J. Reid for Alexander Donaldson, 1735), vol. 2, pp. 1, 2–3.
25. Ibid., vol. 1, p. 202.
26. W. Webster, *An Essay on Book-Keeping, According to the True Italian Method of Debtor and Creditor, by Double Entry* (London: D. Browne, C. Hitch and L. Hawes, 1755), Ed. 12, pp. 11–12; original italics.
27. M. de La Porte, *La science des négocians et teneurs de livre, ou instruction générale pour tout ce qui se pratique dans les Comptoirs des Négocians, tant pour les affaires de banque, que pour les Marchandises, & chez les Financiers pour les Comptes* (Rouen: P. Machuel et J. Racine, 1782). The book is a rewriting of an earlier version from 1685, the *Guide des négocians*, already a smashing success.
28. Ibid., p. vii. 'La Science des Négocians consiste en deux points: I° A connoître toutes les qualités & les circonstances des choses dont ils font commerce: 2° A savoir faire les écritures nécessaires pour conduire ce commerce dans un ordre exact, qui en donne une parfaite connoissance en tout tems. La connoissance renfermée dans le *premier* point, s'acquiert plus par l'usage que l'on en fait chez les Négocians, que par les préceptes que

l'on en pourroit donner. La Science du *second* point, ou des Ecritures qui se pratiquent dans les Comptoirs des Négocians, se peut réduire à des principes, ou règles certaines'.

29. Ibid., p. viii–ix. 'Il faut néanmoins convenir qu'un marchand qui achète tout comptant, qui n'emprunte ni marchandises, ni .argent pour son Commerce, & qui ne prête rien a personne , se pourrait dispenser d'avoir &. de tenir aucun Livre, parce qu'il ne peut tomber dans les cas prévus par l'Ordonnance. Il n'a ni dettes actives, ni dettes passives; ainsi il ne craint point les faillites &: banqueroutes, & n'est point dans le cas de manquer lui-même, ni de faire perdre à ses Créanciers puisqu'il n'en a point. La chose n'est pas sans exemple, & j'ai vu un Marchand (en détail à la vérité) qui pendant plus de soixante ans de boutique ouverte, quoique mêmeil ait fait des affaires assez fortes, n'a rien emprunté ni rien prêté, & qui par conséquent n'a eu aucun Livre: cependant il a conduit son négoce avec beaucoup d'honneur & de probité, & sans aucun embarras. Mais la chose est très-rare, & ne pourroit pas être dans un Marchand qui feroit un négoce un peu considérable. Il est donc nécessaire que celui qui emprunte & qui prête tienne les Livres exactement, afin de voir en tout tems l'état de ses Affaires. Ses Livres lui apprendront quelles affaires & quelles négociations lui ont été à profit ou à perte, il saura quels sont ses Débiteurs & ses Créanciers, pour satisfaire aux uns & se faire payer des autres, & outre cela il sera en état de rendre compte de sa conduite, en cas que par malheur ses affaires venant à manquer, il n'ait pas de quoi satisfaire à ses Créanciers'.
30. F. Barrême, *Traité des Parties Doubles ou Methode aisée pour apprendre tenir en Parties Doubles les Livres du Commerce & des Finances* (Paris: Chez Jean-Geofroy Nyon Libraire, 1721), pp. 26–7, 59, 83. Barrême also opened a 'Household Expenses', account, which he closed into Profits and Losses when balancing his books.
31. Ibid., p. 238; original capitals and italics. 'CAPITAL est le compte chef auquel tous les autres comptes sont subordonnés, auquel tous les autres comptes sont obligez de compter de leur *recette* & de leur *dépense*. CAISSE est un Caissier auquel CAPITAL a confié le maniement de ses deniers. Le compte des Billets de l'Etat est un Commis auquel CAPITAL confie les Billets de l'Etat. Le compte des Eaux-de-vie est un Commis auquel CAPITAL confie ses Eaux-de-vie'.
32. Again, I owe thanks to Yannick Lemarchand, who pointed out to me this identity between *Comptes du Chef* and Mair's 'incomplete' accounts.
33. P. Butel, 'La croissance commerciale bordelaise dans la seconde moitié du XVIIIe siècle' (PhD dissertation, University Paris I, 1973). On the Gradis family, see R. Menkis, 'The Gradis Family of Eighteenth Century Bordeaux: A Social and Economic Study' (PhD dissertation, Brandeis University, 1988); M. Martin, 'Correspondance et réseaux marchands: la maison Gradis au dix-huitième siècle' (MA dissertation, Université Paris I, 2008); S. Marzagalli, 'Opportunités et contraintes du commerce colonial dans l'Atlantique français au XVIIIe siècle: le cas de la maison Gradis de Bordeaux', *Outre-mers*, 362–3 (2009), pp. 87–111; J. de Maupassant, 'Un grand armateur de Bordeaux. Abraham Gradis (1699?–1780)', *Revue historique de Bordeaux et du département de la Gironde*, 6 (1913), pp. 175–96, 276–97, 344–67, 423–48 (on Gradis's career until 1760).
34. Fonds Gradis, Centre d'Archives du Monde du Travail, Roubaix, 'Journal, 20 août 1751–14 mai 1755', 181 AQ 6* (hereafter referred to as 'AN 181 AQ 6*'; 'Journal, 1 June 1755–26 October 1759', 181 AQ 7* (hereafter referred to as 'AN 181 AQ 7*'). I would like to thank the Gradis family, who granted me access to their archives. I analyse in details Gradis' account structure in Gervais, 'Mercantile Credit and Trading Rings'; see also P. Gervais, 'A Merchant ot a French Atlantic? Eighteenth-Century Account Books as Narratives of a Transnational Merchant Political Economy', *French History*, 25:1 (2011), pp. 28–47, over a slightly different timespan (October 1754–September 1755, instead of January–December 1755).

35. Besides Cash, general credit accounts were as follows: Bills Payable, Bills to broker, Bills receivable, Protested Bills, Suspense accounts (disputed transactions), Contracts of sale, Bottomry loans, Bottomry Loans in Cadiz, Freight due by His Majesty, Freight due by Sundries, and two accounts with bankers Chabbert & Banquet, and Gaulard de Journy.
36. See for instance AN 181 AQ 6*, 2 March 1755, 'Marchandises Genérales Dt a Arnaud Gouges & Comp.e £ 2496.17 p 100 Barrils farine qu'ils nous ont envoyé p[esan]t net 17975# a £ 12.10, & 50s par Barril'.
37. AN 181 AQ7*, 3 March 1755 (sals of sugar), and 11 September 1755 (closing of the three accounts).
38. AN 181 AQ 6*, 29 April 1755: 'Marchandises envoyées à Quebec p n/C dans divers navires Dt, a Divers £ 11780.7.7 p les Suivantes Chargées dans le N.e Le st Nicolas Cap Vincent Suivant Le Livre de factures a f° 135 à Marchandi. Generales p Cordage & Beure £ 4783.7.7 à Vins achetés p 15 th.x a 40# 1800 à la Ve La Roche de Girac pr du Papier 4040 à la Ve Brun p fraix au d.t Papier 340 à Primes d'assurance p £ 11000 a 3 3/4 p C.t 412.10 à Caisse pour fraix 404.10'.
39. AN 181 AQ 7*, 18 August 1755, 'Gains & Pertes Dt, a Jacob Mendes £ 237.5 pour 4 tables qu'il a fait venir de Hollande'.
40. AN 181 AQ 6*, 9 December 1754: 'Gains & Pertes Dt a Vins de Compte a 1/2 avec Baillet £ 1298.2.6 pour 7 th(x) 3 Bq. qu'il nous a cy devant Livré p notre 1/2 debitons a Gains & Pertes atendu que Le Compte des Vins achetés a été Solde Sans y avoir debité cet article'.
41. On the lack of metallic currency, cf. Baxter, *The House of Hancock*.
42. Hollingsworth Fund, Collection 289, Historical Society of Pennsylvania, Philadelphia, Series 2a, vol. 86, Journal L, 1786–1788 (herafter 'Journal L'), p. 295.
43. Hollingsworth Fund, vol. 113, Flour Journal, 1784–86 p. 317. The 1787–8 Flour journal is unfortunately lost.

3 Villain, 'Terms of Payment in Retailing: A Tool for Fostering Customer Loyalty or a Form of Managerial Constraint? A Few Observations Based on Accounting from Lorraine in the Eighteenth Century'

1. B. S. Yamey, 'The "Particular Gain or Loss upon Each Article we Deal In:" An Aspect of Mercantile Accounting, 1300–1800', *Accounting, Business & Financial History*, 10:1 (2000), pp. 1–12.
2. C. Muldrew, *The Economy of Obligation: The Culture of Credit and Social Relations in Early Modern England* (New York: St Martin's Press, 1998); also C. Muldrew, 'Credit and the Courts. Debt Litigation in a 17th Century Urban Community', *Economic History Review*, 46 (1993), pp. 23–38, and C. Muldrew, 'Interpreting the Market. The Ethics of Credit and Community Relations in Early Modern England, *Social History*, 18:2 (1993), pp. 163–84; M. C. Finn, *The Character of Credit: Personal Debt in English Culture, 1740–1914* (Cambridge: Cambridge University Press, 2003).
3. N. Coquery, *Tenir boutique à Paris au XVIIIe siècle. Luxe et demi-luxe* (Paris: Editions du CTHS, 2012), p. 180; M.-L. Carlin, *Un Commerce de détail à Nice sous la Révolution* (Aix-en-Provence: Presses Universitaires, 1965), on the Widow Colombo's shop; L. Petit, 'Stratégies d'innovation et développement commercial de la boutique à Paris dans la deuxième moitié du XVIIIe siècle' (MA2 thesis, University Paris 1, 2008);

A. Laroche, 'Le marché du luxe à Paris à la veille de la Révolution' (MA2 thesis, Université Paris 1, 2010).

4. J. Hoppit, *Risk and Failure in English Business 1700–1800* (Cambridge: Cambridge University Press, 1987).
5. F. Braudel, *Civilisation matérielle, économie et capitalisme*, 2 vols (Paris: Armand Colin/ Le Livre de Poche, 1993), vol. 2, pp. 54–72.
6. 'Journaux de vente de Jean–François Leléal (1706 à 1708)', Archives Départementales de Meurthe-et-Moselle (hereafter 'AD 54'), 49 B 290; 'Grand livre des ventes (1698 à 1717)', AD 54, 49 B 293.
7. 'Livre journal des ventes de Dominique Leléal (September 1722–December 1725)', AD 54, 49 B 345; 'Grand Livre (1722 à 1726)', AD 54, 49 B 355.
8. 'Journal des ventes de Germain Empereur (October 1752 – July 1756)', AD 54, 49 B 561; 'Grand Livre des ventes de Germain Empereur' (1750s), AD 54, 49 B 567. The analysis and digitization of Germain Empereur's accounting for the period from 1751 to 1754 is ongoing, and is part of the research project MARPROF (Comptes et profits marchands d'Europe et d'Amérique 1750/1815) financed by *Agence Nationale de la Recherche* (France).
9. There were no 'conditional sales' however of the type identified by N. Coquery (*Tenir boutique*, p. 195) and L. Petit ('Stratégies d'innovation') in Parisian shops.
10. See the conclusions N. Coquery (*Tenir boutique*) and L. Petit ('Stratégies d'innovation') draw from the Parisian merchants' bankruptcy archives. One finds the same kind of approach to sales books in England, Paris, Lorrraine and Nice (the widow Colombo), proof of a high level of consistency in the accounting practices of the Western world in the eighteenth century, not only in long-distance trade but also in shop-keeping. The very frequent absence of any recording of terms of payment by merchants in the retail business thus suggests that their accounting was not meant to determine a rate of profit – which would imply taking into account the delay within which repayments were made – but rather was used to keep a memorandum of credit relations.
11. N. Coquery, 'Les écritures boutiquières au XVIIIe siècle', in N. Coquery, F. Menant, F. Weber (eds), *Ecrire, compter, mesurer. Vers une histoire des rationalités pratiques* (Paris: Editions Rue d'Ulm, 2006), pp. 163–80.
12. R. K. Marshall, *The Local Merchants of Prato. Small Entrepreneurs in the Late Medieval Economy* (Baltimore, MD: Johns Hopkins University Press, 1999), pp. 79–88.
13. The category 'crafstmen' (CRAFT) includes all of the members of 'the trades' for whom an activity was listed in the books. In the absence of other details, all merchants have been allocated to the 'merchant' category (MERCH). These two groups together include most of the less affluent clientele of our merchants. One would have to add to these a few buyers from a more modest background who are likely to be found among the clients categorized as 'Not specified' (NSPEC), due to a complete lack of information on them. Among the elite commoners, I distinguished the 'better sort' without mention of a profession (BETT) from what would be later called the 'capacités' (PROF), a category which includes all non-manual professions. I have also grouped together all the nobles not linked specifically to the judiciary or military service of the Duke or the King under the heading 'nobility' (NOB). The category 'Clergymen' (CLERG) does not require explanations. Judges and officers are listed as 'Administrators' (ADM). The development of the State apparatus, especially in its military, repressive or regulating capacities, manifested istelf through the presence of military people, sometimes noblemen, of brigadiers from the

Gendarmerie ('brigadiers de la Maréchaussée'), as well as of other servants and personnel of the State of lesser importance, all of whom I listed in a separate category (STAT).

14. The noble 'bad payer' is perhaps primarily a cliché of the period, reinforced by the admittedly disastrous financial situation of some segments of the court aristocracy in the eighteenth century.
15. For similar analyses for the Middle Ages, see in particular F. Melis, 'La Compagnia "Parazone e Donato" di Pisa e i conti correnti di correspondenza', *La banca pisana e le origini della banca moderna* (Florence: Le Monnier, 1987), pp. 82–109.
16. Muldrew, *The Economy of Obligation*, pp. 200–1.
17. Originally, 'au bout de 15 jours ou un mois, la page de droite du registre constate que le débiteur s'est libéré'. Carlin, *Un Commerce de détail à Nice*, p. 19.
18. D. B. Thorp, 'Doing Business in the Backcountry: Retail Trade in Colonial Rowan County, North Carolina', *William and Mary Quarterly*, 3rd series, 48:3 (1991), pp. 387–408, on p. 406.
19. Coquery, *Tenir boutique à Paris*, p. 206.
20. These figures agree with observations I have made elsewhere about wholesale trade in Lorraine in the eighteenth century; see J. Villain, 'Espaces et filières d'un commerce de gros et de demi-gros au XVIIIe siècle: les activités commerciales des "marchands-magasiniers" lorrains (années 1750 et 1760)', in C. Maitte, P. Minard and M. De Oliveira (eds), *La gloire de l'industrie XVIIe-XIXe siècle. Faire de l'histoire avec Gérard Gayot* (Rennes: Presses Universitaires, 2012), pp. 127–44.
21. 'Nous avons été très surpris à l'ouverture de l'honneur de la vôtre du 21 du courant à y voir que vous trouviez nos rubans plus chers que ceux que vous dites tirer de Bâle. Nous ne pouvons le concevoir vu que *nous cotons les prix au plus juste et que nous ne gagnons que l'intérêt de notre argent*;' '*je trouve que le profit y est si borné qu'il serait plus avantageux de mettre son argent sur la place*'. Veuve Navière, Incoming correspondence (1757 to 1759), AD 54, 49 B 718 and 719.
22. These extended terms of payment granted to customers having no account, and which differ from the general tendency observed, were mentioned explicitly in the journal: Pierre Thillier from Pagny-sur-Moselle purchased on 15 November 1752, 27 liv. l. 2 s. worth of merchandise – muslinette ('etamette'), North Cloth ('Drap du Nord'), muslin ('étamine') from the Mans, and netting ('Voile') – 'delivered to his wife and to be paid at the grape-harvest' ('délivré[es] à sa femme pour payer aux vendanges proch[aines]' ('Journal des ventes de Germain Empereur', AD 54, 49 B 561, p. 36).
23. T. S. Willan, *An Eighteenth Century Shopkeeper: Abraham Dent of Kirkby Stephen* (Manchester: Manchester University Press, 1970), pp. 26–7. All this also fits with the indications provided by D. A. Kent, 'Small Businessmen and their Credit Transactions in Early 19th Century Britain', *Business History*, 26:2 (1994), pp. 47–64, esp. p. 51ff.
24. J. Savary, *Le Parfait Négociant*, 2 vols (Paris: Chez les frères Estienne, 1757/70), vol. 1, chap. IV, § 8, p. 342.
25. Originally, 'de payer aux fêtes de Pâques prochaines'. 'Journal des ventes de Germain Empereur', AD 54, 49 B 561, p. 40.
26. In AD 54, twenty-two complete inventories for retailers are listed under call number 49 B 162 à 164.
27. As in the case of Michel Durafort from Lunéville (1728; AD 54, 49 B 163), Dominique Maurice from Saint-Mihiel (1726; AD 54, 49 B 162), Joseph Cressand from Nancy (1726; AD 54, 49 B 162), Jean Michel from Toul (1724; AD 54, 49 B 162), or Jean Semelle from Nancy (1728; AD 54, 49 B 163).

28. As in the case of Claude Esmonnier from Vézelise (1728; AD 54, 49 B 163), Jacques Humbert from Charmes (1725; AD 54, 49 B 162) or Nicolas Lerouge from Pont-à-Mousson (1729; AD 54, 49 B 164).
29. Here I corroborate the analyses of Hervé Piant concerning the use of the *prévôtale* court by parties subject to it in an area close to the one I study here. H. Piant, *Une justice ordinaire. Justice civile et criminelle dans la prévôté royale de Vaucouleurs sous l'Ancien Régime* (Rennes: Presses Universitaires, 2006), pp. 143–51.
30. 'Grand Livre des ventes de Germain Empereur', AD 54, 49 B 567, f° 135 recto.
31. 'Grand Livre des ventes de Germain Empereur', AD 54, 49 B 567, f° 141 verso.
32. 'Journal des ventes de Germain Empereur', AD 54, 49 B 561, p. 111 (5 March 1753): 'Mr. Sheldon came to live as a boarder at my house for 62 liv. a month' ('M. Sheldon est entré chez moi le 13 février en pension à 62 liv. par mois').
33. At the shopkeeper Humbert's, 11.5 % of his 1890 £L worth of debts were owed by contract (AD 54, 49 B 162); at Durafort's, the percentage of contracts reached 22.4 % on the 22.000 £L due to him (AD 54, 49 B 163).
34. In many cases, merchants resorted to the courts primarily in order to force the client to acknowledge his debt, hence avoiding any risk of prescription (Piant, *Une justice ordinaire*, p. 144).
35. At Esmonnier's, the proportion was down to 3.7 % (AD 54, 49 B 163), 4.0 % at Maurice's (AD 54, 49 B 162), while at Semelle'es it reached 11.7 % (AD 54, 49 B 163).
36. Trial Notes (1725), AD 54, 11 B.
37. Such was the case for Esmonnier (AD 54, 49 B 163), or, in the 1740s and 1750s, for Duparge from Nancy (1750; AD 54, 49 B 171), Gillot from Nancy (1752; AD 54, 49 B 173) or the Widow Saladin from Neufchâteau (1755; AD 54, 49 B 177).
38. See for instance Cressand (AD 54, 49 B 162) or, in the 1740s, Michelant from Rambervillers (1742; AD 54, 49 B 167), or Henry from Neufchâteau (1752; AD 54, 49 B 174).
39. The same conclusions were already reached in New England by C. Clark, *The Roots of Rural Capitalism. Western Massachusetts 1780–1860* (Ithaca, NY: Cornell University Press, 1990), pp. 28–38.
40. R. Grassby, 'The Rate of Profit in 17th Century England', *English Historical Review*, 84 (1969), pp. 721–4.
41. These rough estimates, valid for Lorraine, are in agreement with the obervations made in Marseilles by C. Carrière, *Négociants marseillais au XVIIIe siècle*, 2 vols (Marseille: Institut Historique de Provence, 1973), vol. 2, pp. 688–5.
42. The commercial paper notebooks of Dominique Leléal when he was a exchange broker in Nancy in the 1750s show that commercial paper on Paris was often negotiated at a discount of 1 % charged to the seller.
43. Chot, '*timbalier des Plaisirs du Duc*', thus purchased goods worth 471 liv. 8 s. on 7 May 1708, and only paid off in May 1713 (AD 54, 49 B 290, f° 205 recto for the waste-book of sales; AD 54, 49 B 293, f° 107 for the accounts current of sales).
44. F. Braudel and E. Labrousse (eds), *Histoire économique et sociale de la France*, 3 vols (Paris: Presses Universitaires de France, 1993), vol. 2, pp. 521–3.
45. Unlike long-distance maritime trade, where the profit on any operation was extremely hazardous and difficult to control; see G. Daudin, *Commerce et prospérité. La France au XVIIIe siècle* (Paris: Presses universitaires Paris-Sorbonne, 2005), pp. 281–335.
46. J.-Y. Grenier, *L'économie d'Ancien Régime. Un monde de l'échange et de l'incertitude* (Paris: Albin Michel, 1996), pp. 102–3.

4 Grant, 'The Wings of a Butterfly: Private Creditor Strategies in the "Chinese Debts" Crisis of 1779–80'

1. E. H. Pritchard, 'The Crucial Years of Early Anglo-Chinese Relations, 1750–1800', *Research Studies of the State College of Washington*, 4:3–4 (1936), pp. 200–1, 204; J. Hanser, 'Mr. Smith Goes to China: British Private Traders and the Interlinking of the British Empire with China, 1757–1793' (PhD dissertation, Yale University, 2012), pp. 42, 100, 151, 156–7, 171.
2. Pritchard, 'The Crucial Years', pp. 200–1, 204; L. Dermigny, *La Chine et L'Occident: Le Commerce A Canton Au XVIIIe Siècle 1719–1833*, 4 vols (Paris: Service de Vente des Publications Officielles de l'Education Nationale, 1964), vol. 2, pp. 822–6.
3. Dermigny, *La Chine et L'Occident*, vol. 2, p. 823; 'En effet, tout subrécargue n'a qu'un désir: s'enricher le plus rapidement afin de raccourcir d'autant la durée de l'exil à Canton, et, dans ce but, disposer d'une mise initiale assez considérable pour engendrer en quelques années un avoir de plusieurs centaines de milliers de livres'.
4. Pritchard, 'The Crucial Years', pp. 200–1, 204; Hanser, 'Mr. Smith Goes to China: British Private Traders', pp. 29–31, 34, 40, n. 107 and 61. See Dermigny, *La Chine et L'Occident*, vol. 2, pp. 891–4.
5. Hanser, 'Mr. Smith Goes to China: British Private Traders', p. 32.
6. Ibid., pp. 45, 64, 209.
7. Ibid., p. 14.
8. A. K. Ch'en, *The Insolvency of the Chinese Hong Merchants 1760–1843* (Nankang: Institute of Economics, Academia Sinica, 1990), pp. 275–6, 297–302; H. B. Morse, *The Chronicles of the East India Company Trading to China, 1635–1834*, 5 vols (Oxford: Oxford University Press, 1926–9), vol. 2, pp. 255, 261–2.
9. O. Ng, 'Ch'ing Management of the West: A Study of the Regulations, Homicide Cases and Debt Cases, 1644–1820' (MA thesis, University of Hong Kong, 1979), pp. 170–1.
10. Hanser, 'Mr. Smith Goes to China: British Private Traders', p. 39.
11. Pritchard, 'The Crucial Years', pp. 200–1, 204; Dermigny, *La Chine et L'Occident*, vol. 2, pp. 822–6.
12. Pritchard, 'The Crucial Years', pp. 200–1, 204; Dermigny, *La Chine et L'Occident*, vol. 2, pp. 822–6; Hanser, 'Mr. Smith Goes to China: British Private Traders', pp. 36, 47, 58–9, 62–3, 77, 82, 151, 181. See Dermigny, *La Chine et L'Occident*, vol. 2, p. 824 (quoting a letter dated 6 January 1768 from Achille de Robien to Louis-Joseph de Robien, which states, in part: 'L'intérêt de la place chez les marchands chinois faisant le commerce avec toutes les nations européennes est de 18 % par an; quelqu'un qui auriot à luy 100.000 francs pourroit en retirer 18 mille la première année et la seconde placer les 118.000 qui luy renderoient l'année suivante 18 % d'intérêt, de sorte que dans quatre années il pourroit doubler à quelque chose prèt ses fonds'.
13. Hanser, 'Mr. Smith Goes to China: British Private Traders', p. 36, citing H. Furber, *Rival Empires of Trade in the Orient, 1600–1800* (Minneapolis: University of Minneapolis Press, 1976), p. 291.
14. Hanser, 'Mr. Smith Goes to China: British Private Traders', p. 83.
15. Ibid., pp. 50–1 (George Smith [of Canton] complained of slow payments by hong debtors in 1772 and again in 1773).
16. S. Y. Tsai, 'Trading for Tea: A Study of the English East India Company's Tea Trade with China and the Related Financial Issues, 1760–1833' (PhD dissertation, University of Leicester, 2003), p. 295.

17. Ch'en, *The Insolvency of the Chinese Hong Merchants*, pp. 181–2, 186–90, 195, 200; W. E. Cheong, *The Hong Merchants of Canton: Chinese Merchants in Sino-Western Trade* (Richmond: Curzon Press, 1997), pp. 257, 262; Pritchard, 'The Crucial Years', p. 201; A. B. White, 'The Hong Merchants of Canton' (PhD Dissertation, University of Pennsylvania, 1967), pp. 67–9; Ng, 'Ch'ing Management of the West', pp. 144–6.
18. Morse, *The Chronicles of the East India Company Trading to China*, vol. 5, p. 96; L. Fu, *A Documentary Chronicle of Sino-Western Relations (1644–1820)* (Tucsonm, AZ: University of Arizona Press, 1966), p. 225.
19. *The Great Qing Code*, trans. W. C. Jones (Oxford: Clarendon Press, 1994), p. 161 (Art. 149, § 1); J. Junjian, 'Legislation Related to the Civil Economy in the Qing Dynasty', in K. Bernhardt and P. C. C. Huang (eds), *Civil Law in Qing and Republican China* (Stanford, CA: Stanford University Press, 1994), pp. 42–84, on pp. 72 (Qing Code Art. 149) and 77 (origins of the statutory rule of *yi ben yi li*).
20. Hanser, 'Mr. Smith Goes to China: British Private Traders', p. 83.
21. Ch'en, *The Insolvency of the Chinese Hong Merchants*, pp. 264–5, 409 n. 68, 422 n. 30; Cheong, *The Hong Merchants*, pp. 85, 88, 257, 260; Morse, *The Chronicles of the East India Company Trading to China*, vol. 2, p. 55.
22. Pritchard, 'The Crucial Years', pp. 201–2; Hanser, 'Mr. Smith Goes to China: British Private Traders', pp. 59–60.
23. Pritchard, 'The Crucial Years', p. 206; Morse, *The Chronicles of the East India Company Trading to China*, vol. 2, pp. 44–5.
24. Hanser, 'Mr. Smith Goes to China: British Private Traders', p. 77.
25. Cheong, *The Hong Merchants*, p. 258; Dermigny, *La Chine et L'Occident*, vol. 2, pp. 826, 898–9, 908.
26. Their debts to British creditors were: $1,354,713 (Yngshaw), $1,151,299 (Coqua), $634,784 (Seunqua III) and $438,735 (Kewshaw). Ch'en, *The Insolvency of the Chinese Hong Merchants*, pp. 199, 200, 203; Morse, *The Chronicles of the East India Company Trading to China*, vol. 2, p. 45.
27. Ch'en, *The Insolvency of the Chinese Hong Merchants*, p. 199.
28. Hanser, 'Mr. Smith Goes to China: British Private Traders', pp. 25–6 (footnotes omitted).
29. J. Quincy, *The Journal of Major Samuel Shaw, The First American Consul at Canton* (Boston, MA: William Crosby & H. P. Nichols, 1847), pp. 314–5.
30. Abraham Leslie, a junior surgeon employed by the British EIC, had lent much of his savings to Coqua at high interest, and stood to lose $11,000 in his insolvency. On 4 October 1779, with loaded pistols in hand, and the support of several Lascars and large dogs, he seized Coqua's hong and all its contents. Leslie posted his name above the door and raised a blue flag reading 'Leslie, an English merchant, has taken possession of this hong until he is paid', in English and in Chinese. He then remained in possession for two years, refusing orders by Chinese officials to vacate the premises, and orders by the British EIC to return to quarters. After debt proceedings were commenced against Yngshaw, Leslie broke the official seals that secured the door to Yngshaw's shuttered hong and seized it on 22 September 1780, now as agent for a third party creditor. Again, he posted signs, stating that possession had been taken until the creditor was paid. He took down the lanterns marked with the name of Yngshaw's hong (Taihe) and replaced them with lanterns marked with his name in Chinese. The Chinese carpenter who helped Leslie prepare the signs was put in irons for the translation offense. Leslie put up a sign in English advertising rooms for rent, the income to be applied to reduce debt, and rented a room in the

Taihe hong to an English captain from a private ship. He defied Chinese and British EIC demands to vacate both hong premises, and posted Lascar guards to prevent approach. The Chinese authorities grew increasingly frustrated that the British either would not or could not control their own employee. '[S]carcely a month passed in which the Chinese authorities did not demand angrily why the supercargoes did not coerce him into being obedient to the laws and doing right and justice'. At the end of 1780, the incumbent Governor, Li Hu, offered $17,500 as a lump sum in satisfaction of the Coqua, Yngshaw and Kewshaw debts, to induce Leslie to yield up the premises. Leslie accepted, and the money was paid through Puankhequa on 17 January 1781, but he then refused to leave. Abraham Leslie was finally arrested, delivered to Macao, imprisoned there for a period of time, and deported. Morse, *The Chronicles of the East India Company Trading to China*, vol. 2, p. 66 (text quoted); Ch'en, *The Insolvency of the Chinese Hong Merchants*, pp. 207–8; Cheong, *The Hong Merchants*, p. 259; Hanser, 'Mr. Smith Goes to China: British Private Traders', pp. 25, 87–94; P. A. Van Dyke, *The Canton Trade: Life and Enterprise on the China Coast, 1700–1845* (Hong Kong: Hong Kong University Press, 2005), p. 98.

31. Hanser, 'Mr. Smith Goes to China: British Private Traders', p. 83.
32. Ibid. To further complicate matters, at least three distinct types were noted among the creditors themselves: the first group 'made it their profession to gain from the difference between a large interest which they gave to others and a still larger they received from the merchants. 2ndly those who are agents for persons they did not know. And 3rdly those who acting for their friends and connections ... But because Smith, Hutton, and Crichton alone possessed 'merchants bonds to near three fourths of the whole debt', the [local] supercargo-creditors suggested that Captain Panton's representation had really been undertaken on account of those three men'. Hanser, 'Mr. Smith Goes to China: British Private Traders', p. 84.
33. Pritchard, 'The Crucial Years', pp. 203–5.
34. Ch'en, *The Insolvency of the Chinese Hong Merchants*, p. 196; Pritchard, 'The Crucial Years', pp. 205–8; Morse, *The Chronicles of the East India Company Trading to China*, vol. 2, pp. 47–8; Quincy, *The Journal of Major Samuel Shaw*, pp. 307, 310–11.
35. Ch'en, *The Insolvency of the Chinese Hong Merchants*, p. 198; quoted text from Hanser, 'Mr. Smith Goes to China: British Private Traders', p. 74; Pritchard, 'The Crucial Years', p. 207; Quincy, *The Journal of Major Samuel Shaw*, pp. 312–3; Morse, *The Chronicles of the East India Company Trading to China*, vol. 2, pp. 48–9.
36. Hanser, 'Mr. Smith Goes to China: British Private Traders', p. 74.
37. Ch'en, *The Insolvency of the Chinese Hong Merchants*, p. 198; Hanser, 'Mr. Smith Goes to China: British Private Traders', pp. 74–5; Pritchard, 'The Crucial Years', p. 207; Quincy, *The Journal of Major Samuel Shaw*, pp. 312–3; Morse, *The Chronicles of the East India Company Trading to China*, vol. 2, pp. 48–9; Dermigny, *La Chine et L'Occident*, vol. 2, p. 912.
38. Quincy, *The Journal of Major Samuel Shaw*, p. 312.
39. Ch'en, *The Insolvency of the Chinese Hong Merchants*, p. 198; Pritchard, 'The Crucial Years', p. 207; Quincy, *The Journal of Major Samuel Shaw*, p. 312; Morse, *The Chronicles of the East India Company Trading to China*, vol. 2, pp. 48–9.
40. Morse, *The Chronicles of the East India Company Trading to China*, vol. 2, pp. 53–54; Pritchard, 'The Crucial Years', pp. 208–9.
41. Pritchard, 'The Crucial Years', p. 209.
42. Morse, *The Chronicles of the East India Company Trading to China*, vol. 2, p. 55; Pritchard, 'The Crucial Years', p. 209.
43. Hanser, 'Mr. Smith Goes to China: British Private Traders', p. 87.
44. Cheong, *The Hong Merchants*, pp. 165, 167, 172, 223, 242 n. 116; Ch'en, *The Insolvency of the Chinese Hong Merchants*, pp. 201, 308.

45. Ch'en, *The Insolvency of the Chinese Hong Merchants*, p. 204; Cheong, *The Hong Merchants*, p. 260; Hanser, 'Mr. Smith Goes to China: British Private Traders', pp. 80–1.
46. Cheong, *The Hong Merchants*, pp. 206–7, 262; Ch'en, *The Insolvency of the Chinese Hong Merchants*, pp. 88–9, 92–102; M. Greenberg, *British Trade and the Opening of China 1800–42* (Cambridge: Cambridge University Press, 1951), p. 52 n. 3; Pritchard, 'The Crucial Years', pp. 140, 210; Morse, *The Chronicles of the East India Company Trading to China*, vol. 2, p. 69; White, 'The Hong Merchants of Canton', pp. 75, 192–5.
47. Cheong, *The Hong Merchants*, pp. 143, 172, 259; Ch'en, *The Insolvency of the Chinese Hong Merchants*, pp. 226–7, 271–2, 409 n. 69.
48. Cheong, *The Hong Merchants*, pp. 211, 228; Pritchard, 'The Crucial Years', p. 210; Morse, *The Chronicles of the East India Company Trading to China*, vol. 2, pp. 58–9.
49. Ch'en, *The Insolvency of the Chinese Hong Merchants*, pp. 96, 203, 205–7, 272; Pritchard, 'The Crucial Years', p. 210.
50. Morse, *The Chronicles of the East India Company Trading to China*, vol. 2, p. 56; Pritchard, 'The Crucial Years', pp. 209–11 (quotation at p. 211), 240–1.
51. Hanser, 'Mr. Smith Goes to China: British Private Traders', p. 74. Crichton, a commission merchant, was a leader of the Madras group of hong merchant creditors. A former business partner of George Smith [of Canton], Crichton had resided and traded in Canton from 1768 to 1774, leaving for Madras with two-thirds of his fortune outstanding as loans to hong merchants. Hanser, 'Mr. Smith Goes to China: British Private Traders', pp. 37, 66–9; Dermigny, *La Chine et L'Occident*, vol. 2, pp. 907, 910–11.
52. Hanser, 'Mr. Smith Goes to China: British Private Traders', pp. 143–4.
53. Ibid., pp. 25–6, 55–7, 99–103, 144–7.
54. Ibid., pp. 110, 114, 126–44, 215–21.
55. Pritchard, 'The Crucial Years', pp. 43, 99–103, 144–7, 156–9, 171–2, 176, 180–2, 191, 248.
56. Ibid., pp. 177–8.
57. Hanser, 'Mr. Smith Goes to China: British Private Traders', p. 241.
58. F. D. Grant, Jr, 'The Chinese Cornerstone of Modern Banking: The Canton Guaranty System and the Origins of Bank Deposit Insurance 1780–1933' (PhD dissertation, Leiden University, 2012), p. 158.
59. Grant, 'The Chinese Cornerstone of Modern Banking', p. 168 (Table 4.1).
60. Quincy, *The Journal of Major Samuel Shaw*, pp. 314–5.
61. R. R. Edwards, 'Ch'ing Legal Jurisdiction Over Foreigners', in J. A. Cohen, R. R. Edwards and F. C. Chen (eds), *Essays on China's Legal Tradition* (Princeton, NJ: Princeton University Press, 1980), pp. 222–69, on pp. 237–8.
62. Grant, 'The Chinese Cornerstone of Modern Banking', pp. 187–204.
63. Ibid., pp. 205–13.

5 Lamikiz, 'The Transatlantic Flow of Price Information in the Spanish Colonial Trade, 1680–1820'

1. See, for example, J. J. McCusker, 'The Demise of Distance: the Business Press and the Origins of the Information Revolution in the Early Modern Atlantic World', *American Historical Review*, 110:2 (2005), pp. 295–321; J. J. McCusker and C. Gravesteijn, *The Beginnings of Commercial and Financial Journalism: The Commodity Price Currents, Exchange Rate Currents, and Money Currents of Early Modern Europe* (1979; Amsterdam: Nederlandsch Economisch-Historisch Archief, 1991).
2. For two exceptions that deal with the eighteenth century, see J. Baskes, 'Communication Breakdown: Information and Risk in Spanish Atlantic World Trade during an Era of

"Free Trade" and War', *Colonial Latin American Review*, 20:1 (2011), pp. 35–60; and X. Lamikiz, 'Patrones de comercio y flujo de información comercial entre España y América durante el siglo XVIII', *Revista de Historia Económica-Journal of Iberian and Latin American Economic History*, 25:2 (2007), pp. 231–58.

3. Lamikiz, 'Patrones de comercio', pp. 231–58.
4. In the years 1717–38 a yearly average of 10,483 tons of merchandise was shipped to Spanish America. In 1739–54 the average was 13,893 tons, and that figure rose to 25,132 tons in 1755–78. A. García-Baquero, *Cádiz y el Atlántico, 1717–1778: El comercio colonial español bajo el monopolio gaditano*, 2 vols (Seville: Escuela de Estudios Hispano-Americanos, 1976), vol. 1, pp. 172–3.
5. S. J. Stein and B. H. Stein, *Edge of Crisis: War and Trade in the Spanish Atlantic, 1789–1808* (Baltimore, MD: Johns Hopkins University Press, 2009), p. 17.
6. J. Campillo y Cosío, *Nuevo sistema de gobierno económico para América* (Oviedo: GEA, 1993, 1st ed. 1789), pp. 274–5.
7. 'Testimonio de las diligencias hechas en Veracruz sobre ajuste de precios de una feria', Archivo General de Indias, Seville (hereafter AGI), Consulados 87, nº 15.
8. For a more detailed description of these sources, see X. Lamikiz, *Trade and Trust in the Eighteenth-Century Atlantic World: Spanish Merchants and their Overseas Networks* (Woodbridge: Boydell Press / Royal Historical Society, 2010), pp. 21, 100–7.
9. J. Savary, *Le Parfait Négociant, ou Instruction Générale pour ce qui regarde le commerce des Marchandises de France & des Pays Etrangers*, 2 vols (Paris, 1675), vol. 2, pp. 77–8.
10. A. C. Loosley, 'The Puerto Bello Fairs', *Hispanic American Historical Review*, 13:3 (1933), pp. 314–35, on p. 328.
11. Ibid., p. 329.
12. G. J. Walker, *Spanish Politics and Imperial Trade, 1700–1789* (London: Macmillan, 1979), p. 196.
13. B. Álvarez Nogal, 'Mercados o redes de mercaderes: el funcionamiento de la feria de Portobelo', in N. Böttcher, B. Hausberger and A. Ibarra (eds), *Redes y negocios globales en el mundo ibérico, siglos XVI–XVIII* (Madrid/Frankfurt: Iberoamericana, 2011), pp. 53–86, on p. 78.
14. 'Testimonio de las diligencias hechas en Veracruz sobre ajuste de precios de una feria', AGI, Consulados 87, no. 15, f. 2r. See also A. M. Bernal, *La financiación de la Carrera de Indias: Dinero y crédito en el comercio colonial español con América* (Seville: Fundación El Monte, 1992), pp. 224–6.
15. Upon the arrival of the 1706 fleet, similiar negotiations to those of 1683 again produced no agreement. See I. Escamilla González, 'La nueva alianza: El Consulado de México y la monarquía borbónica durante la Guerra de Sucesión', in G. Valle Pavón (ed.), *Mercaderes, comercio y consulados de Nueva España en el siglo XVIII* (Mexico City: Instituto Mora, 2003), pp. 41–63. See also G. Valle Pavón, 'La lucha por el control de los precios entre los consulados de México y Andalucía', *Revista Complutense de Historia de América*, 32 (2006), pp. 41–62.
16. The following discussion is taken from X. Lamikiz, 'Flotistas en la Nueva España: diseminación espacial y negocios de los intermediarios del comercio transatlántico, 1670–1702', *Colonial Latin American Review*, 20:1 (2011), pp. 9–33.
17. Vicente Ros de Ysava to Pedro de Munárriz, Veracruz, 6 February 1799, The National Archives, Kew, Surrey, High Court of Admiralty (hereafter TNA, HCA) 30/231.
18. Ysava to Munárriz, Veracruz, 9 August 1700, ibid.
19. Francisco de Preen y Castro to Munárriz, Mexico City, 7 December 1699, ibid.

20. For problems at the Portobelo fairs see G. R. Dilg, 'The Collapse of the Portobelo Fairs: A Study in Spanish Commercial Reform, 1720–1740' (PhD dissertation, Indiana University, 1975).
21. Prices were clearly more volatile under the more regulated fleet/fair system than under this new system. As Sheilagh Ogilvie states, 'in so far as merchant guilds and privileged companies were able to prevent individual knowledge from contributing to price formation, they probably increased the 'noise' of price signals in pre-modern trade'. S. Ogilvie, *Institutions and European Trade: Merchant Guilds, 1000–1800* (Cambridge: Cambridge University Press, 2011), pp. 402–3. However, Spanish merchants perceived price volatility as more damaging with less regulated, more frequent unscheduled exchanges, simply because these were far less predictable than the commercial fleets.
22. Walker, *Spanish Politics*, p. 211. Licensed ships appear to have been fewer in number. Over the period 1740–56, Madrid officials licensed 164 *registros sueltos* (119 to Spaniards and forty-five to non-Spaniards). In addition, twenty-four mail-boats were sent in the same period. S. J. Stein and B. H. Stein, *Silver, Trade, and War: Spain and America in the Making of Early Modern Europe* (Baltimore, MD: Johns Hopkins University Press, 2000), p. 194.
23. The most significant examples can be found in two boxes: TNA, HCA 30/250 and 32/124.
24. Lamikiz, *Trade and Trust*, p. 91.
25. Ibid., p. 92.
26. Ibid.
27. J. J. McCusker, *European Bills of Entry and Marine Lists: Early Commercial Publications and the Origins of the Business Press* (Cambridge, MA: Harvard University Library, 1985), p. 8.
28. McCusker and Gravesteijn, *Beginnings of Commercial and Financial Journalism*, pp. 171–3.
29. 'The first American business newspaper', notes McCusker, 'was a commodity price current published at Philadelphia starting in the middle of 1783'. McCusker, 'The Demise of Distance', p. 312.
30. James Comerford to Wargent Nicholson, Cádiz, 30 Jan. 1752, TNA, Chancery 111/200.
31. Stein and Stein, *Silver, Trade, and War*, p. 192.
32. For the Jalapa fairs see J. J. Real Díaz, *Las ferias de Jalapa* (Sevilla: Escuela de Estudios Hispano-Americanos, 1959).
33. See S. J. Stein and B. H. Stein, *Apogee of Empire: Spain and New Spain in the Age of Charles III, 1759–1789* (Baltimore, MD: Johns Hopkins University Press, 2003), pp. 119–42; and J. Baskes, 'Risky Ventures: Reconsidering Mexico's Colonial Trade System', *Colonial Latin American Review*, 14:1 (2005), pp. 27–54.
34. Lamikiz, *Trade and Trust*, p. 93.
35. Ibid. The ship papers and the intercepted mail can be found in TNA, HCA 32/124/25.
36. Juan Cranisbro to Tomás Núñez, Lima, 1 March 1759, Archivo General de la Nación, Lima, TC-GR1, caja 119, doc. 644, f. 45r-v. Similar remarks in Cranisbro to Tomás Cantillón, ibid., ff. 46v–47r; Cranisbro to Pedro Cranisbro, ibid., f. 47r–v; Cranisbro to Francisco José del Rivero, ibid., ff. 49v–51v.
37. Correspondence from *La Perla* is distributed among eight boxes: TNA, HCA 30/275, 30/276, 30/311, 30/312, 30/313, 30/314, 30/315 and 30/316. See Lamikiz, *Trade and Trust*, pp. 100–7.

38. Joaquín Manuel Azcona to Juan Martín Aguirre, Lima, 30 March 1779, TNA, HCA 30/315/2, no. 279.
39. José Antonio Lavalle to Lorenzo Asunsolo, Lima, 29 March 1779, TNA, HCA 30/314/1, no. 278.
40. Joaquín Tajonar to Juan Francisco Vea Murguía, Lima, 10 May 1779, TNA, HCA 30/315/18, envelope without number.
41. In 1791, for instance, the sixteen ships that set sail from Spain for Buenos Aires and Montevideo carried a cargo valued at 1.1 million pesos, whereas six ships bound for Callao (Lima's seaport) carried a cargo worth 4.65 million. J. R. Fisher, 'El impacto del comercio libre en el Perú, 1778–1796', *Revista de Indias*, 48:182–183 (1988), pp. 401–20, on p. 403.
42. For a lucid assessment of the overall impact of *comercio libre*, see J. Baskes, *Staying Afloat: Risk and Uncertainty in Spanish Atlantic World Trade, 1760–1820* (Stanford, CA: Stanford University Press, 2013), pp. 71–109.
43. Lamikiz, *Trade and Trust*, p. 181.
44. Baskes, 'Communication Breakdown', p. 49.
45. Stein and Stein, *Edge of Crisis*, pp. 14–19.
46. Baskes mentions one coming from Veracruz to Cádiz in August 1798. Baskes, 'Communication Breakdown', p. 49.
47. For works that emphasize the importance of business networks and merchant letters see K. Morgan, 'Business Networks in the British Export Trade to Northern America, 1750–1800', in J. McCusker and K. Morgan (eds), *The Early Modern Atlantic Economy* (Cambridge: Cambridge University Press, 2001), pp. 36–62; F. Trivellato, 'Merchant Letters Across Geographical and Social Boundaries', in F. Bethencourt and F. Egmond (eds), *Cultural Exchange in Early Modern Europe*, vol. 3: *Correspondence and Cultural Exchange in Europe, 1400–1700* (Cambridge: Cambridge University Press, 2007), pp. 80–103; and S. Aslanian, '"The Salt in a Merchant's Letter": The Culture of Julfan Correspondence in the Indian Ocean and the Mediterranean', *Journal of World History*, 19:2 (2008), pp. 127–88.
48. Miguel Ventura Osambela to Francisco Miguel Lombardo, Lima, 27 October 1804, TNA, HCA 32/942, envelope G37.
49. In Mexico City and Veracruz, for example, *Correo Semanario*, *Diario Mercantil de Veracruz*, *Journal Económico Mercantil de Veracruz* and *Gaceta de México*. P. Pérez Herrero, 'Comercio y precios en la Nueva España: Presupuestos teóricos y materiales para una discusión', *Revista de Indias*, 44:174 (1984), pp. 467–88, on p. 487.
50. J. Adelman, *Sovereignity and Revolution in the Iberian Atlantic* (Princeton, NJ: Princeton University Press, 2006), pp. 104–15.
51. As Jeremy Baskes puts it, '[w]ar increased substantially the potential for profits since the difference in price between markets for commodities grew significantly'. Baskes, *Staying Afloat*, p. 151.
52. Usually the most affluent merchants had wealth tied up in fixed assets such as buildings and land, but also experienced shockingly high levels of debtor default. At the time of his death in 1796, Guatemala's wealthiest merchant, the Navarrese Juan Fermín de Aycinena, was worth 2,196,029 pesos (assets plus liabilities); his receivable debts amounted to 1,500,696 pesos of which a staggering 795,675 (or 53 %) were deemed dubious or lost. R. F. Brown, 'Profits, Prestige, and Persistence: Juan Fermín de Aycinena and the Spirit of Enterprise in the Kingdom of Guatemala', *Hispanic American Historical Review*, 75:3 (1995), pp. 405–40, on p. 415. The case of the Cádiz merchant Miguel Sánchez de la

Vega (d. 1769) points in the same direction. Although not as rich as Aycinena, his estate's net worth of 264,675 pesos included 146,688 receivable debts of which 77,377 (or 52 %) were considered lost or doubtful. García-Baquero, *Cádiz y el Atlántico*, vol. 1, pp. 505–6.

6 Margairaz, 'Product Quality and Merchant Transactions: Product Lines and Hierarchies in the Accounts and Letters of the Gradis Merchant House'

1. J.-M. Tuffery, Ébauch*e d'un droit de la consommation: la protection du chaland sur les marchés toulousains aux XVIIème et XVIIIéme siècles* (Paris: LGDJ, 1998); G. Béaur, H. Bonin and C. Lemercier (eds), *Fraude, contrefaçon et contrebande de l'Antiquité à nos jours* (Genève: Droz, 2006); A. Stanziani, *Histoire de la qualité alimentaire XIXe–XXe siècles* (Paris: Seuil, 2005).
2. J. Styles, 'Product Innovation in Early Modern London', *Past & Present*, 168 (2000), pp. 124–69; M. Berg, 'From Imitation to Invention: Creating Commodities in Eighteenth-Century Britain', *Economic History Review*, 55 (2002), pp. 1–30, and M. Berg, *Luxury and Pleasure in Eighteenth Century Britain* (Oxford: Oxford University Press, 2005); L. Hilaire-Pérez, '"Techno-esthétique." De l'économie smithienne: valeur et fonctionnalité des objets dans l'Angleterre des Lumières', *Revue de Synthèse*, 133 (2012), pp. 495–523.
3. L. Thévenot et al., 'L'économie des conventions', *Revue économique*, 40:2 (1989), pp. 141–400; A. Orléan (ed.), *L'analyse économique des conventions* (Paris: PUF, 1994); F. Eymard-Duvernay (ed.), *L'économie des conventions. Méthodes et résultats*, 2 vols (Paris: Éditions de La Découverte, 2006).
4. A. Appadurai, *The Social Life of Things* (Cambridge: Cambridge University Press), 1986.
5. J. Bourdieu, M. Bruegael and A. Stanziani (eds), *Nomenclatures et classifications: approches historiques, enjeux économiques* (Paris: Presses de l'INRA, 2004); J.-Y. Grenier, 'Une économie de l'identification. Juste prix et ordre des marchandises dans l'Ancien Régime', in Stanziani (ed.), *La qualité des produits*, pp. 25–53; A. Conchon and D. Margairaz, 'De l'idiome mercantiliste à l'idiome libéral: classement, déclassement, reclassement des produits (XVIIIe –début XIXe siècles)', in M. Cassan (ed.), *Classement, déclassement, reclassement de l'Antiquité à nos jours* (Limoges: PULIM, 2011), pp. 334–58. On the strained relationships between similarity and singularity, see M. Callon, C. Meadel and V. Rabeharisoa, 'L'économie des qualités', *Politix*, 13:52 (2000), pp. 211–39.
6. On dictionaries and textbooks for the use of merchants, see *Ars Mercatoria : Handbücher und Traktate für den Gebrauch des Kaufmanns, 1470–1820*, 3 vols (Paderborn: Schöningh, 1991–2001); also the clarification by J. Hoock, 'Information économique de l'*Encyclopédie commerciale* à la presse économique, 1680–1820', *L'information économique XVIe–XIXe siècles* (Paris: CHEFF, 2008), pp. 63–70.
7. P. Jeannin, 'Distinction des compétences et niveaux de qualification: les savoirs négociants dans l'Europe moderne', in F. Angiolini and D. Roche, *Cultures et formations négociantes* (Paris: Éditions de l'EHESS, 1995), pp. 363–97.
8. See A. Conchon, 'Penser l'ordre des échanges / classer les produits: les tarifs de péages au XVIIIe siècle', in Bourdieu, Bruegel and Stanziani (eds), *Nomenclatures et classifications*, pp. 57–68; also D. Margairaz, 'Qualité et fiscalité dans l'économie d'Ancien Régime', in J. Vögle and R. Salais (eds), *Qualitätspolitik. Die Qualität der Produkte in historischer Perspektive* (Berlin: Campus, 2014, forthcoming).

9. The collective construction of 'Madeira wine' by producers, consumers and import and export merchants, as well as the various adaptations of the ideal-type of the good to local tastes shows that in the particular case of the 'invention' of a product, consumers and producers are actually joint-initiators. See D. Hancock, 'Commerce and Conversation in the Eighteenth-Century Atlantic. The Invention of Madeira Wine', *Journal of Interdisciplinary History*, 39 (1998), pp. 197–219 and D. Hancock, 'L'émergence d'une économie de réseau (1640–1815). Le vin de Madère', *Annales. Histoire, Sciences Sociales*, 58:3 (2003), pp. 649–72. For a more exhaustive approach, see D. Hancock, *Oceans of Wine: Madeira and the Emergence of American Trade and Taste* (New Haven, CT: Yale University Press, 2009).
10. A. Wegener-Sleeswijk, 'Du nectar et de la godaille : qualité et falsification du vin aux Provinces-Unies, XVIIIe siècle', *Revue d'histoire moderne et contemporaine*, 51:3 (2004), pp. 20–5, and A. Wegener-Sleeswijk, 'Les vins français aux Provinces-Unies au XVIIIe siècle: négoce, dynamique institutionnelle et la restructuration du marché' (PhD dissertation, École des Hautes Études en Sciences Sociales, 2006).
11. A. Wegener-Sleeswijk, 'La relation problématique entre principal et agent dans la commission: l'exemple de l'exportation des vins vers les Provinces-Unies au XVIIIe siècle', in S. Marzagalli and H. Bonin (eds), *Négoces, ports, océans, XVIe–XVIIIe* siècles (Pessac: Presses universitaires de Bordeaux, 2000), pp. 29–45, especially p. 32; and L. Pineau-Defois, 'Sphères d'approvisionnement. Grands négociants nantais en denrées d'exportation (fin XVIIIe siècle)', *Histoire urbaine*, 30 (2011), pp. 87–107, especially pp. 101–2.
12. From October 1754 to May 1756. Cf. Arch. Nat., Gradis Fund, Centre d'Archives du Monde du Travail, Roubaix, 'Journal, 20 août 1751–14 mai 1755', 181 AQ 6* (hereafter 'Journal, 181AQ6*'), and 'Journal, 1 June 1755–26 October 1759', 181 AQ 7* (hereafter 'Journal, 181AQ7*'); also 'Lettres commerciales d'Europe, 1755–1795' 181 AQ 57, May 1755–May 1756 (hereafter 'Correspondence, 181AQ57').
13. The fund we have from the Chaurands does not cover the same dates: accounting was treated from October 1773 to December 1774, and for the first three months of 1784, and correspondence only partly for the first period. See Y. Lemarchand, C. McWatters and L. Pineau-Defois, 'The Current Account as Cognitive Artefact: Stories and Accounts of *La Maison Chaurand*', this volume pp. 13–31.
14. On the Gradis, see P. Butel, *Les négociants bordelais, l'Europe et les îles au XVIIIe siècle* (Paris: Aubier, 1974); J. Cavignac, *Les israélites bordelais de 1780 à 1850* (Paris: Publisud, 1991); J. Schwob d'Héricourt, *La maison Gradis de Bordeaux et ses chefs* (Argenteuil: s. ed., 1975); R. Menkis, 'The Gradis Family of Eighteenth Century Bordeaux: A Social and Economic Study' (PhD dissertation, Brandeis University, 1988). On Chaurand, see J. Meyer, *L'armement nantais dans la deuxième moitié du XVIIIe siècle* (Paris: Éditions de l'École des hautes études en sciences sociales, 1999); L. Pineau-Defois, 'Les grands négociants nantais du dernier tiers du XVIIIe siècle. Capital hérité et esprit d'entreprise (fin XVIIe–début XIXe siècles)' (PhD dissertation, Université de Nantes, 2008).
15. Correspondence, 181AQ57, 27 January 1756, 3 and 27 February 1756, f° 207, 213 and 235.
16. Beginning in 1774, Honoré-Anne and Pierre-Louis Chaurand were associates under the corporate name 'Chaurand Frères'. They combined ship fitting-out, direct trade with the colonies as well as the slave trading ventures, through operations for their own account or in participation (goods traded on joint account, shares in ships, pacotille merchandise, insurance, and bottomry loans).

17. A. Forestier, 'Principal-Agent Problems in the French Slave Trade: The Case of Rochelais Armateurs and their Agents, 1763–1792' (PhD dissertation, London School of Economics, 2005). Available at http://www.lse.ac.uk/economicHistory/Research/GEHN/GEHNPDF/WorkingPaper13AF.pdf [accessed 6 October 2013].
18. 'Marchandises pour la Société Dt a Robert, Antoine £ 3982.12.6 pour *diverses* qu'il nous a envoyé', Journal, 181AQ6*, 11 March 1755; italics added.
19. P. Gervais, 'Crédit et filières marchandes au XVIIIe siècle', *Annales HSS*, 67 (2012), pp. 1011–48.
20. As in the following entry, for instance: 'Mr Moïse Gradis Dr. to Sundries £ 10081 for the Following merchandise we Delivered for the Carg. of the sh.p le Jean P.re captain P.re Daignan Accord.g to the acc.t agreed upon Today between Them, That is *to General Merchand. for 250 Barrels flour £ 5492*' ('Mr Moïse Gradis Dt a Divers £ 10081 p les marchandises Suivantes que nous luy avons Livré p la Carg. du n.re le Jean P.re cap P.re Daignan Suiv.t le c.te arreté ce Jour entre Eux Sçavoir *a Marchand. Generales pr 250 Barrils farine £ 5492*'). Journal, 181AQ7*, 30 November 1755; italics added.
21. 'Marchandises pr La Société Dt a Horutener & Cie £ 12561 p. leur envoy de 14 Balles, 1 th[onneau] et 2 Caisses Suiv.t fact.e & Connoissem.t du 29 Janvier'. Journal, 181AQ6*, 9 February 1755.
22. Originally, 'pour 6 th[onneaux] à divers prix'. Journal, 181AQ6*, 23 March 1755.
23. Journal, 181AQ6*, 'to wines purchased for the Following That is f. 10 Barr.ls *from Monferand* £ 2100 10 barr.ls of [?] 1260 3 of *White* £ 300' ('à vins achetés pour les Suivants Sçavoir pr 10 thon.x de Monferand £ 2100 10 th.x d. 1260 3 d. Blanc £ 300'), 2 January1755; 'to Wines bought for 5 b[arrels] and a 1/3 *in bottles* £ 1663.6.8' ('à Vins achetés pour 5 th[onneau]x et 1/3 en Bouteilles £ 1663.6.8'), 22 March 1755; 'to Wines bought for 20 b[arre]ls 3 H[ogshea]ds *in Le Neptune*; 49 *in the n^tre^ dame de la Garde*; 69 b[arrels] 3 H[ogshea]ds *at 40 W* £ 8370' ('à Vins achetés pr 20 th[onneau]x 3 B[arri]q[ues] dans Le Neptune; 49 dans le n^tre^ dame de la Garde; 69 th. 3 B[arri]ques a 40W £ 8370'), 21 April 1755; 'to Wines bought pr. 3 b[arrel]s *Red at 70 W* £ 360' ('à Vins achetés pr 3 th.x Rouge a 70 W £ 630'), 21 April 1755. Italics ours; 'W' means *Livre de compte*, worth 3 *livres tournois*.
24. In about one quarter of entries, the sender appears as the only mark of qualification.
25. Gervais, 'Crédit et filières marchandes', p. 1024.
26. Correspondence, 181AQ57. The incoming ('passive') correspondence has not been kept. The letters we have are those concerning Europe, those concerning America are not publicly available.
27. Correspondence, 181AQ57, 30 January 1756, f° 211 (letter to Mr le chevalier de Beaufremond).
28. Originally, 'pour les 30 barils de farines de Moissac, la chose ne sera pas possible, il faut les demander sur les lieux. Si cependant j'en trouvais qui soient bonnes de quelque autre fabrique et une autre occasion prompte pour vous les expédier, nous le ferons'. Correspondence, 181AQ57, 29 October 1755, f° 125 (letter to Mr Chauverau).
29. For instance: 'Here is a small memorandum of prices for articles we payed for fifteen days ago for supplies. *Good wines from Monferan* [*sic*] will cost around 180# the barrel for a first purchase, those of Capri around 240 to 270#, *the good old wine from Graves* 300 à 320, *white wine from Graves* 400' ('Voici un petit mémoire des prix des articles que nous avons payé il y a 15 jours pour des provisions. Les *bons vins de Monferan* [*sic*] coûteront aux environs de 180# le tonneau de premier achat, ceux de Capri aux environs de 240 à

270# *le bon vin vieux de Graves* 300 à 320 le *vin blanc de Graves* 400'. Correspondence, 181AQ57, 2 December 1755, f° 162 (letter to Mr Le M. Le Gardeur).

30. 'Nous vous avons mandé qu'il n'y avait pas ici de bon vin d'Alicante. J'en ai que je dois faire *qualifier* et que nous venons de recevoir, nous verrons de vous en faire passer quelque bouteille qui est très vieux et fort bon'. Correspondence, 181AQ57, 27 November 1755, f°156 (letter to Mr Asselin). Italics ours.
31. A town situated in the wineyards covering the hillsides on the right bank of the Garonne, south-east of Bordeaux, and producing sweet white wines.
32. 'Nous avons occasion d'une trentaine de tonneaux de vin de chez vous tout ce qu'il y a de plus parfait et de meilleur, ce que nous vous prions de choisir pourvu que le prix ne passe par de 34 à 35 tout au plus ... envoyez-nous une bouteille avec quelques autres *montres* ... ici nous avons goûté ceux de madame de Loupes desquels nous n'avons pas été du tout satisfaits. Depuis que nous les avons, ils ont perdu de leur couleur et sont venus petits comme de l'eau et ils ont avec cela bien de la verdure'. Correspondence, 181AQ57, 15 December 1755, f° 171 (letter to Mr Roux aîné).
33. Hancock, *Oceans of Wine*, and Wegener-Sleeswijk, 'Du nectar et de la godaille'.
34. Originally, 'nous ne vous enverrons pas les deux tonneaux de vin de Cahors que porte votre mémoire, n'étant pas d'une trop bonne qualité de cette année, mais nous les remplacerons par pareil nombre d'excellent vin de Montferrand dont sûrement vous aurez lieu d'être content'. Correspondence, 181AQ57, 25 January 1756, f° 203 (letter to Mr le Marquis de Goutte). Wines from Monferand were Languedoc wines, not to be confused with the Italian wines from Montferrat.
35. Originally, 'toute la difficulté sera pour les vins de Cahors première qualité et les autres vins des palus, n'en voulant pas de Monferat ni de ceux de Capri ... pour les vins de palus, la plus grande partie de ceux de la dernière récolte sont d'une mauvaise qualité ... le besoin où vous nous témoignez être d'avoir vos provisions viennent de nous déterminer à acheter une partie de vos *grands* vins rouges qui nous ont paru bons pour l'année dernière et sur lesquels nous comptons pour leur conservation'. Correspondence, 181AQ57, 18 October 1755, f°112 (letter to Mr Chauvereau; italics added). *Palus* wines ('vins de palus') were Bordeaux-area wines produced on sandy soils bordering the Gironde or from former seaside marshes, drained and reclaimed; these wines were considered mediocre, and had long been used for coupage.
36. Originally, 'chargez le Sr Lareguy d'en faire la vente [de toiles de Morlaix] et le recouvrement et l'emploi en beaux cafés. Il le fera plus avantageusement que ne le feront les commissionnaires et bien plus fidèlement, même à meilleur marché, car il se contentera pour vente et achat de 5 p% au lieu que les commissionnaires vous en feront payer 10 p% et que d'ailleurs ils vous fourniront de mauvais cafés et même à un plus haut prix que le bon'. Correspondence, 181AQ57, 23 December 1755, f°184 (letter to Mr le marquis de Vienne).
37. 'Les cafés que vous nous avez fait Passer Par le navire Le Patriarche (Capitaine Combal) sont encore invendus, la qualité en est très mauvaise en partie, nous ferons en sorte de nous en défaire le plus tôt qu'il nous sera possible', Correspondence, 181AQ57, 13 septembre 1755, f° 78; 'il est sûr que celui qui vous a vendu les cafés que vous nous avez adressés par le navire Le Patriarche vous a très mal servi, étant de très mauvaise qualité. Cependant nous venons de les vendre ce jour à 18ˢ la [livre] ce qui est un bon Prix vu leur défectuosité. S'ils eussent été bons nous en aurions pu obtenir 20ˢ ou 20ˢ 6d', Correspondence, 181AQ57, 31 September [*sic*], f°83 (letters to Mr Dupradel, Paris).

38. As Michel Morineau has shown, commercial profit on direct Transatlantic trade was generated by incoming cargoes. See 'Quelques recherches relatives à la balance du commerce extérieur français au XVIIIe siècle: où cette fois un = deux', in *Pour une histoire économique vraie* (Lille: Presses universitaires de Lille, 1985), pp. 277–93.
39. This cloth had a variety of sub-categories such as 'Toile de brin', 'de commun', 'de beau fort', 'herbée', etc., to which one would frequently add Holland cloth shipped from Rouen.
40. This is the structure described for instance by Silvia Marzagalli, 'Stratégies marchandes et organisation du monde du négoce en Europe et aux Amériques (fin XVIIe-début XIXe siècle)' (HDR dissertation, Université de Paris Panthéon-Sorbonne, 2004).
41. For instance the widow Tirand, in Lille, who was a well-known trader in cloth and household linen.
42. See for instance Correspondence, 181AQ57, 11 October 1755, f° 106, an order which included '500 chaudières de cuivre rouge étamées les couvertes en casseroles de 8. 10. & 12. Points, 150 chaudières idem depuis 2 jusques à 4 Points, 600 Couvertes de 2 points, 2000 idem de 2 points ½, 2000 idem de 3 points, 500 idem de 4 points, 1200 idem à berceau, 1500 au siamois en 5/4 tout blanc & à petites raies, 6000 au coton en ½ au jolie couleur, 30 milliers grosses aiguilles à coudre, 6 douzaines épingles N° 17, 30 gros peignes de bois et de buis assortis, 10 gros peignes de corne, 12 Douzaines gallon à l'aumonne, 2000 Cornes à poudre bien faites, 2000 Cornes pour lanterne de la grande sorte, 4 barils fer blanc assorti, 200 Carreaux de verre de 11/12, 2000 au Siamois en ¾, 2400 Carreaux de 8/9, 2000 idem de 7/8, 1500 au Gingas & bontin, 4 Gros dés à coudre, 22 Pièces flanelle assorties'500 chaudières de cuivre rouge étamées les couvertes en casseroles de 8. 10. & 12. Points, 150 chaudières idem depuis 2 jusques à 4 Points, 600 Couvertes de 2 points, 2000 idem de 2 points ½ , 2000 idem de 3 points, 500 idem de 4 points, 1200 idem à berceau, 1500 au siamois en 5/4 tout blanc & à petites raies, 6000 au coton en ½ au jolie couleur, 30 milliers grosses aiguilles à coudre, 6 douzaines épingles N° 17, 30 gros peignes de bois et de buis assortis, 10 gros peignes de corne, 12 Douzaines gallon à l'aumonne, 2000 Cornes à poudre bien faites, 2000 Cornes pour lanterne de la grande sorte, 4 barils fer blanc assorti, 200 Carreaux de verre de 11/12, 2000 au Siamois en ¾, 2400 Carreaux de 8/9, 2000 idem de 7/8, 1500 au Gingas & bontin, 4 Gros dés à coudre, 22 Pièces flanelle assorties'). Also Correspondence, 181AQ57, 20 décembre 1755, f° 176, a similarly diverse order: '400 livres de grosses éponges 200 livres de noix de Galles depuis 30# à 60#, 12 paires balances plateaux de cuivre fléaux de fer, 50 douzaines vrilles assorties, 100 têtes de fromage à croûte rouge, 100 fil de laiton, 100 lampes de fer pour caserne 50 livres de fils de fer assorties 25 quintaux d'acier d'Allemagne en petites barres, un quintal idem à ressort 1000 livres tôle mince,12 quintaux clous à bardeaux'.
43. Originally, 'ci-joint Mrs le mémoire des marchandises qu'il nous faut *cette année* de chez vous', Correspondence, 181AQ57, 9 October 1755, f° 103 (letter to Mssrs Raully frères and letter to Mssrs Mariette et Dumas); italics added.
44. Correspondence, 181AQ57, 18 octobre 1755, f°104 (letter to Mssrs Ferregeau & fils).
45. '77 pièces de molleton dont la moitié de blancs, un quart rouge et un quart bleu;' 'à l'égard des articles des molletons, l'on ne nous en fait pas d'explication dans la qualité dans les demandes qu'on nous fait, ainsi nous ne pouvons rien vous dire à cet égard, nous vous prions *de faire au mieux*'. Correspondence, 181AQ57, 25 December 1755, f° 186 (letter to M. Payes); italics added. The order was dated from the 18th, and the request for a clarification from the 21th, which proves that Payes, at least, was quick to react.

46. See for instance Correspondence, 181AQ57, 6 January 1756, f° 194 (letter to Mr Horutener: 'as for the 20 pieces of white flannel, they must also be of a quality *more or less the same that you have sent heretofore*' ('à l'égard des 20 pièces de flanelle blanche, elles doivent être aussi de la qualité à peu près de celle que vous m'avez ci-devant envoyée'). See also Correspondence, 181AQ57, n.d. [February 1756], f° 231 (letter to Mr Guillaume Nayrac: 'Send us at the first opportunity a crate of writing paper *similar to the one you sent us heretofore*' ('Nous envoyer par la première occasion une caisse de papier à lettres *comme celle que vous nous avez ci-devant envoyée*'). Also Correspondence, 181AQ57, 14 January 1756, f° 199 (letter to Mr David Alexandre): '15 to 20 days from now, I will have the opportunity for a hundred or so pieces of silk handkerchiefs *like the ones you sent us last year*' ('j'aurai occasion d'ici à 15 ou 20 jours d'une centaine de pièces de mouchoirs de soie *comme ceux que tu nous envoyas l'année dernière*'); italics added.
47. 'Ayez agréable madame, d'apporter vos attentions à ce qu'il n'y ait point de retardement à l'expédition comme par le passé aussi bien qu'à la belle et bonne qualité du papier sans quoi nous serons obligés de nous pourvoir ailleurs'. Correspondence, 181AQ57, 18 October 1755, f° 111 (letter to Mad. Vve La Roche). This papermaker dated back to the beginning of the eighteenth century. In 1806, the heir of the widow La Roche won a prize at the national fair for industrial products; the paper manufactory later took the name of Laroche-Joubert.
48. Marked in the correspondence through the following formula: for payment, *you can draw on us* at Mssrs Chabert & Banquet' ('pour le paiement, *vous pouvez vous prévaloir sur nous* chez Mrs Chabert et Banquet'); italics added.
49. 'Il nous a fallu payer presque tout comptant et même avant que la livraison de la plus grande partie nous ait été faite, ayant donné des forts acomptes *pour être mieux servi* et pour obtenir la marchandise à meilleur marché', Correspondence, 181AQ57, 18 July 1755, f° 76 (letter to Mr Le Proux de la Rivière); italics added.
50. *Carises* were a type of coarse woollen cloth; 'petit barillage' included low-capacity barrels and other containers for wine.
51. 'Il y a longtemps que nous n'avons eu l'honneur de vous écrire faute d'occasion, nous avons celui de le faire ce jour'. Correspondence, 181AQ57, 18 December 1755, f° 174 (lettrer to Mr Antoine Robert, in Toulouse).
52. 'À l'égard des 20 douzaines de serviettes que nous vous avons demandées avec leurs nappes, lesquelles sont si chères, il faudra rayer notre ordre et ne point en faire l'achat. Nous n'avons absolument nulle connaissance à Gand, nous nous informerons à quelqu'un pour voir si l'on pourra nous indiquer une personne afin de voir s'il y aura quelque chose à faire'. Correspondence, 22 October 1755, 181AQ57, f° 223 (letter to Mr David Alexandre).
53. 'Nous avons le mémoire des fournitures que vous nous avez remis qui est différent du premier que vous nous avez ci devant envoyé. Nous travaillerons de toutes nos forces pour pouvoir l'accomplir du mieux qu'il nous sera possible quoique nous prévoyons bien de la difficulté pour cet excédent, *ayant bien peu de temps pour cela*'. Correspondence, 181AQ57, 17 December 1755, f° 172 (letter to M. Bréard).
54. 'Nous vous donnons la préférence pour *la plus grande partie* de notre mémoire, l'attachement et l'estime que nous vous avons n'exige pas moins de notre part'. Correspondence, 181AQ57, 9 October 1755, f° 103 (letter to Mssrs Raully frères).

55. Correspondence, 181AQ57, 9 October 1755, f° 103 (letters to Mr Payes and to Mssrs Mariette et Dumas). Gradis was ordering cloth and blankets which he shared as follows:

	Raully frères	Payes	Mariette & Dumas
Dourgne* curly and purple to blue ('frisé et violet à bleu')	75. Pieces	38 Pieces	37. Pieces
Mazamet* curly and brown to burgundy ('frisé brun et vineux')	65. Pieces	35 Pieces	30. Pieces
Molleton red blue and white	100. Pieces	50 Pieces	50. Pieces
Cadis* of Aignan curly, assorted ('frisé assorti')	20. Pieces	10 Pieces	10. Pieces
Cadis montaigne	25. Pieces	12. Pieces	13. Pieces
Couvertes of Toulouse blue and green	50	25	25.

* A kind of small woollen cloth named after the places of production, namely the town of Mazamet and the village of Dourgne. This product was mostly sold at the Pézenas fair, and exported to Canada. See L. Dutil, *L'état économique du Languedoc à la fin de l'Ancien Régime, (1750–1789)* (Paris: Hachette, 1911), and R. Cazals (ed.), *Histoire de Castres, Mazamet, la montagne, Toulouse* (Paris: Privat, 2004). *Cadis* were coarse cloth used in lower-class clothing. *Cadis* from Aignan were made in Montauban, and derived their name from its first manufactory, which had been started in 1626 by Jean and David d'Aignan. See P. Desfontaines, 'Montauban', *Annales de Géographie*, 38 (1929), pp. 460–9, and more generally on Languedoc cloth and its commercialization, J.-M. Minovez, *L'industrie invisible. Les draperies du Midi XVIIe-XXe siècles* (Paris: CNRS-éditions, 2012), and R. Descimon, 'Structures d'un marché de draperie dans le Languedoc au milieu du XVIe siècle', *Annales E.S.C.*, 30 (1975), pp. 1414–46.

56. On this little-researched issue, see D. Woronoff, *Envelopper les objets: Pour une histoire de l'emballage en France du XVIIIe siècle à nos jours, n. p., 2011.*
57. 'Nous avons été obligés de prendre un baril de sucre entier ... ce sucre se conservera mieux en baril que si on l'eût mis en sac, c'est ce qui nous a déterminé à vous en envoyer plus que ce que votre mémoire ne portait'. Correspondence, 181AQ 57, 7 November 1755, f° 131 (letter to Mr le marquis de Vienne).
58. 'Observez que tout soit bien emballé et bien conditionné pour que rien ne se gâte ni se brise dans le voyage'. Correspondence, 181AQ57, 30 January 1755, f° 210 (letter to Mr Guérin, goldsmith).
59. Originally, 'attention de faire emballer ces carreaux [de verre] mieux que la fois passée dont il s" est trouvé plus de la moitié de cassés'. Correspondence, 181AQ57, 20 December 1755, f° 174 (letter to Mssrs Horutener et Cie).
60. Originally, 'nous avons pensé qu'il convenait de vous faire cet envoi séparé soit pour partager vos risques soit pour que vous fussiez assuré en cas de retardement de vos vins d'avoir du moins de vos autres provisions'. Correspondence, 181AQ57, 7 November 1755, f° 131 (letter to Mr le marquis de Vienne).
61. Originally, 'nous vous avons seulement prié d'en suspendre l'envoi jusques à de nouveaux ordres de notre part non pour vous les laisser sur les bras mais uniquement pour vous marquer au juste si vous nous les expédierez pour ici en droiture ou pour quelqu'autre

port par terre que nous vous marquerons incessamment'. Correspondence, 181AQ57, 15 November 1755, f° 138, 15 novembre 1755 (letter to Mad. La veuve Baptiste Tirand).

62. F. Eymard Duverney, 'Conventions de qualité et formes de coordination', *Revue économique*, 40:2 (1989), pp. 329–59.
63. On this issue see J. Gadrey, 'The Characterization of Goods and Services: An Alternative Approach', *Review of Income and Wealth*, 46:3 (2000), pp. 369–87.
64. É. Serverin, 'La sécurité des produits sur la scène juridique', in Stanziani, *La qualité des produits*, pp. 241–70. This is the model of expected qualities for every actor for a given product, as produced by the actors' coordination.
65. See J.-P. Hirsch, *Les deux rêves du commerce. Entreprise et institutions dans la région lilloise 1760–1840* (Paris: Editions de l'EHESS, 1991). For a detailed case study, see P. Minard, 'Le bureau d'essai de Birmingham, ou la fabrique de la réputation au XVIIIe siècle', *Annales HSS*, 65 (2010), pp. 1117–46.

7 Deschanel, 'The Pinet Family of Gap and their Business Relations, 1785–1816: Official Activities and the Issue of Commercial Risk'

1. D. Hume, *Essays and Treatises on Several Subjects* (1752; London: Printed for A. Millar, 1758), p. 157.
2. A thesis developed in F. Knight, *Risk, Uncertainty and Profit* (1921; New York: Cosimo, Inc., 2006), pp. 197–232.
3. J. Schumpeter, *Capitalism, Socialism and Democracy* (1943; London: Routledge, 2012), p. 131.
4. P.-C. Pradier, *La notion de risque en économie* (Paris: La Découverte, 2006), pp. 8–15.
5. On this point, see the conclusions of Jean-Yves Grenier and the distinction he introduces between 'profit 1' and 'profit 2' in his *L'Economie d'Ancien Régime: un monde de l'échange et de l'incertitude* (Paris: Albin Michel, 1996), pp. 133–8. Profit 2 was linked to risk-taking and uncertainties in the economic context (p. 134). Moreover, Grenier points out that 'profit 2, being unstable and economic in nature, was starkly opposed to the morally acceptable and accordingly regulated immobility of profit 1' ('*au profit 2, instable et de nature économique s'oppose la fixité moralement acceptable et donc normée du profit 1*', *Economie d'Ancien Régime*, p. 138).
6. The family documents, mostly unpublished, are kept in the Archives départementales of Isère, under call number 14 J, and have recently been sorted. Our observations are based mainly on the analysis of the outgoing correspondence (1785–1816), of accounting documents (journals and inventories of debts, 1788–93), and of papers concerning military supplies (1792–1813).
7. R. Favier, 'Un grand bourgeois à Gap à la fin de l'Ancien Régime: Pierre-Daniel Pinet', in M. Vovelle (ed.), *Bourgeoisies de province et Révolution* (Grenoble: Presses Universitaires de Grenoble, 1987), pp. 43–53.
8. D. Margairaz, 'L'invention du "service public:" entre "changement matériel" et "contrainte de nommer"', *Revue d'histoire moderne et contemporaine*, 52:3 (2005), pp. 10–32, on p. 13.
9. A regional administrative district during the Ancien Régime [translator's note].
10. Favier, 'Un grand bourgeois à Gap', p. 46.
11. *Journal de Paris*, n° 207, 15 July 1784.

12. 'Précis pour Jean-Joseph-André Pinet contre les frères Gayde', AD Isère 14 J 24 (printed document, 1813).
13. D. Woronoff, 'Économie de guerre et intervention de l'État', *État, finances et économie pendant la Révolution française; colloque de Bercy 12–14 octobre 1989* (Paris: CHEEFF, 1991), pp. 283–93.
14. 'Mr. Pinet the father had at all times been responsible in the military procurement administration for supplying the strongholds in Haut-Dauphiné. This speculation was suitable for him because of the employment he exercised as *Receveur des tailles* in the Gap élection, while at the same time it benefited his region, for by supplying the goods for which he was responsible, he was able to use within the region itself the product of the *tailles*, and thus the money did not leave the region' ('Le sieur Pinet père s'était de tout tems chargé auprès de l'administration des vivres, de l'approvisionnement des places de guerre du Haut-Dauphiné. Cette spéculation lui convenait, à raison de l'emploi qu'il exerçait de receveur des tailles de l'élection de Gap, en même tems qu'elle profitait à son pays, car par les fournitures de denrées dont il se chargeait, il trouvait à employer dans le pays même le produit des tailles, et ainsi l'argent n'en sortait pas'). AD Isère 14 J 24, 'Précis pour Jean-Joseph-André Pinet contre les frères Gayde'.
15. Favier, 'Un grand bourgeois à Gap', p. 44.
16. AD Isère 14 J 11 'Grand livre, 1782–1783'.
17. Around the same time, the Chauvet and Lafaye company, started by two young tradesmen from Haut-Dauphiné, but established in Cap-Français, totalled a yearly volume of business of *c.* 300,000 lt. (Archives de la CCIMP, L 19/62/03). Similarly, Étienne Cornud's firm, in the Rhône area of Dauphiné, showed a volume inferior to 50,000 lt. per year in the 1780's (AD Drôme, 37 J 15).
18. The accounting archives of the family were indeed spread over several distinct volumes, of which some seem to have been lost.
19. As a number of enquiries show, whether they concern a specific firm or a specific commercial centre. See for example P. Butel, *Les négociants bordelais, l'Europe et les Îles au xviiie siècle* (Paris: Aubier, 1974), pp. 325–80.
20. See in particular the examples of Abel (AD Hautes-Alpes, 38 J 12), Borel du Bez (Archives Nationales F 3484), Chauvet (Arch. de la CCIMP, L 19/62), Jacques (AD Hautes-Alpes, L 1623) and Tanc (AD Hautes-Alpes, 77 J).
21. G. Daudin, 'Profits du commerce intercontinental et croissance dans la France du xviiie siècle', *Revue économique*, 57:3 (2006), pp. 605–13.
22. AD Hautes-Alpes, 3 M 6.
23. AD Isère, 14 J 9, liasse 1; Arch. de la CCIMP, L 19/62/11.
24. L. Dupré d'Aulnay, *Traité général des subsistances militaires* (Paris: Prault Père, 1744), pp. 3–8.
25. Favier, 'Un grand bourgeois à Gap', pp. 43–4.
26. R. Szramkievicz, *Les régents et censeurs de la Banque de France* (Genève: Droz, 1974), pp. 4–6. See also the archives of the Ithier family (AD Hautes-Alpes, 15 J 1, 4, 5, 7, 21 et 31). Jean-Joseph-Paul Ithier, Barrillon's nephew, was a former officer turned trader in association with his uncle.
27. The sources available to us are mostly incomplete, and some refer to an earlier period. An accounting journal nonetheless exists for 1788–93, but it focuses on the family's Gap business and the transfers of money from Lyon without giving details on the origins of the profit made. The many documents generated by the lawsuit between Jean-Joseph-André and his former associates, the Gayde brothers, allude to an even greater number of

other documents which have been lost or perhaps not yet sorted, and which therefore we were not able to consult (AD Isère 14 J 23–24).

28. In addition to a fixed income, the office of *receveur* (tax collector) [translator's note] also generated income which was indexed on the volume of taxes collected, and thus fluctuated from one year to the next.
29. Concerning the various forms of profit and their complementarity, see especially Grenier, *L'économie d'Ancien Régime*, pp. 103–4.
30. AD Isère 14 J 221 (incoming correspondance). Letter of 15 April 1789 from the *receveur général des finances* Anson, Paris.
31. Strategies different in form, but similar in their logic can be found, for example, among merchants active in the transoceanic and slave trades. See O. Pétré-Grenouilleau, *Les traites négrières. Essai d'histoire globale* (Paris: Gallimard, 2004), pp. 327–31.
32. Dupré d'Aulnay, *Traité général des subsistances militaires*, p. 8.
33. 'Vous aurez reçu [de M. Sain Costard et Pinet frères de Lyon] une nouvelle remise qui réduira mon débit à 300 400 lt., que je ne puis vous remettre dans ce moment, n'ayant pu me procurer encore assez de fonds pour faire face aux engagements que j'avais été obligé de prendre à Lyon ... Pour parvenir à vous payer pendant tout le temps du bouleversement de notre province, nos recouvrements, malgré toute mon exactitude, sont encore arriérés en plus de 60 000 lt. N'ayant pas compté sur cet inconvénient au commencement de l'année, je n'avais pas pu prendre des précautions'. AD Isère, 14 J 6, letter from December 1788 to Paris de la Bollardière, Paris.
34. Favier, 'Un grand bourgeois à Gap'.
35. AD Isère 14 J 5 et 6 for the period concerned (1785–9).
36. AD Isère 14 J 17.
37. AD Isère 14 J 23.
38. The ratio between the amount of the debt and the speed of its collection was extremely variable. Only 10 % of debts yielded a ratio of 2 lt. 2 s. per day or more.
39. AD Isère, 14 J 26, 'Fragments de comptes'.
40. L. Fontaine, *L'économie morale. Pauvreté, crédit et confiance dans l'Europe préindustrielle* (Paris: Gallimard, 2008), p. 51.
41. Favier, 'Un grand bourgeois à Gap', p. 47.
42. These proportions have been calculated from samples, each containing the same number of letters (665), equivalent to 10% of the total correspondence from 1785 to 1815.
43. We have not found any trace of references to urban riots in the correspondence, even to the *Journée des Tuiles* in June 1788. Many letters were sent to the Periers during this period, but there was no particular mention of the Grenoble events.
44. 'Les troubles survenus depuis deux ou trois jours dérangent entièrement nos projets ... Nous sommes tous au désarroy. Ce qu'il y a de plus dangereux, c'est la mauvaise intention des paysans envers leurs seigneurs'. AD Isère 14 J 06, letter dated August 1789.
45. In another letter from 15 April 1789, Pinet declared: 'Il y a une si grande levée chez le peuple qu'aucun citoyen honnête n'est en sécurité chez lui: j'ai craint plusieurs jours de voir ma caisse enlevée' ('There is such a great uprising of people that no honest citizen is safe in his own home: I feared for several days that my cashbox would be taken away').
46. Most of the known examples are found in Bas-Dauphiné and the Rhône valley. See especially P. Léon, *La naissance de la grande industrie en Dauphiné (fin du XVIIe–1869)*, 2 vols (Paris: Presses Universitaires de France, 1954), vol. 1, pp. 144–55; F. Bouchardeau and P. Bouchardeau, *Histoire de la chambre de commerce de Valence. La formation du*

patronat drômois au XIXe siècle (Grenoble: Université des sciences sociales de Grenoble, 1981), pp. 18–19.

47. 'Que Dieu alarme les esprits sur les vrais devoirs et soumissions envers le roi'. AD Isère 14 J 06, letter dated 21 July 1789.
48. AD Hautes-Alpes, 1 Q 218.
49. Jean-Joseph-André personally intervened in order to protect his brother's properties (AD Hautes-Alpes, 1 Q 296).
50. 'Le sieur [Jean-Joseph-]André aîné étant devenu, après son père, receveur des tailles, continua la même spéculation. Ayant reçu dans l'année 1792 une immense quantité d'assignats en remboursement de la finance de ses charges ou de ses créances assez considérables, il dut chercher à en faire un emploi, et il n'en trouva pas de plus avantageux, et qui l'exposât moins à la persécution qui s'attachait à ceux qui paraissaient riches, que de faire, dans des moments d'abondance, des achats de denrées pour les placer ensuite dans les administrations ou dans les entreprises publiques, lorsque le besoin de l'État l'exigerait, et que cependant il pourrait faire de tels placements avec sûreté pour le remboursement de ses fonds'. AD Isère14 J 24, 'Précis pour Jean-Joseph Pinet contre les frères Gayde'.
51. On this point, see V. Azimi, 'Heur et malheur des "salariés publics" sous la Révolution', *État, finances et économie pendant la Révolution française*, pp. 159–200.
52. The Pinets (of Manteyer) and their relatives (Blanc) would go on to play an important part in the political and administrative activities of the *département* throughout the nineteenth century. See V. Wright, *Les préfets de Gambetta* (Paris: PUPS, 2007), p. 108.
53. This statistical analysis was built from the electoral lists drawn up around 1810. See Archives Nationales F/1/cIII.

8 Sarson, '"The Way to Make a Huge Fortune, Easily and Without Risk": Economic Strategy and Tactics among Tobacco-South Planters in the Early National United States'

1. The pioneering work on colonial tobacco planters is A. C. Land, 'Economic Behavior in a Planting Society: The Eighteenth Century Chesapeake', *Journal of Southern History*, 33 (1967), pp. 467–85, and A. C. Land, 'Economic Base and Social Structure: The Northern Chesapeake in the Eighteenth Century', *Journal of Economic History*, 25 (1965), pp. 639–54. For overviews see A. Kulikoff, *Tobacco and Slaves: The Development of Southern Cultures in the Chesapeake, 1680–1800* (Chapel Hill, NC: University of North Carolina Press, 1986) and L. S. Walsh, *Motives of Honor, Pleasure, and Profit: Plantation Management in the Colonial Chesapeake* (Chapel Hill, NC: University of North Carolina Press, 2010). For the early national era see B. E. Marks, 'Economics and Society in a Staple Plantation System: St. Mary's County, Maryland, 1790–1840' (PhD, University of Maryland, 1979); F. J. Teute, 'Land, Liberty and Labor in the Post-Revolutionary Era: Kentucky as the Promised Land' (PhD thesis, Johns Hopkins University, 1988); J. B. Lee, *The Price of Nationhood: The American Revolution in Charles County* (New York: Norton, 1994); E. A. Perkins, *Border Life: Experience and Memory in Revolutionary Ohio Valley* (Chapel Hill, NC: University of North Carolina Press, 1998); and S. Sarson, *The Tobacco Plantation South in the Early American Atlantic World* (New York: Palgrave Macmillan, 2013).
2. See the Introductory essay to this volume by P. Gervais, Y. Lemarchand and D. Margairaz, pp. 1–12; T. Burnard, *Creole Gentlemen: The Maryland Elite, 1691–1776*

(New York: Routledge, 2002), esp. ch. 2; D. C. Klingaman, 'The Significance of Grain in the Development of the Tobacco Colonies', *Journal of Economic History*, 29 (1969), pp. 268–78; E. C. Papenfuse, Jr, 'Planter Behavior and Economic Opportunity in a Staple Economy', *Agricultural History*, 46 (1972), pp. 279–312; L. G. Carr, 'Diversification in the Chesapeake: Somerset County, Maryland, in Comparative Perspective', in L. G. Carr, P. D. Morgan and J. B. Russo (eds), *Colonial Chesapeake Society* (Chapel Hill, NC: University of North Carolina Press, 1988), pp. 342–88.

3. See especially J. Habermas, *The Structural Transformation of the Public Sphere: An Inquiry into a Category of Bourgeois Society* (Cambridge, MA: MIT Press, 1989).
4. See especially P. Bourdieu, *Distinction: A Social Critique of the Judgement of Taste* (1984; Cambridge, MA: Harvard University Press, 2006).
5. M. L. Callcott (ed.), *Mistress of Riversdale: The Plantation Letters of Rosalie Stier Calvert, 1795–1821* (Baltimore, MD: Johns Hopkins University Press, 1991), p. 20. Rosalie Calvert acculturated successfully into southern Maryland's elite, broadly conforming to the model of plantation mistresses described by E. Fox-Genovese in *Within the Plantation Household: Black and White Women of the Old South* (Chapel Hill, NC: University of North Carolina Press, 1988), p. 35, pp. 37–145. She was more economically active than most planters' wives, but seems thereby to have assimilated planter economic and social values all the more. I thank Robert J. Brugger of Johns Hopkins University Press for permission to use the letters, Ann B. Wass of the Riversdale Historical Society for sending me samples of the originals and for a guided tour of Riversdale, and Nathalie Morello of Swansea University for assessing the (excellent) translations from French. Prince George's County Register of Wills (hereafter PGCRW) (Benedict Calvert), February 18, 1788, T 1, 258–62. Prince George's County Tax Assessments (hereafter PGCTA), Personal Property, 1793, 39. Ibid., Real Property, 1804, 23, 25, 30. Prince George's County Land Records (hereafter PGCLR), Charles John [*sic*] Stier to Rosalie Eugenie Calvert, Deed, 2 April 1816, JRM 15, 612–16. Federal Direct Tax, Prince George's County, Maryland (hereafter FDTPG), Rock Creek and Eastern Branch Hundreds, Particular List of Lands, Lots, Buildings, and Wharves, 2; Horsepen and Patuxent Hundreds, Particular List of Lands, Lots, Buildings, and Wharves, 5, Particular List of Slaves, 2; Upper Marlboro, Charlotte, and Mount Calvert Hundreds, General List of Lands, Lots, Buildings, and Wharves, 1. PGCTA, Personal Property, 1818, 25, 31, 35; 1821, 27, 33, 37; Real Property, 1834, 9, 17; 1835, 9, 17; Personal Property, 1834, 8, 16; 1835, 8, 16.
6. Rosalie Eugenia Calvert (hereafter REC) to Henri Joseph Stier (hereafter HJS), 8 July 1804, Callcott (ed.), *Mistress of Riversdale*, p. 91
7. REC to HJS, 22 September 1805, 26 March 1807, Callcott (ed.), *Mistress of Riversdale*, pp. 128, 160.
8. REC to HJS, 14 May 1804, Callcott (ed.), *Mistress of Riversdale*, pp. 84, 106; Mobberly quoted in Marks, 'Economics and Society in a Staple Plantation System', pp. 166–7, 168.
9. REC to HJS, 19 November 1803, Callcott (ed.), *Mistress of Riversdale*, p. 59.
10. REC to HJS, 26 March 1807, 5 May 1808, 9 July 1808, 17 March 1812, REC to Charles Jean Stier [CJS], 18 February 1814, Callcott (ed.), *Mistress of Riversdale*, pp. 161, 184, 191, 250, 261.
11. REC to HJS, 30 August 1810, Callcott (ed.), *Mistress of Riversdale*, 229. Charles Varlo, *The Essence of Agriculture, being a Regular System of Husbandry, through All its Branches; Suited to the Climate and Lands of Ireland ... With the Author's Twelve Months Tour thro' America: ... With an Address to the Legislature and Gentlemen of Ireland. How to Levy*

Taxes on Luxury ... In Two Books, Bound in One Volume (London, 1786), quoted in Marks, 'Economics and Society in a Staple Plantation System', p. 82. The calculations about livestock and food crops are from Marks, p. 127.

12. REC to HJS, 26 March 1807, 31 March 1814, Callcott (ed.), *Mistress of Riversdale*, pp. 161, 265.
13. REC to HJS, 10 September 1808, 1 April 1809, Callcott (ed.), *Mistress of Riversdale*, pp. 191–2, 201.
14. Marks, 'Economics and Society in a Staple Plantation System', pp. 109, 465–9.
15. REC to HJS, 30 August 1810, 20 March 1815, Callcott (ed.), *Mistress of Riversdale*, pp. 229, 279.
16. REC to HJS, 11 November 1815, Callcott (ed.), *Mistress of Riversdale*, p. 285.
17. REC to HJS, 20 March 1816, Callcott (ed.), *Mistress of Riversdale*, pp. 291–2.
18. REC to CJS, 8 April 1816, Callcott (ed.), *Mistress of Riversdale*, pp. 295–6.
19. This is Margaret Law Callcott's calculation, Callcott (ed.), *Mistress of Riversdale*, p. 293 n. 1; REC to HJS, 20 March 1816, REC to CJS, 8 April 1816, Callcott (ed.), *Mistress of Riversdale*, p. 296.
20. REC to HJS, 29 October 1816, Callcott (ed.), *Mistress of Riversdale*, p. 307.
21. Marks, 'Economics and Society in a Staple Plantation System', pp. 92–3, lists Baltimore tobacco prices for every year from 1784 to 1850.
22. REC to HJS, 28 June 1803, REC to HJS and Mary Louise (née Peeters) Stier (hereafter MLS), 12 August 1803, REC to HJS, 19 January 1807, 20 August 1805, Callcott (ed.), *Mistress of Riversdale*, pp. 52, 55, 156, 126.
23. REC to HJS, 23 June 1807, 5 June 1820, Callcott (ed.), *Mistress of Riversdale*, pp. 169, 360.
24. REC to HJS, 20 August 1805, 1 April 1809, Callcott (ed.), *Mistress of Riversdale*, pp. 126, 201–2; Marks, 'Economics and Society in a Staple Plantation System', pp. 125–6.
25. Prince George's County Register of Wills, Inventories, 3 April 1838, PC 1, 411–7.
26. Marks, 'Economics and Society in a Staple Plantation System', pp. 176, 129, 84–5.
27. REC to HJS, 22 September 1805, 7 October 1805, 19 January 1807, Callcott (ed.), *Mistress of Riversdale*, pp. 128, 129, 156. 'The Mick' refers to the Stiers's eighteenth-century country home, the Château du Mick, at Brasschaat, in modern-day Belgium. Marks, 'Economics and Society in a Staple Plantation System', p. 122.
28. REC to HJS, 22 September 1805, 9 June 1809, Callcott (ed.), *Mistress of Riversdale*, pp. 128, 206.
29. REC to HJS, 1 April 1809, REC to HJS and MLS, 12 August 1803, REC to HJS, 19 November 1803, Callcott (ed.), *Mistress of Riversdale*, pp. 202, 55, 60; George Calvert to Thomas Ewell, Lease, Prince George's County Land Records, JRM 15, 25 February 1812, 575–7; to Thomas Ferrall, Lease, AB 1, 18 July 1820, 383–7; Lease, 1 April 1826, AB 2, 285–7.
30. REC to HJS, 17 March 1812, 5 June 1820, 30 August 1810, Callcott (ed.), *Mistress of Riversdale*, pp. 250, 360, 229.
31. REC to CJS, 23 July 1810, REC to HJS, 12 December 1808, 12 April 1813, Callcott (ed.), *Mistress of Riversdale*, pp. 222, 198, 256. The toll charges are listed by Margaret Law Callcott in *Mistress of Riversdale*, p. 258 n. 1. Rosalie Calvert's list of investments and projection of profits are from REC to HJS, 12 April 1813, pp. 256–7, and 29 October 1816, p. 307. See also Prince George's County Levy Court, Proceedings, 25 February 1815, 523, Deed, 4 March 1834, AB 8, 393–7.

32. This is also Margaret Law Callcott's calculation, *Mistress of Riversdale*, pp. 183–4 n. 1. REC to HJS, 13 June 1805.
33. REC to HJS, February [no date], 1811, Callcott (ed.), *Mistress of Riversdale*, p. 235.
34. REC to HJS, 12 May 1817, Callcott (ed.), *Mistress of Riversdale*, pp. 317–18.
35. REC to HJS, 13 March 1819, November [no date], 1810, Callcott (ed.), *Mistress of Riversdale*, pp. 242, 230.
36. REC to HJS, 22 September 1805, 12 May 1808, 1 April 1809, March [no date] 1810, 15 June 1810, 30 August 1810, REC to Isabelle van Havre, 11 January 1819, Callcott (ed.), *Mistress of Riversdale*, pp. 127, 190, 201, 217, 221, 228, 340.
37. REC to HJS, 6 September 1806, Callcott (ed.), *Mistress of Riversdale*, pp. 146, 147–8. Prince George's County Register of Wills, Inventories, 3 April 1838, PC 1, 411–7. See also Marks, 'Economics and Society in a Staple Plantation System', p. 377.
38. J. T. Main, *The Social Structure of Revolutionary America* (Princeton, NJ: Princeton University Press, 1965); R. R. Menard, 'From Servant to Freeholder: Status Mobility and Property Accumulation in Seventeenth-Century Maryland', *William and Mary Quarterly*, 3rd series, 30 (1973), pp. 37–64; R. R. Menard, P. M. G. Harris and L. G. Carr, 'Opportunity and Inequality: The Distribution of Wealth on the Lower Western Shore of Maryland, 1638–1705', *Maryland Historical Magazine*, 69 (1974), pp. 169–84; L. Gr. Carr and R. R. Menard, 'Immigration and Opportunity: The Freedman in Early Colonial Maryland', in T. W. Tate and D. L. Ammerman (eds), *The Chesapeake in the Seventeenth Century: Essays on Anglo-American Society* (Chapel Hill, NC: University of North Carolina Press, 1979), pp. 206–42; L. S. Walsh, 'Servitude and Opportunity in Charles County, Maryland, 1658–1705', in A. C. Land, L. G. Carr and E. C. Papenfuse, Jr (eds), *Law, Society, and Politics in Early Maryland* (Baltimore, MD: Johns Hopkins University Press, 1977), pp. 111–33; W. F. Bliss, 'The Rise of Tenancy in Virginia', *Virginia Magazine of History and Biography*, 58 (1950), pp. 427–41; G. A. Stiverson, *Poverty in the Land of Plenty: Tenancy in Eighteenth-Century Maryland* (Baltimore, MD: Johns Hopkins University Press, 1977); L. S. Walsh, 'Land, Landlord, and Leaseholder: Estate Management and Tenant Fortunes in Southern Maryland, 1642–1820', *Agricultural History*, 59 (1985), pp. 373–96.
39. For more detail, see S. Sarson, 'Distribution of Wealth in Prince George's County, Maryland, 1800–1820', *Journal of Economic History*, 60 (2000), pp. 847–55; S. Sarson, 'Landlessness and Tenancy in Early National Prince George's County, Maryland', *William and Mary Quarterly*, 3rd series, 57 (2000), pp. 569–98; S. Sarson, '"Objects of distress:" Inequality and Poverty in Early Nineteenth-Century Prince George's County', *Maryland Historical Magazine*, 96 (2001), pp. 141–62; S. Sarson, 'Yeoman Farmers in a Planters' Republic: Socioeconomic Conditions and Relations in Early National Prince George's County, Maryland', *Journal of the Early Republic*, 29 (2009), pp. 63–99; Sarson, *The Tobacco Plantation South*, esp. 'Appendix: A Statistical Analysis of Wealth Distribution and Mobility', and tables, pp. 169–202. For inequality elsewhere in the tobacco South, see S. S. Hughes, 'Elizabeth City County, Virginia, 1782–1810: The Economic and Social Structure of a Tidewater County in the Early National Years' (PhD dissertation, College of William and Mary, 1975); Marks, 'Economics and Society in a Staple Plantation System'; L. Soltow, 'Land Inequality on the Frontier: The Distribution of Land in East Tennessee at the Beginning of the Eighteenth Century', *Social Science History*, 5 (1981), pp. 275–91; L. Soltow, 'Kentucky Wealth at the End of the Nineteenth Century', *Journal of Economic History*, 43 (1983), pp. 617–33; F. J. Teute, 'Land, Liberty, and Labor in the Post-Revolutionary Era'. For a national perspective see L. Soltow, *Dis-*

tribution of Wealth and Income in the United States in 1798 (Pittsburgh, PA: University of Pittsburgh Press, 1989).

40. W. Kilty, *Laws of Maryland, 1776–1818, Revised and Collected under the Authority of the Legislature* (Annapolis, 1820), 1817, c. 192; Prince George's County Levy Court, Proceedings, 21 February, 1 March, 17 March, 19 May, 7 July 1817, 603, 604–16, 621–4, 626–9, 639–40. For more detail, see Sarson, '"Objects of Distress:"', pp. 141–62, and Sarson, *The Tobacco Plantation South*, pp. 159–68.

DuPlessis, 'Conclusion: Reorienting Early Modern Economic History: Merchant Economy, Merchant Capitalism and the Age of Commerce'

1. European languages have, in fact, proliferated words to capture the nuances of profit. To list only the most frequently used nouns in two languages, ancient Greek had ἆρος, κέρδος, λυσιτέλεια, ὄνειαρ, and ὄνησις, while English employs *advantage*, *benefit*, *bottom line*, *earnings*, *fruit*, *gain*, *profit*, *proceeds*, *return*, *revenue*, *surplus*, *yield*.
2. Mark 8:36 (King James Version).
3. These examples, chosen at random from many others, come from É. Littré, *Dictionnaire de la langue française* (Paris: Hachette, 1872–7), s.v. 'profit', 'Dictionnaires d'autrefois' at http://artfl-project.uchicago.edu/node/17 [accessed 20 September 2013].
4. These citations are from, respectively, *OED*, s.v. 'profit', and Littré, *Dictionnaire de la langue française*, s.v., 'profit', 'Dictionnaires d'autrefois' at http://artfl-project.uchicago.edu/node/17 [accessed 20 September 2013].
5. See above, 'Introduction', p. 2.
6. I am borrowing the formulation that the United States Securities and Exchange Commission requires all financial firms to attach to reports and prospectuses: 'Returns represent past performance and are not a guarantee of future performance'.
7. The quoted term comes from the title of a 1974 conference that focused on these two cases, and its subsequently published themes and findings merit another look: F. Krantz and P. M. Hohenberg (eds), *Failed Transitions to Modern Industrial Society: Renaissance Italy and Seventeenth Century Holland* (Montréal: Interuniversity Centre for European Studies, 1975).
8. I have obviously borrowed this phrase from J. Burckhardt, *The Civilization of the Renaissance in Italy* (1859; New York: Harper and Row, 1929), part II, c. 1, whose famous formulation proposes that 'the early development of the Italian' made him 'the first-born among the sons of modern Europe'. Burckhardt attributes this primacy to a calculating mentality – engendered, however, not by economic precocity but by politics, notably the need by city-states to maintain power and develop legitimacy.
9. See, for example, P. Gervais, 'Neither Imperial, nor Atlantic: A Merchant's Eye View of International Trade in the 18th Century', *History of European Ideas*, 34:4 (2008), pp. 465–73.
10. See, for example, K. N. Chaudhuri, *The Trading World of Asia and the English East India Company 1660–1760* (Cambridge: Cambridge University Press, 1978), pp. 280–1 and passim.
11. P. Aspers, *Markets* (Cambridge: Polity Press, 2011), p. 80.
12. A. Carlos and F. Lewis, *Commerce by a Frozen Sea. Native Americans and the European Fur Trade* (Philadelphia, PA: University of Pennsylvania Press, 2010), p. 75.

13. K. Pomeranz, *The Great Divergence. Europe, China, and the Making of the Modern World Economy* (Princeton, NJ: Princeton University Press, 2000).
14. K. N. Chaudhuri, *Trade and Civilisation in the Indian Ocean: An Economic History from the Rise of Islam to 1750* (Cambridge: Cambridge University Press, 1985); A. Reid, *Southeast Asia in the Age of Commerce*, 2 vols (New Haven, CT: Yale University Press, 1988–93), vol. 1, ch. 1.
15. C. Shammas, 'The Revolutionary Impact of European Demand for Tropical Goods', in J. J. McCusker and K. Morgan (eds), *The Early Modern Atlantic Economy* (Cambridge: Cambridge University Press, 2000), pp. 162–85; K. Morgan, *Slavery, Atlantic Trade and the British Economy, 1660–1800* (Cambridge: Cambridge University Press, 2000).
16. For the best introductions to the vast literature on the subject, see S. Ogilvie and M. Cerman (eds), *European Proto-industrialization* (Cambridge: Cambridge University Press, 1996); and J. de Vries, *The Industrious Revolution. Consumer Behavior and the Household Economy, 1650 to the Present* (Cambridge: Cambridge University Press, 2008).
17. Cf. P. Maw, 'Yorkshire and Lancashire Ascendant: England's Textile Exports to New York and Philadelphia, 1750–1805', *Economic History Review*, 63:3 (2010), pp. 734–68, esp. p. 761.
18. K. Marx, *Das kapital: Kritik der politischen oekonomie*, 3 vols (1867–94; London: Penguin, 1981); M. Weber, *General Economic History* (New York: Greenberg, 1927); M. Weber, *The Protestant Ethic and the Spirit of Capitalism* (1904; London: G. Allen & Unwin, 1930); W. Sombart, *Der moderne kapitalismus* (Leipzig: Duncker & Humblot, 1902).
19. P. M. Sweezy (ed.), *The Transition from Feudalism to Capitalism* (London: NLB, 1976); R. S. DuPlessis, 'From Demesne to World-System: A Critical Review of the Literature on the Transition from Feudalism to Capitalism', *Radical History Review*, 4:1 (1977), pp. 3–41; T. H. Aston and C. H. E. Philpin (eds), *The Brenner Debate* (Cambridge: Cambridge University Press, 1987).
20. See, respectively, Marx, *Das kapital*, vol. 1, c. 20, 36, 47; P. Deyon and F. Mendels (eds), *La protoindustrialisation: théorie et réalité: rapports* (Lille: Université des arts, lettres et sciences humaines de Lille, 1982); E. Williams, *Capitalism and Slavery* (Chapel Hill, NC: University of North Carolina Press, 1944); I. Wallerstein, *The Modern World-System*, 3 vols (New York and San Diego, CA: Academic Press, 1974–89).
21. J. E. Inikori, *Africans and the Industrial Revolution in England: A Study in International Trade and Development* (Cambridge: Cambridge University Press, 2002).
22. B. Solow (ed.), *British Capitalism and Caribbean Slavery: The Legacy of Eric Williams* (Cambridge: Cambridge University Press, 1987); B. Solow (ed.), *Slavery and the Rise of the Atlantic System* (Cambridge, MA: Harvard University Press, 1991).

INDEX

For Product Safety Concerns and Information please contact our EU
representative GPSR@taylorandfrancis.com
Taylor & Francis Verlag GmbH, Kaufingerstraße 24, 80331 München, Germany

www.ingramcontent.com/pod-product-compliance
Ingram Content Group UK Ltd.
Pitfield, Milton Keynes, MK11 3LW, UK
UKHW021615240425
457818UK00018B/579

* 9 7 8 1 1 3 8 6 6 3 1 7 6 *